TOYS FOR EARLY CHILDHOOD DEVELOPMENT

Selection Guidelines for Infants, Toddlers, and Preschoolers

Berenda W. Abrams

Nancy Allen Kauffman

Illustrations by Linda Howe

THE CENTER FOR APPLIED
RESEARCH IN EDUCATION
West Nyack, New York 10995

Library of Congress Cataloging-in-Publication Data

Abrams, Berenda.
  Toys for early childhood development : selection guidelines for
infants, toddlers, and preschoolers / Berenda Abrams and Nancy
Kauffman ; illustrations by Linda Howe.

      p. cm.
    ISBN 0–87628–924–3
    1. Toys—United States. 2. Play. 3. Child development—United
States. I. Title.
  HQ784.T68A27 1990
  649′.55—dc20
                                                    90–2218
                                                      CIP

ISBN 0-87628-924-3

**THE CENTER FOR APPLIED
RESEARCH IN EDUCATION**
BUSINESS & PROFESSIONAL DIVISION
A division of Simon & Schuster
West Nyack, New York 10995

PRINTED IN THE UNITED STATES OF AMERICA

Our sincere thanks go to our loving families for their forbearance and encouragement, to members of the dedicated scientific community on whose work our suggestions are based, and to our young clients who continually inspire and teach us.

ABOUT THIS BOOK

The purpose of *Toys for Early Childhood Development* is to give you useful and practical ideas for choosing toys that will benefit young children at different stages of development and at different ages. Selecting toys often creates a dilemma for the parents of young children, as well as for teachers, therapists, and administrators. This book will enhance your skills as a knowledgeable toy consumer, qualified to observe children as they play, and then to select and use the best toys. (Please note that we will alternate the sex of the child from one chapter to the next to that you will not be distracted by the repeated use of he/she and him/her.)

This book explores the following three themes to help you review important concepts of child development that are essential to making the most appropriate choices in toy selection:

1. Eight of the major aspects of child development are stimulated by play. They are introduced in Chapter 1, "Why Children Play," and expanded upon in greater detail throughout the book.

2. Development occurs in normal, orderly sequences. Developmental sequences for infants, toddlers, and preschoolers ages three to five are introduced in Chapter 2, "How Children Develop," and then are discussed in depth in Chapters 4, 5, and 6. Each of these chapters includes specific suggestions for promoting a child's progress. For the most part, the suggestions are listed in developmental order.

3. Toys stimulate development. The toy chart provided at the end of each age chapter (4 through 6) gives examples of what toys can accomplish for each of the eight major aspects of child development. The charts can help you plan your toy purchases and can also serve as a gift-buying guide. We do not represent any toy manufacturer, nor do we sell toys. Each toy included in the charts was chosen solely on our evaluation of its merit.

Dozens of practical suggestions for encouraging play and development are included in every age chapter. Look for the light bulb symbol. In Chapter 3, "Toy Tips," pointers are given for play value, selection, storage, and creating play environments. Safety and health concerns are also emphasized.

We have been using toys in our work for a total of over forty-five years to enhance the development of children. We hope that the information and suggestions in this book will help you choose toys that will provide engrossing and stimulating play experiences for the youngsters in your care.

Berenda W. Abrams

Nancy Allen Kauffman

ABOUT THE AUTHORS

Berenda Abrams has a Bachelor of Science degree in Education from the University of Pennsylvania, a degree from the Philadelphia School of Occupational Therapy, certification from Sensory Integration International, and is licensed by the Commonwealth of Pennsylvania. She has been in private practice working with children for over twenty-five years, is a speaker at local nursery schools, and a regular consultant at a group home for the mentally retarded, and the Quaker School at Horsham, Pa. for learning disabled children. She was the Director of Occupational Therapy at a children's hospital, a member of the state and district boards of the Pennsylvania Occupational Therapy Association in her capacity as chairperson of the state conference, and the recipient of two study grants from the Easter Seal Society for Crippled Children and Adults.

Ms. Abrams has served on the board or as president of many community organizations and has chaired various cultural fund-raising projects, especially music and art events. She was on the board of the Playhouse Nursery School, an early cooperative, and was a parent volunteer for three years. She chaired and contributed to three township directories and compiled a county leisure-time facilities directory. She has been listed in *Who's Who of American Women*. She is married to a physician-scientist and has four grown children and three young grandsons.

Nancy Kauffman has a Bachelor of Science degree in Occupational Therapy from the University of Pennsylvania and a Master of Education degree from Temple University, certification from Sensory Integration International, and is licensed in the Commonwealth of Pennsylvania. Following eight years of work in a public school for the learning disabled, she reopened a hospital pediatric outpatient program, and then entered private practice working with children. She is also an educational consultant at the Pennsylvania School for the Deaf. She is a regular contributor to recent editions of the textbooks *Willard and Spackman's Occupational Therapy* (therapists in the school-setting chapter) and *Neurological Rehabilitation* (visual-perception chapter). She has also coauthored occupational therapy research articles and has written school curricula, child development charts, and learning disability assessments.

Ms. Kauffman has taught children in church and Scout programs and is a member of the volunteer board at the Melmark Home for the mentally retarded. She plays the violin in the Delaware County Symphony and serves on the orchestra's board. She is past president of her community association and is active in her Friends (Quaker) Meeting. She has two grown children.

FOREWORD

Play is the work of early childhood. To learn to work effectively in later life, a child must learn to play effectively in earlier life. It is through play that children have an opportunity to exercise so many relevant brain functions while developing and refining skills that will promote social, behavioral, and academic success during the school years.

For proper education, as children proceed through the school years, they require judiciously selected textbooks, curricula, and teaching methods. No one would pretend that a child could learn to read, write, or understand scientific phenomena just by perusing randomly selected books and being taught in a haphazard, unsystematic manner. Ironically, it is that random haphazard approach that is all too often characteristic of efforts to optimize develoment before age five. Since early education is so intimately bound to play activities, there is justification for parents and other interested adults to become systematic and thoughtful in the ways that toys are selected at particular periods. Encountering the right toy or game at the right time can lead children to acquire a sense of the intense satisfaction associated with new discoveries and confirmations of insights. The early acquisition of this delight in discovery can ultimately evolve into authentic intellectual curiosity, academic motivation, and a sense of entrepreneurialism all of which can reap enormous benefits for children on into adulthood.

Through toys children can extend newly acquired capabilities. They can discover opportunities to apply new skills at the same time that they learn some hard lessons regarding the limitations of such abilities. New ways of being effective keep appearing. While they may seem rather obvious to us adults, the discoveries that children make about themselves during the earliest years of life are, in fact, quite revolutionary from their perspectives. A few examples might illustrate this point:

Rather early in their infantile educational experience, babies acquire sophisticated knowledge about the visual-spatial world. They learn about changes that they can effect in that realm. They learn that the sides of their bodies can cooperate to achieve these changes. They learn that the objects in their spatial world are truly permanent, they they even exist when you can't see them! Games like peek-a-boo and toys like a jack-in-the-box keep confirming this extraordinary realization!

Very early in life children become introduced to the dimensions and properties of time and sequence. They learn that many routines occur in a predictable order. Ultimately they come to appreciate time-laden vocabulary, words such as "before," "after," "yesterday," "today," etc. This early understanding of time and sequence may be thought of as critical preparation for the later onslaught of demands requiring performing tasks in the correct order, organizing time, learning practical sequences (such as the alphabet, the days of the week, and the months of the year), and remembering multistep instructions. Many of the games and toys which children play require an appreciation of sequential ordering, so that their explicit use during early childhood has the potential for increasing awareness of serial order and the often confusing time parameters in life.

Play activities can also enhance language skills. Following verbal directions in play can prepare a child for the far more complex language inputs he or she will need to succeed academically and socially in later life. Communication skills can develop rapidly within the arena of play. Verbal interactions between children sharing recreational pursuits can serve to bolster a child's language fluency while at the same time teaching collaboration, social effectiveness, and even negotiation. Many play activities in early childhood require children to integrate language inputs with motor responses. This kind of linkage needs to be facilitated, so that students can become adept at using language to understand and implement a wide range of motor procedures in their later activities.

Play involves repetition, and that very repetition enhances playing skill. As this process of repeated play unfolds, children are actually making excellent use of a variety of memory skills. Learning, remembering and applying rules of play may comprise excellent preparation for the heavy load of rule-based memory learning that children are to encounter subsequently in their educations.

Perhaps one of the most important early childhood avocational endeavors is the pursuit of imaginary play. There is reason to believe that in contemporary society, children overindulged in television and highly structured activities, have a paucity of experience in imaginary play. There is now abundant evidence to suggest that engaging in imaginary games during preschool and the early school years can enable children to become first rate brainstormers later on. Through imaginary play, creativity and highly divergent thinking become paramount, so that children gain proficiency in formulating original ideas and displaying unique perspectives. Such creativity can obviously reap benefits throughout later life.

Another critical life acquisition involves a child's ability to make use of selective attention. Children engaged in play activities during early childhood are likely to strengthen the various mechanisms needed to sustain concentration, to filter out irrelevant distractions, to think about what they are doing while they are doing it, and to remain focused on an activity until that activity reaches a reasonable stage of completion or closure. Sustained and selected attention is so fundamental for learning and life adjustment that the development of these capacities needs to be a major goal as one observes or supervises the play of very young children.

Play so often involves toys, just as the later academic curriculum involves books. This is not to say that books are unimportant in early childhood (to the contrary they themselves are critical toys), nor should we believe that older children need not have play, but it is true that the toys of infants, toddlers, and preschoolers provide vital channels and directions for play. By choosing the right toy and and the right variety of toys at the right times in life, the early education and experience of children can be dramatically heightened. We all want to make sure that as children acquire new skills and insights, they develop their abilities to the greatest possible extent and their understandings to the profoundest possible depths. There exist many children who proceed through early childhood and their school years with a series of what might best be called "tenuous grasps" on skills and concepts. Many of these youngsters struggle to succeed; many become frustrated and many underachieve. Such underachievement can take its toll on self-esteem and motivation. With the proper selection of toys early in life, it is possible to minimize the tendency toward the tenuous or incomplete development of skills and understandings.

The kinds of acquisitions enumerated above need to be experienced and deployed to the greatest possible extent in early childhood. It is truly exciting therefore that Berenda Abrams and Nancy Kauffman have collaborated to create *Toys for Early Childhood Development*. As a developmental pediatrician and a professional who has observed so many children in the process of growing up, I can say that this book fills a most conspicuous gap in the practical knowledge so acutely needed by early childhood educators and, even more, by parents. In reading this book, all of those concerned with optimal development during early childhood are likely to be much more informed about the wise selection of toys and about their richest applications in play. Hopefully, this volume will be read and applied widely to enrich the early years of the lives of many children. I believe that such youngsters will come to the realization that little in life is as fulfilling as the remarkable chain of processes that links exploring to discovering, discovering to learning, learning to applying, applying to mastering, mastering to succeeding, and succeeding to feeling like a fulfilled person, a person motivated to explore incessantly.

Melvin D. Levine, M.D.
Professor of Pediatrics, University of North Carolina
Director of Center for Development and Learning
Author of *Keeping A Head in School*

CONTENTS

Toys for Early Childhood Development
List of Figures

1

WHY CHILDREN PLAY

Play is a natural and necessary part of childhood that is a common denominator among people everywhere. Through play and the use of toys, children enthusiastically participate in activities that help shape personality and intelligence. Play allows children to experiment with their own capabilities and should not be thought of as "just play."

Play has been called "exploratory learning" by play expert Mary Reilly. As we watch youngsters completely absorbed in play, we can see that they are exploring new things and striving to develop new levels of competence. Learning takes place automatically as children playfully encounter and master new challenges. Finally, the play experience results in the achievement of new physical or social standards they find satisfying. The new standards may have been created by the players, or may have been adopted from a model suggested by someone else. Without the presence of this opportunity for mastery, most children will not be motivated to continue the play activity.

As children explore and strive during play, they voluntarily repeat actions just for the fun of it—just for the pure pleasure and satisfaction. To be the most beneficial and engrossing, play must be directed toward a goal chosen by the youngsters.

Play provides an outlet for a child's natural curiosity and creativity. It offers stimulation for the inventiveness that is characteristic of the early years.

Play occupies a majority of the young child's time and has often been called "the work of children." Both play and work are associated with achieving proficiency, and both are important for establishing a sense of purpose and identity.

Play is an essential activity, necessary to help children organize and understand themselves and their world. It helps them interact with and master their environment. It helps them adapt to their culture. By the school years, exploratory learning experience begins to be structured into the framework that becomes, as the child approaches adulthood, more work-oriented.

Details of how children play at each level of development will be presented in the age chapters (4 through 6). A few general principles about play will be presented here.

IMPORTANCE OF TOYS IN PLAY

Toys are the essence of play. They are intrinsically motivating. The right toys available at the right time can spontaneously guide children to new heights of accomplishment. It is the role of the adults in their lives to provide toys, other playthings, and a play environment that are appropriately stimulating while at the same time safe. These may range from simple playthings handmade from household items to the most elaborate and expensive toys. It is the appropriateness that counts.

From among the toys made available to them by discriminating adults, children spontaneously figure out which ones to play with and how. The bright-eyed toddler or eager preschooler during play enthusiastically selects a toy with a firm sense of purpose. The selection is no accident. Play does not occur randomly. The child knows instinctively what will probably be interesting and fun. The toddler will not select a two-wheeled bicycle. The first grader will not select a teething ring.

If a toy provides the right kind of stimulation and the right amount, it will arouse the developing youngster's innate curiosity. Children are attracted to toys that provide just the right amount of challenge to encourage them to learn and expand their world. Toys should have both familiar and unexplored features. Just the right degree of novelty is necessary.

If a toy is too different from one that has already been mastered, it may be too confusing or uninteresting to be attractive. If it is too similar, it may provide no new challenge and will soon be cast aside as boring.

PLAY TESTS REALITY AND FOSTERS DEVELOPMENT

A child's understanding of the physical world is at first quite general. Later it becomes more specific. The same is true of her understanding of people and feelings. Through play, she examines a variety of actions as well as emotions, relationships, and roles. She reflects on her observations and forms guesstimates regarding the outcome of future behavior. Then she tests facts and misinformation against what is real, slowly working out a harmony between her understandings and reality. Play even helps her accept truths that may be in conflict with her own wishes of what she would like reality to be. The play experience provides clarification.

We believe children should not be pushed to learn advanced skills beyond their stage of readiness. If conditions are right, play can develop new skill levels in a variety of areas by stimulating each child's intrinsic inner drive. This may broaden a child's general adaptability, which is much more important than speeding up the rate of development in one or two obvious areas. New skill levels occur in natural sequences, which will be discussed more fully in the next chapter.

Wise selection of toys for the child at each stage can go a long way toward enhancing the learning process. Toys help to motivate the trial-and-error period that usually occurs in the early stages of learning. Play often provides the "ah-ha" experience that brightens the child's awareness—like a light bulb of understanding that suddenly clicks on inside her brain.

As new awareness dawns, play provides the opportunity for practice and repetition of the newly acquired concept or skill. After a lengthy period of practice to integrate and become accustomed to using the new skill, the child moves on to mastering an even higher level. At each level, the child needs a variety of toys and opportunities.

One day an infant may suddenly discover that frantically wiggling her whole body causes a crib toy suspended overhead to provide a delightful sound and sight response. This remarkable "ah-ha" experience is followed by hours, even days, of repetition of the purposeful whole-body movement. Gradually this practice period ends, and the child seeks new and slightly novel ways of playing with the suspended toy. Perhaps she accidentally or purposefully wriggles into a position to reach the toy with her hands for more accurate manipulation. A new level of understanding occurs.

Forward progress is not easy and smooth but requires concentration and effort during play. It may be accompanied by a healthy degree of stress. This stress calls forth more familiar, lower-level behaviors, too, that allow the child to concentrate on the new accomplishment. When the new skill becomes automatic and the child no longer has to think through each step, the earlier behaviors disappear. This up and down, "three steps forward and one step back" process characterizes learning at many stages.

Here is an example of how babies automatically return to lower levels of development in one area while, at the same time, mastering a new higher level in another. A baby who can walk while holding onto things for support will play with toys at the level of low tables and chairs for days, maybe even weeks, while learning her new "cruising" skill. Finally the skill will become so automatic that she dares to let go briefly. With a delighted grin, she realizes she has just taken those important first steps of walking.

As she earnestly practices her new walking skill, she stops using her hands for playing with toys. Now the stress of trying to walk makes it necessary to use her hands and arms for helping with balance, and she holds them in the air closer to her shoulders to gain stability (high-guard position). She may also drop back to practicing sitting balance. This helps stabilize her upper trunk for the balance she needs to stand erect without holding onto furniture. Only gradually does she acquire enough stability in this new position to again use her hands to play with toys while walking. By this time, she learns to use push-toys and, later, pull-toys.

With each day of practice and new experimentation, the play gradually becomes more precise and more complicated. As confidence and learning grow with each successful play experience, the play becomes more diverse. New toys and playthings are tried, and old familiar toys are used in new ways. The effect of play action on a toy and/or a play companion—even on her own body—tells the child what works most effectively to bring her satisfaction. As she monitors these responses, she chooses to change her next play action adaptively to gain even greater satisfaction. She begins to understand cause/effect relationships.

The play itself provides increasingly varied experiences and expands the child's repertoire of behaviors. This opportunity for variety provides a basis for the adaptability necessary for emotionally healthy and mature living.

Throughout this book, we are going to highlight eight aspects of child development to help you to accurately identify why children choose to play as they do. A brief description of each aspect is introduced in Figure 1–1 to familiarize you with the concepts we want to emphasize. The eight aspects overlap considerably and are all a basic part of a child's learning process, existing from birth. They will be referred to in greater detail in later chapters.

PLAY BUILDS RELATIONSHIPS

Babies love to play affectionately when approached by familiar adults or by other children. Often, however, they play alone, absorbed in their own movements or in the response of the toys they handle. Slowly they become interested in passively watching other children play. By toddler age, they play near each other but with separate toys. Only later do children begin to play cooperatively with friends—pretending, imagining, and establishing rules.

The play environment should include people as well as toys. Growing children need far more than food, clothing, and shelter from adults. Without time set aside for social interaction, playfulness, and being handled tenderly, normal development will falter. Without these positive experiences, children may fail to thrive or to establish social attachments or basic trust in others. Adults provide role models of adult behavior that children mimic in play and slowly incorporate into their own personalities.

In play experiences with other children, they reaffirm their own impression of themselves and learn social skills that do and do not provoke favorable responses from peers. If toys are at the right level to foster success, play helps to build the confidence they need as a basis for getting along with other people.

Figure 1–1 EIGHT ASPECTS OF CHILD DEVELOPMENT

1. *Awareness of Sensations.* This includes an understanding of sound, sight, smell, taste, and touch. It includes recognition of being moved and also of moving all or parts of the body. Memory of these sensations is included, and the ability to resist being distracted by them.

2. *Balance and Big Movements.* This incorporates general coordination and ability to plan new movements. It incorporates balance and posture and the automatic reflexes that work together to synchronize them. Small movements of one or several parts of the body will be included when they are essential to achieve an overall big movement.

3. *Dexterity and Hand/Eye Coordination.* This refers to grasp, coordinating the fingers, and manipulating small objects. It includes drawing and writing. It also refers to the use of hands and eyes together, and to the establishment of hand dominance.

4. *Vision.* This covers sight, eye movements, and perception. Perception means understanding the distinguishing characteristics of what is seen. Vision also covers visual memory and recognizing colors.

5. *Space/Time Awareness.* This encompasses the awareness of personal and environmental space, and the passage of time. It also includes cause/effect relationships, sequencing, and logic.

6. *Personality/Socialization.* This involves building character and independence as well as learning participation and cooperation. It involves acknowledging and expressing feelings, and developing self-awareness.

7. *Language.* This means listening to, understanding, remembering, and communicating sounds and symbols. It also means grammar, vocabulary, inflection, discriminating and articulating sounds, and categorizing meanings.

8. *Imagination/Creativity.* This incorporates imitating and pretending previous experiences, and anticipating or inventing new ones. It also incorporates fantasy and the creating of unique concepts and solutions to problems. It helps lay a foundation for abstract thought.

PLAY PREPARES FOR ADULTHOOD

Play is not a frivolous pastime. It is the serious business of children learning about themselves and accommodating to the people and things in the world around them. Play can be instrumental in helping to enhance the quality of life. Each of the eight aspects of development mentioned earlier in this chapter plays a major role in determining how a child, as she grows and develops, will adjust to the demands of adolescence and adulthood. It is not the rate of learning any single skill that is important. It is the overall ability of the developing youngster to accommodate to her environment in each of these aspects that will help determine her happiness and contribution to society as an adult.

Here are some examples. The infant who learns to be aware of and comfortable with a variety of *sensations* is likely to grow into the grade-schooler who is not afraid to handle guinea pigs or frogs, and the adolescent who delights in walking barefoot in the sand or grass, holding hands comfortably with a romantic companion. In adulthood, this appropriately aware person may thrive comfortably in the close confines of a crowded shopping mall or commuter train, easily disregarding both the noise and the feel of people lightly bumping into her. Yet she can quickly discriminate the feel of coins from the keys in her pocket when she needs to pay her bill and can focus on the sound of the public address system that gives information she wants. Her keen awareness of tactile sensations can contribute to a satisfying sexual relationship.

The adult whose *balance and big-movement* skills have received a firm foundation is likely to stand without undue effort during a jerky subway ride. She can neatly fold a contour sheet or learn to serve a tennis ball. Her movements will be sure and confident as she weaves her shopping cart among crowded, unsteady grocery displays or walks down uneven flagstone stairs after dusk.

The adult with adequately developed *dexterity and hand/eye coordination* will use handwriting that is fast and legible enough not to impair her on the job. If she wants to, she will be able to learn how to touch-type on a computer keyboard, do crewel embroidery, or demonstrate skillful catching to her child's Little League baseball team.

Visual skills of the well-rounded adult include more than a consideration of whether she has 20/20 vision. Can she quickly select the correct size film from a confusing photography display or follow the diagram in the "easy-to-assemble" toy she has bought her children? These perceptual skills first began to develop during childhood play experiences. How about the visual memory skill of remembering where a car is parked in the huge shopping center? Coordinated eye movements required for speed reading and watching a sporting event without losing track of the ball are also vision tasks.

The preschooler who uses toys effectively to help build an accurate awareness of *space and time* may grow into the adult who can use a map to find a destination in a new city—by subway! She may be able to back a Jeep down a winding mountain road. She may have the skills to judge how long it will take to pack for a vacation so that she can be ready with time to spare.

Happy play experiences in childhood can help prepare for the *personality and socialization* skills necessary for developing close, intimate adult relationships while retaining the ability to stand up for one's rights. In addition, many well-adjusted adults can confidently and appropriately give a speech, run a meeting, or recognize the authority of someone else in the room. Playing independently, and later cooperatively, sets the stage for the give-and-take of important friendships. Good work habits are gradually established as children learn to deal with frustrations, finish what they start, ask for help when they really need it, and have the satisfaction of completing games they have invented themselves.

Play skills help create an adult who understands the *language* innuendoes that tell when a friend is kidding or serious and can relate jokes or personal incidents with clarity. Many people will want to be able to write a report for work or for the club newspaper, or to use a foreign language well enough to ask directions during a vacation abroad.

Although few babies in the nursery will grow up to be great painters or authors of novels, many will grow up to demonstrate their *imagination* or *creativity* in other ways. Many adults will plan and carry out a sewing project, design and plant a garden, invent a recipe, or find an innovative solution to a weighty business problem. Others will find the right words to comfort a distressed friend, to try a novel approach to balancing the family time or financial commitments, or to reorganize a company so that it operates out of the red. Many will have at least an avocational interest in music, movement, art, or literature. Most will provide critical analyses of TV shows and movies. These and other forms of creative thinking are the basis for change and progress in every society.

Play, the business of children, begins to prepare youngsters for the years ahead. It lays the groundwork for each person to make a unique contribution in the adult world.

2

HOW CHILDREN
DEVELOP

Children develop in orderly, sequential steps that are similar across cultures, regardless of basic personality and intellectual differences. Adults everywhere recognize in children the importance of first words, first steps, and learning to share a toy without fighting.

When children acquire a major new skill, adults take note with joy. Parents whip out the family camera and phone the grandparents. Teachers in child-care centers and nursery schools note it in the daybook. Adults realize the value of the new achievement as a major step toward growing up. This type of accomplishment is a developmental milestone.

Such milestones are, by definition, clearly observable new skills, indicating that the child has reached an important new level of learning. However, they do not come out of the blue. They do not suddenly crop up from nowhere. The major milestones follow logically after the child has acquired many small, obscure developmental steps. Slowly, but steadily, the child has been moving toward accomplishing the major milestone that finally occurs one day.

You may wish to think of these big, major developmental milestones as maxi-milestones. Think of the small, less obvious steppingstones that lead to those big successes as mini-milestones.

MINI-MILESTONES

If you are a caretaker who nurtures growing children, you can benefit from recognizing the mini-milestones that are pre-requisites for accomplishing major milestones. They are likely to be taken for granted by the adults caring for children. However, they are just as important as the maxi-milestones during the process of growing up. They lay the groundwork. In Figure 2–1 are a few examples of the many discrete little developmental progressions, or mini-milestones, necessary to achieve independent sitting, a maxi-milestone clearly evident to everyone. The mini-milestones begin in the infant's earliest days in the crib or bassinet.

Other little developmental accomplishments and progressions would, of course, lead to different maxi-milestones. Recognition of mini-milestones will help you gain more pleasure from watching children play and better understand how to make skillful decisions about purchasing toys. It will also help you know how to use toys and play activities to gently stimulate and encourage mini-milestones to develop. Then the maxi-milestones will seem to blossom automatically.

MAXI-MILESTONES

Listed in Figure 2–2 is a series of children's maxi-milestones that occur at various ages in each of the eight aspects of child development that we have chosen to focus on in this book. These examples, listed sequentially, are

Figure 2–1 MINI-MILESTONES LEADING TO SITTING

1. Controls head steadily so that it doesn't wobble.

2. From prone position on tummy, uses arms to push chest and head up off the mattress and hold that position.

3. Rolls over by coordinating back and tummy muscles to work together.

4. Balances on one hand/arm while reaching out for a barely attainable toy.

5. Once placed in a sitting position, maintains position by sitting with legs wide apart and using hands on the floor to maintain balance.

6. Sits erect independently, adjusting posture as needed, hands free to play with toys.

provided as an overview. They will be expanded and discussed more fully in later chapters.

Child growth and development is very complex, and this list is not exclusive. We have chosen to include only those aspects and milestones most closely related to how and why a child plays with toys. In this way, we hope to expand awareness of the developmental process and increase understanding of how to observe children and their play.

The eight aspects of child development focused on in this chapter are interdependent. Children progress in all eight simultaneously, but not all at the same rate. The milestones reached in one aspect of development often foster and support the acquiring of new skills in another. Occasionally children acquire skills in a different sequence from that listed here.

Every child has an instinctive need and ability to develop new skills, to try new challenges, to achieve new milestones. A child is remarkably adaptable and has a degree of plasticity and flexibility unequaled in adult life. The developmental process is stimulated by many factors that interact simultaneously. Some occur automatically because of innate influences the child inherits. These will be discussed next. Later, we will mention other factors that contribute to development but are environmental and depend largely on things that happen in the child's life after birth. The relative importance of "nature versus nurture" has been debated often. Each plays a vital role.

AUTOMATIC INFLUENCES ON DEVELOPMENT

Certain of the automatic influences on a child's development are inherited from parents. For example, personality characteristics show a trend that is evident from birth. Identical twins, separated in infancy and raised in quite different environments, have often been shown to have remarkably similar interests, temperaments, and behavioral traits in adulthood.

Some automatic influences have a common denominator throughout the human race. Just as an acorn obviously will not grow up to be a rose, humans, too, can be assured of certain qualities. One aptitude that seems to be prewired to unfold automatically in humans is the development of language if the child is exposed to language in his environment.

In acquiring language, the developing child does not just imitate or speak a garbled version of adult language. Children actually gather information from language they hear. Then they automatically begin to form hypotheses about how language is created. (For example, English-speaking children notice that "s" signifies plural.) Finally, they test out their hypotheses by trying new words and sounds, some of which are not a part of adult language at all. (You have probably heard a child say "mouses" or "mices.") All children everywhere apparently use tongue positions and breath control for speaking, use subjects and predicates for expressing ideas, and ask questions or give commands. These language characteristics are universal.

Figure 2–2 EXAMPLES OF MAXI-MILESTONES

1. *Awareness of Sensations.* Stops crying when picked up or rocked. Visually recognizes parents. Turns head to sound. Enjoys range of foods but expresses preference. Dislikes visit to doctor because it reminds him of previous injections. Recognizes food by cooking odors.

2. *Balance and Big Movements.* Rolls over. Sits. Crawls. Stands. Walks. Rides a tricycle. Catches a ball.

3. *Dexterity and Hand/Eye Coordination.* Plays with feet. Plays pat-a-cake. Scribbles. Eats with utensils. Prints name. Manipulates video games with dexterity. Ties bow.

4. *Vision.* Follows movement with eyes. Pats pictures named in book. Matches, then later names, colors.

5. *Space/Time Awareness.* Plays peekaboo and searches for lost toy (i.e., understands "out of sight" concept). Knows approximately when his favorite TV show comes on. Understands morning, afternoon, and evening.

6. *Personality/Socialization.* Smiles responsively. Responds differently to familiar people versus strangers. Says "no" often, sometimes even when means yes. Realizes own sex and that of others. Understands and cooperates with rules of simple games.

7. *Language.* Says first word. Uses phrases and gestures. Can tell story of recent event. Asks questions; says "why" often. Converses clearly and with complex sentence structure.

8. *Imagination/Creativity.* Imitates bye-bye and baby-so-big. Plays trucks, house, tea party. Sings. Invents fantasies (magical thinking). Draws a picture. Tells or acts out simple stories based on books or personal past experience.

The child also has involuntary reflexes and motor reactions that automatically dominate movements during certain periods of the earliest weeks and months. Examples you have probably noticed are the rooting and sucking reflexes that are activated each time an infant's mouth touches a new surface. When the side of his mouth is touched, he will turn his head, open his mouth, and make sucking movements with his lips and tongue, whether or not the object touched is a food source. These reflexes are clearly essential for survival in early infancy. However, they diminish in importance as the child's head control improves so that he can seek food sources with more discrimination. By the toddler years, these reflexes no longer occur, although the child retains the ability to purposefully suck on something when it is appropriate.

Other movement reflexes emerge at just the right time to allow new big-movement capabilities to evolve. During the early months, a variety of automatic movements temporarily dominate. These help to develop and distribute muscle tone and to position his body correctly for developing sitting, standing, and walking. Then they become a less powerful influence so that more mature movements can dominate the baby's actions, allowing him to develop more flexible, purposeful movement responses.

In summary, it can be observed that automatic factors spontaneously encourage the developing child to blossom in much the same way that a healthy flower automatically presses its new shoots up from under the dark earth in springtime. The prewiring encourages the flower's leaves to expand and its petals to unfold gently, one by one, until full bloom is achieved.

IMPORTANCE OF THE ENVIRONMENT

Just as weather and soil conditions encourage or stunt the growth of a new flower, the play environment and nurturing skills surrounding the developing youngster foster or slow down this unfolding process. We know that affection and successful play experiences motivate the child to try new accomplishments. The more things the child is involved in doing—the more positive experiences he has—the more likely he is to accumulate new capabilities.

You cannot predict when the first step will come as a result of reflexes that have worked together, but you should provide plenty of safe space for moving around. Things to hold onto for support while cruising can be provided, as well as toys to motivate walking a few steps to attain an enjoyable play experience. A caretaker can be interested in and pleased with the child's accomplishment, smiling and complimenting him for each step.

Nurturing adults can, in these ways, provide a safe playing and growing environment of appropriate stimuli and social rewards to foster growth and learning. They can also provide toys that are particularly suitable for encouraging a child to acquire new milestones. (See criteria in Chapter 3, "Toy Tips.")

CAUTION: MATCH EXPECTATIONS TO THE CHILD

We will point out in this book many ways that adults can enhance the learning process by encouraging a child to find more challenging and interesting uses for his toys. *However*, it is very important to refrain from trying to push a child ahead to achieve goals before he is ready. The child will quickly feel the emotional pressure, which will take its toll. We do not recommend creating unhealthy stress from a prodding environment that tries to push too hard and too fast toward higher and higher goals and skill levels. Avoid placing unrealistic expectations on a child that are beyond his genetic endowment, beyond the best his inherited strengths and shortcomings can realistically allow him to learn at his age. We also do not recommend overstimulating a child or stifling his creativity and initiative.

Another reason to avoid presenting toys or pushing for skill levels too soon is that a child is likely to lose interest in the activity. Then later, at a more appropriate age, he will not be willing to risk new frustration or failure with the same toy or activity.

On the other hand, it is important not to deprive a child by providing a barren and unrewarding environment. Follow the child's lead in play with toys.

Only after lengthy experimentation by the child himself should the caretaker gently try to draw him into active new exploration, expanding or enhancing the child's own use of a toy. Ideally, we suggest providing surroundings that allow the child freedom to choose from a variety of interesting and stimulating play experiences, with lots of hugs, words of praise, and smiles. Maintain a playful attitude that helps create the security of an atmosphere of fun and acceptance.

In this book, we point out developmental sequences in which children usually acquire new competencies. We do so to help define the role of toys in development. In the text, we only allude to specific ages because the range of normal is wide and we want to de-emphasize exact timetables. Children are unique individuals. Each has his own novel timing that does not always agree with developmental charts. Some deviation from the usual sequence or rate of acquiring new maxi- or mini-milestones is perfectly normal. If you notice a marked disparity between a child's behavior and the age guidelines described in this book, we suggest you advise parents to consult their pediatricians or other pediatric specialists.

3

TOY TIPS

The ultimate goal in selecting appropriate toys is to bring pleasure and growth to children. Toys are an expensive investment, but they are an essential part of childhood and a necessity for preschool educational settings. We will review general criteria for toy selection, as well as information about their storage and use. The intent is to enhance both your skills as a knowledgeable and discriminating consumer in the toy marketplace, and your insight and adaptability in the use of toys in your play environment.

ORGANIZING A PLAN FOR TOY SELECTION

Whether you are selecting toys for one child, a day-care center, or a nursery school, it is a good idea to organize a plan. Provide equipment that safely enriches and promotes each facet of child development. Arrange your investment in the play environment so that it considers both long-term and short-term financial commitments.

Toy catalogs and store displays present toys attractively, but it is important to analyze each toy carefully. The criteria you use in making your final toy selections reflect the philosophy of your facility and your knowledge of both toys and child development.

Toys should be available to foster development in all the eight aspects of child development that are presented in Chapter 1. In addition, you will want to have toys that provide play experiences that are varied and pleasurable. This will motivate an increased interest span for play that develops each of the eight aspects mentioned. Examples of good quality toys are presented in chart form at the end of each age chapter (4 through 6). The charts emphasize not only the eight aspects but also the ten play categories listed in Figure 3–1.

Design your record-keeping so that your toy inventory is carefully documented. Include toys owned, a repair record (to help plan future purchases), and long-range plans for additional purchases as space and income permit. If it helps you, use the ten play categories and the eight aspects of child development as a cross-reference on whether your toy supplies cover a wide gamut of criteria.

PLAY VALUE AND ADAPTABILITY OF TOYS

Toys must be intriguing enough to attract and hold children's attention for perfecting skills that are difficult or newly emerging. In addition, they should delight youngsters as they broaden capability levels in areas that already show advanced skill or avid interest. The qualities of a toy should provide *the* challenge that allows a child to explore, strive, and succeed without undue discouragement. Toys should be attractive, appealing, and fun *for children*. Avoid the temptation to buy toys that appeal more to adults.

Figure 3–1 TEN PLAY CATEGORIES REPRESENTED IN TOY CHARTS

1. Arts and crafts

2. Big equipment

3. Books

4. Construction

5. Games

6. Imitative playthings

7. Manipulative

8. Musical/listening

9. Riding

10. Water play

Diversity. Certain toys are particularly suitable to a wide range of happy play experiences. Examples would be large outdoor climbing equipment and the contents of costume boxes.

Be aware of the many personality differences among children before you make a purchase. Recognize that some children are energetic strivers who thrive on novelty, big movements, and noise. Others are quiet thinkers who prefer to manipulate intricate pieces and can delay gratification for long periods of time. In your toy selection, prepare for fostering children's natural personality tendencies as well as for helping promote a balance in other areas of social development, if needed. Remember that even noisy strivers need quiet time alone. The silent plodder or timid tyke can be stimulated to enjoy active playtime with friends if the right toys are available. Also consider children's intellectual needs, natural talents, and interests. Plan to have toys at all levels to avoid frustration while providing challenge and encouraging diversified play.

Complexity. Some toys (like a rattle or a tiny tricycle) are appropriate for children of a particular age. Other toys are suitable for children of many ages. These are more open-ended toys that can be used many ways rather than just one "right" way. They will withstand the test of time and will retain their appeal. At each age, the child's approach to and use of the toy will change as she achieves higher levels of motor development, perceptual and spatial awareness, socialization, language skills, and imagination.

In Figures 3–2 and 3–3 are examples of toys with lasting play value for children of the ages covered in this book. These toys continue to help the child perfect skills previously learned, while also adding new enjoyment and competencies.

When considering play value for placing toys in areas appropriate to a particular age group, recognize that toys should be carefully graded in their degree of challenge and stimulation. A coloring book with busy pictures may encourage a five-year-old to color carefully, using a charming variety of happy colors. However, the same picture will probably confuse and discourage the novice three-and-one-half-year old, who may cope by scribbling randomly in wide strokes across the page with a single crayon, realizing as she does so that her picture doesn't look good. Instead, choose for the younger child colorful, large, blank paper that encourages successful creative expression with crayons, paints, or felt tipped markers. For the four-year-old, you could find a coloring book with large, single-design pictures on each page—like a football or an ice cream cone. Then her wide strokes will come closer to staying within the lines, and she will be proud to display her successful efforts to visiting parents.

Staff members should be made aware of the location of toys and books for all ages so that they can easily find an appropriate activity in another room if needed by a particularly advanced or delayed youngster. If a child seems frustrated by futile attempts to play with a toy that is too advanced for her, try to avoid her playing with it until she is older. Put it out of reach or in another room if other children in her group are not using it. Avoid having her remember

Figure 3–2 A COLORFUL BALL HAS LASTING PLAY VALUE

Up to four months: Visually regards the colorful object (place it to the side of a newborn, and 6 to 8 inches from her face), and tracks it with her eyes if it moves slowly in close proximity to her. Ball encourages eyes to move across her midline if it rolls sideways in front of her. Learns head control as she turns to watch ball move, especially in prone position (on her tummy).

Four to eight months: Reaches for the ball, and hands come together to play with it (bilateral hand use). Tries a palmar grasp and begins to integrate the feel of roundness. Begins to look for the ball if it is hidden and becomes frustrated because the ball moves away when she tries to get it. Shifts weight, rotates trunk, and improves sitting balance as she plays, sometimes moving her hands across her midline.

Eight months to one year: Crawls after the ball. Delights in a chase-and-retrieve ball game with adult or older child, demonstrating her growing trust of consistency in both the ball's movements and the actions of other people who are significant in her life.

One to two years: Enjoys putting the ball into and out of a box or basket, practicing voluntary release as she drops it. Plays roll-and-catch with another person, often while gesturing and verbally interacting animatedly. Recognizes and names "ball." Begins to integrate spatial and distance concepts as the ball moves and as she moves toward its changing positions. Practices standing balance by adjusting her posture to stoop or run to play with the ball.

Two to three years: Though she parallel-plays with two or three children of her own sex, she prefers to maintain her own autonomy by carrying her ball and playing catch with an adult since she is unlikely to share it with a child. Has developed sufficient balance and coordination to be able to kick the ball when asked.

Three to four years: Moves skillfully to play with the ball, kneeling and squatting as needed. Begins to shift her weight to throw the ball, but catches only with arms extended.

Four to five years: Bounces the ball awkwardly with two hands, and now catches with arms flexed. Throws overhead, purposefully motor planning her movements and coordinating eyes and hands to accurately hit a close target.

Five years: Tosses the ball in the air, and can sometimes catch it after one bounce. Bounces ball one or two times with preferred hand. Talks delightedly in full sentences while planning rules for simple ball games with friends. Names all the ball's colors and its geometric shape decorations.

Figure 3–3 COLORED BLOCKS HAVE LASTING PLAY VALUE

Six to eight months: As she grasps, mouths, and releases blocks, baby develops hand/mouth and hand/eye coordination, and sensations of squareness. Moves toward a tower or arrangement of blocks you have built. Bangs blocks together with lots of noise, repeating this pleasurable action purposefully as she comes to realize she is responsible for the sensations it produces (cause/effect). Transfers blocks from one hand to the other, and now crosses her midline to place or retrieve them.

Eight months to one year: While sitting, she pushes the blocks as far as she can reach if they are in a small wheeled container, and later learns to pull them. Often drops the blocks and looks for them on the floor. Listening to verbal encouragement from care-givers, she plays hide-and-seek with the blocks under a cover, demonstrating her beginning awareness that the blocks are there even if she cannot see them (object permanence).

One to two years: Revels in piling blocks into and dumping them out of a container, unconsciously observing the spatial relationship between the size of the container and the size of the block. Carries blocks across the room or pushes/pulls them on the floor in a small wheeled container as she works on developing mobility. Holds blocks with thumbs/fingertips rather than in palms.

Two to three years: Although play with blocks is often random and without an organized plan, she can *imitate* (not copy) your three-block train or two-block tower, thus beginning to demonstrate sequencing and integration of visual perceptual skills. Sometimes names her own unplanned structures.

Three to four years: With emerging imagination, she creates a variety of original structures and designs. Waits her turn and shares her blocks with playmates.

Four to five years: With more confidence and purposefulness, she creates her building plan and shows great satisfaction after carrying it out. Perseveres even when her tower topples or her plan is unsuccessful.

Five years: Can accurately count ten blocks and copy or create three-dimensional complicated buildings in both vertical and horizontal planes. Usually uses both hands, with her preferred hand leading and the other helping (emerging hand dominance and accommodation).

it later as a "not-very-much-fun" toy so that she will gain maximum benefit from using it when she is more ready.

Success. Other considerations regarding the "just right" challenge of a toy's play value include the feelings of success and amount of self-expression encouraged. Some toys respond to a flip of a switch by doing everything for the child, leaving little to the imagination. Such a toy may make a child feel successful and may be fun to play with briefly, but the novelty soon wears off. An example is a windup toy that responds by performing a complex action. Such a toy could hold a child's interest during a parent interview in the school director's office. However, it is not likely to hold a child's long-term interest and will soon be pushed to the back of the toy shelf.

Toys that provide personal satisfaction and a feeling of accomplishment or involvement maintain the child's interest in a play activity without frustration. For a four-year-old dressed up as a beautiful lady, a glance in the mirror will reflect success in her costuming efforts. It will motivate a continuation of the dexterity necessary for buttoning, pinning, or buckling. That one mirror glance will encourage the big-movement planning necessary for donning or removing additional capes, jackets, or frilly pantaloons. The costume will inspire the imaginative spirit and social interaction that propels the pretend game forward with her friends.

One way to extend a child's interest in a toy is to furnish add-on pieces. These expand and upgrade the toy's complexity and encourage creativity. For example, construction toys often have wheels, roofs, or people figures that can be stored near the basic construction set to add inspiration to the play.

Subliminal Messages. One important factor regarding a toy's play value is the subconscious messages the toy may be imparting. Many adults avoid sexual stereotyping in toy selection by not always giving a girl dolls and tea sets or a boy trucks or sporting equipment. Many little girls automatically choose dolls over trucks, but some well-adjusted adult women do drive trucks. Many adult men like to cook as a hobby or profession. On the other hand, it has been observed that when girls play with a truck, they are likely to put a doll in it and play in a definite, confined space. A boy is more likely to play in a much wider area and may throw the toy and be rough. Follow the children's lead in matching toys to their interest and needs.

Weapons and other toys of violence present a particular problem to many adults who select toys for children. Advertising strategies and sometimes peer pressure encourage children to consider these toys favorably, but we have found that such toys promote aggressive, even hostile behaviors in children.

It is true that children need to feel able to express angry feelings at times as well as to feel in control of their own behavior. They also need opportunities for action and fantasy, and for feeling part of a group. However, we recommend that you keep to a minimum toys that foster vying for power, domination, and pretending injury to another. For example, most preschool centers do not allow children to bring in toy guns. While it is true that some children will still spontaneously use a pointed finger as a weapon, no weapon will be visible later to encourage a return to the game.

Perhaps you can gently influence the children in your care to reconsider whether they need to conform to violent play methods. If a child repeatedly gravitates toward domineering roles in imaginative play, guide her to assume more positive leadership roles or distract her to other, less aggressive forms of play. Help her learn to discriminate between assertiveness and aggressiveness.

One subliminal message that some preschool centers encourage is the valuing by parents of their child's play, creative endeavors, and "work space." When parents arrive for pick up, they are encouraged to spend a few minutes, letting their child demonstrate their school toys and activities. This also gives the adults time to switch roles and be parents again after their busy day of work or household responsibilities. Centers in or close to the workplace sometimes arrange for parents to come in and play with or nurse their children in the middle of the day. Many preschools, when they observe real milestones like baby's first step, prefer to make a general comment ("Your baby looks ready to walk soon"), then allow parents the pleasure of "discovering" that important first step at home. These thoughful little policies help maintain family continuity and give to the child the intuitive message that her play and development are valued by the parents.

TOY SAFETY

While play value is the single most important factor in a toy's appeal, safety features must take precedence during the final selection process. Read safety labels and heed recommendations. All children experience some falls and bruises, and most eat something at least once that they should not eat. However, you would never want the toys you purchase to be the direct cause of harm to a child. Government regulation and voluntary safety standards imposed by toy manufacturers in the 1970s have resulted in great strides toward identifying and eliminating hazardous toys. However, a large measure of the responsibility for toy safety still rests with professionals who work with children.

Tiny Pieces. Small pieces should **never** be included in toys for children under three since small parts can be swallowed or lodged in throats, nostrils, or ears. (One reason infants and young babies automatically put most things in their mouths is because the mouth provides one of baby's best discriminating abilities.) Eliminate small parts that might break off larger toys—for example, wheels, eyes, buttons, and ornaments—and check large toys carefully to be sure their parts are put together strongly.

Check teethers and squeeze toys especially. Look for small parts that could become either separated or compressed so small that they could block the baby's air passages. Pacifiers should be made in one piece, and it is important not to use soft toys that allow a small child to bite off a piece. Even some of the old standard rattles shaped like a small telephone receiver or a dumbell have been found to be dangerous when babies accidently put them down their throats. Avoid toys that break by shattering when dropped from a height. Cute little rattles used as cake decorations at baby showers are nearly always too small to be safely given to a baby afterward. A toddler should always be prevented from running with a toy or a lollipop in her mouth to avoid a problem if she falls.

To eliminate questions about size, Toys To Grow On manufactures a measuring device called "No-Choke Testing Tube" that compares an item's size with that of a baby's mouth and trachea. It is available to toy manufacturers and parents (P.O. Box 17, Long Beach, CA 90801) and is listed in various toy catalogs for about $1.00.

Until recently, it was often difficult to verify whether a baby had swallowed small plastic toy parts. Now barium sulfate is available be to all toy manufacturers. If they add it during the manufacturing process, it makes the plastic radiopaque and allows it to be seen on an X-ray. You may wish to inquire about this feature when making purchases of plastic toys. Also inquire about potentially hazardous chemicals like nitrosamines in rubber products and DEHP in soft plastics. Toy manufacturers can choose not to use DEHP because of concern that it might be absorbed into a baby's mouth, and some companies substitute a safer chemical to make plastic soft. Pacifiers and soft plastic teething rings especially should not contain this substance. According to 1985 research by Herb Denenberg of WCAU-TV, Philadelphia, Rock-a-Stack® plastic donuts and Snap-lock® Beads, both by Fisher-Price®, and nipples by Gerber® and Evenflo,® and Playtex® pacifiers are among the products that contain no DEHP. Johnson & Johnson has stopped using it.

Suspended Toys. These toys can be dangerous if they are used too long. Avoid crib gyms when a baby begins to sit or gets on her hands and knees so that she will not get her neck caught on strings or her clothing entrapped in the wooden bar apparatus. Do not use toys with cords, ribbons, or strings that could become wrapped around a baby's neck, waist, wrist.

Other potential causes of strangulation or suffocation include uninflated or broken balloons and certain baby furniture. Injuries to children have dictated that slats on the sides of cribs should have no more than 2⅜ inches between them, and there should be no cutouts on the endboards or space between the mattress and endboards. New regulations state that no projection longer than ⅝ inch is allowed on any crib. Baby gates with wide accordion- or scissor-folded slats should be avoided because children's necks can become caught in the wooden folds. The old play enclosure made by encircling this kind of expandable gate is particularly lethal and is no longer made. Playpens made of mesh netting with holes of less than ¼ inch are recommended as a substitute.

Falls. Riding toys for toddlers should have wide, stable bases. As a baby rides on such toys, however, be aware that vision of floor obstacles may be limited, and the toy's widely spread feet may inadvertently slip over the edge of unprotected stairs. High chairs and baby swings should have crotch straps to prevent babies from slipping, and many have seat belts as well. Car seats must meet federal safety standards.

Sharp Points and Rough Edges. Toys with sharp points and rough edges should be avoided for children of all ages, especially young children. This includes wires inside of stuffed toys, which may become exposed with use. It also includes wood splinters and rough surfaces on exposed hardware, bolts, and screws.

Projectiles. Toys that are pointed or made of metal, such as darts, play bullets, or rockets should be forbidden in sporting or play equipment. These can, and often do, cause eye damage or other injury. Of course, darts for children should always have Velcro® or suction tips. Because such toys require constant supervision, we do not recommend them for young children.

Flammable Materials. Toys made of flammable materials are dangerous and hard to detect without putting a match to them before purchasing! However, the manufacturers can tell you if their toys are flameproof, and you may wish to inquire about this safety feature. Of course, it is important for the staff not to smoke or use matches near the children.

Electrical Toys. These toys should be treated cautiously. If you choose to make available a record player, tape recorder, or other piece of electrical equipment, be sure it remains permanently plugged in so that the preschooler will not be tempted to use the wall plug. Of course, electrical toys that heat pose a hazard that should be avoided for children under eight. Electrical outlet covers should be plugged into all exposed outlets.

Noisy Toys. Toys such as caps and guns that produce loud noises must now be labeled by the manufacturer if they produce a noise above a certain level. New research suggests they may cause damage to hearing—even to a developing fetus in a pregnant mother standing near the sound.

Secondhand Toys. Toys from thrift stores or parents' attics might have play appeal and an attractive price tag, but beware of concealed safety hazards before considering old toys as gifts or bargains. Older plastic toys probably will not be visible on an X-ray. Paint may not be lead-free to make it nontoxic, and cloth items may not be flame-resistant. Safety pointers may have been discarded along with the original packaging. Beware also of using hand-me-down cribs, door gate barriers, and accordion-folded play corrals that might not have modern safety dimensions or paint. Also be particularly cautious when selecting handcrafted toys whose creators may not be as familiar with potential hazards as are major toy manufacturers. All secondhand toys should be washed thoroughly with soap before being added to the play areas.

Safe Storage. Storage should be an important consideration. When children of several ages have access to your toy collection, be sure you are providing a safe environment. Store toys with tiny parts or long cords high enough so that babies cannot have access to them. Place heavy toys low enough so that older children will not be injured when trying to remove them from their storage location.

Select toy shelves that cannot tip over if a young mountain climber tries to reach the top shelf. If you are particularly enamored of toy chests (we are not!), be certain yours has a support mechanism that will prevent the lid from slamming down on unsuspecting little heads, necks, or fingers. Modern toy chests do not close completely, so the chance of suffocation is reduced. Many preschool programs use plastic milk crates or colored utility baskets for storage instead.

Think carefully about protecting a developing explorer from poisons and hazardous wastes. Obviously you will want to store these high out of reach. Be particularly cautious about rodent-repellent food, mothballs, and cleaning supplies that might be mistaken for food treats. Valuables and other less dangerous forbidden objects may be stored in cabinets and drawers equipped with a safety latch. This makes them inaccessible to children but allows them to be opened easily by adults just far enough to squeeze a finger inside and depress the latch. Kiddie Locks also restrict children's access by providing a plastic clasp that curves through handles of double-door cabinets and refrigerators, fastening them together. Door access also can be limited by Kiddie Knobs, plastic sleeves that slip over doorknobs and require squeezing in addition to rotating. (These restricting devices are available from Belwith International, Ltd., 18071 Arenth Avenue, City of Industry, CA 91748. Telephone 818-965-5533.)

Health Concerns. To reduce the occurrence of illness, adults should be instructed to wash their hands frequently and keep their hands away from their mouths and eyes. Soapy water in the water-play table can be used to promote hand cleanliness. Children should always wash their hands before meals and snacks, and after using the bathroom. Play surfaces should be washed often.

Sick children should stay home or be separated from the group. For minor colds, boxes of tissues should be readily available with trash receptacles nearby. Be sure to sterilize or wash with soap a toy used by a sick child or sat upon by a child with soiled pants. If this is impossible in the middle of a busy day, remove the toy to a temporary storage basket and clean the contents at the end of the day. This precautionary step may also help cut down illness of staff, particularly those working with groups of children for the first time. Their resistance to childhood germs may be minimal at first.

One concern that has recently surfaced is the increased incidence of thrush reported in children who use pacifiers. The Candida organism that causes this yeast infection remains on the pacifier and can reinfect the baby. Always be sure to wash pacifiers carefully after each use, and be sure children do not inadvertently exchange them. If a baby has recurrent thrush, it is recommended that her pacifier be discarded or boiled.

Some preschool centers have discovered lice in their costume box if one youngster happens to be infected. They have treated the problem successfully by washing the costumes in soapy water and disinfecting the inside of the box. Check children's heads and the costumes periodically to rule out spreading this highly contagious condition.

Remind parents that many eye specialists advise that children should have had at least one, if not two, vision examinations before they start school. A three-year-old is not too young to be examined. Modern eye test materials do not require reading skills, letter recognition, or even language.

Language development is likely to be delayed if a partial loss of hearing is present in a child. Therefore, suggest to parents that they consult their doctor at once if you observe any of the following recurrent signs often seen in young children with hearing impairment:

1. Plateauing of how rapidly language is acquired.

2. Frequent requests for you to repeat your words or to increase the volume of tapes, records, or videos louder than others prefer.

3. A pronounced need for her to face you or watch you point when you are giving directions.

4. Generally unintelligible speech or dropping off end sounds in words by the third birthday.

If a child avoids play with nearly all playground equipment, even when encouraged, consider whether her development of big-movement skills is delayed. This could interfere with interpersonal relationships for the next several years since these relationships so often blossom on the playground. For a while, try dropping back to an easier level of play equipment—on the ground, or less movable. Give her time to develop skill and confidence at this level. Then slowly introduce her to the more advanced equipment again. If after several months she still cannot happily make it work for her and looks particularly awkward or precarious in her attempts, discuss your observations with her parents and gently suggest they ask their pediatrician or other pediatric health-care specialist to check her.

*Water Play. **Always carefully supervise children in water.*** If your program has a pool available periodically, take special precautions even for children who are swimmers or who have received instruction. Learning to swim is a safety precaution as well as a source of lifetime recreational enjoyment. However, make sure the children have a healthy respect for water safety. Children who swim early tend to take more chances and have less supervision than do other children. Also be aware that infants repeatedly dunked in a swimming pool for "fun" or instruction may swallow more water than is good for them. Water intoxication, a condition known as hyponatremia, or salt dilution, may result.

Also be cautious about watching children engaging in nonswimming activities around water, such as fishing, wading, walking on rocks, and skipping stones across creeks. A sudden dunking may accompany one false step.

Never allow inflatable water toys to serve as life preservers for nonswimming children. They tend to float away, support the child in an *inverted* position, or leak air unexpectedly. This can force a child to have to fend for herself, sometimes in water over her head or at least deep enough to be a hazard. Real life preservers are individual flotation devices that fasten securely around the torso and assure upright floating.

Other Safety Considerations. Kiddie Bumpers (available from Belwith International) fit over sharp corners of furniture or counters and may help prevent bumps and bruises. Kindergard makes a Child Protection Kit which contains kitchen cabinet latches, outlet plug covers, and cushion strips to cover sharp corners and edges. Order item 520 from Kindergard Corporation, Dallas, TX 75234.

White paste is a safe substitute for rubber cement and airplane glue, which are known to have noxious fumes. Many preschool centers prefer to keep the temperature of the water heater moderate so that children cannot be accidently scalded by tap water. Further information about toy safety is listed in Figure 3–4.

We have included these safety tips not to scare you, but to heighten your awareness of your legal responsibilities in safeguarding the children in your care. Act on the precautions mentioned here and notice new warnings as they come out in professional publications, newspapers, and magazines. However, let your caution be unobtrusive. Enjoy your time with the children, and do not superimpose any anxiety onto them. First make the play environment as safe as possible, and then let them happily explore their world and their toys.

COST VERSUS QUALITY

Toy construction is an important consideration. Look for sturdy, durable toys suitable for rough, enthusiastic handling. The quality of how a toy or piece of play equipment was manufactured will have a large impact on its ability to stand up against weather and many years of play by children of all ages. Poorly constructed toys are frustrating when they do not work right, and they are not much fun when they are sitting on the repair bench. They may be dangerous as well. If small pieces are an intended factor in a toy's construction, keep in mind the safety considerations mentioned earlier, as well as storage policies that will prevent the frustration of lost parts (see storage section below).

Materials. Toys made of hardwoods like oak and hickory that have been thoroughly varnished or painted tend to last well through the years. They can be

Figure 3–4 SOURCES OF TOY SAFETY INFORMATION

Toy Quality and Safety Report (Revised annually)
(Lists recommendations regarding best and worst toys.)
Published by:
Consumer Affairs Committee of Americans
for Democratic Action
1511 K Street—Suite 941
Washington, DC 20005
202-638-6447

U.S. Consumer Product Safety Commission (CPSC)
(Founded in 1973)
5401 Westbard Avenue
Bethesda, MD 20207
301-492-6550

National Safety Council
Public Relations Department
444 North Michigan Avenue
Chicago, IL 60611
312-527-4800

Arts Hazards Information Center
Center for Safety in the Arts
5 Beekman Street—Suite 1030
New York, NY 10038
212-227-6220

refinished periodically. Avoid leaving them out in the rain unless their finish is specifically intended to resist water.

In plastic toys, look for strength, regardless of whether the material is pliable or firm. Beware of the fact that some soft plastics can be chewed or dented by young babies, and some firm plastics are brittle in exuberant little hands. Sturdiness of a toy's joints is also important because soft joints are susceptible to breaking with repeated bending, and firm ones must be well constructed in order to withstand heavy pressure during play. Inflatable toys are likely to be punctured at least once in their lifetime. Ask for a good mending kit to accompany such toys even if you have to purchase one separately.

In metal toys, select firm, heavy construction and good quality, smooth finish. Examine potential stress points carefully before making purchases because toys may break and leave jagged or sharp edges that can be dangerous. In addition, remember that metal toys rust if left outdoors.

Some toys are made of unusual or interesting textures, for example, fuzzy-cloth building blocks or infant toys with rounded plastic spines. This adds interest to the play, and texture can be an excellent feature as long as it does not add frustration. (Do the building blocks stack without falling over often?)

For very young children, look for reading materials that are chew-proof (cloth with lead-free paint), drool-proof (cloth or sturdy plastic), or wrinkle-proof (no-iron cloth, sturdy plastic or plasticized cardboard).

Cost. Once you have evaluated a toy's safety, construction, and play value (considering immediate enjoyment and adaptability through the years), it is usually necessary to weigh these factors against cost before making a final decision. Do not allow cost to be the only or the primary consideration. Toys intended to last for years, through many levels of child development, are not short-term investments.

If your budget is limited, major purchases can be augmented with less expensive toys intended for short-term or seasonal use. Occasionally discount outlets or other stores will market last year's style of a well-made toy at a bargain price. Be sure the quality of low-budget toys is not so compromised that play value is restricted. Cheaply made toys are not a bargain, since their survival rate will be short.

Try adding some carefully selected, clean, sturdy, secondhand toys to your toy collection. (However, remember the warnings mentioned under "Secondhand Toys.") Parents or neighbors may be glad to cooperate with your search for playthings by raiding their homes and attics. In addition to toys, they may turn up pans and measuring utensils for your kitchen play area and clothes to encourage creative dress-up play. Watch out for high-heeled shoes because of twisted ankles or falls. Another good source of inexpensive playthings is a neighborhood garage sale or a nearby thrift shop. Secondhand playthings should be investigated carefully for loose, fragile, or missing parts before purchasing.

Whether you choose to invest in costly or in modestly priced toys, be discriminating and careful about their care. Elegant stuffed toys may make a good impression on parents as they shop around for a day-care center or a nursery, but they are impractical for everyday use in a preschool setting. Display the more fragile plush animals or dolls on shelves until children are old enough to play creatively and socially with them without damage that is out of proportion to the play value gained. When infants are in the mouthing stage or are burping up food often, use washable toys or dolls.

Whatever the construction material, gently encourage a child to treat toys with care (for example, reading books are not for tearing or scribbling; metal trucks cannot be left out in the rain). This helps to instill in the child a respect and responsibility for caring for personal belongings of their own and of others throughout childhood and into the adult years. On the other hand, do not expect a child to compensate for poorly constructed toys or for toys designed for older children's more dextrous fingers. Play should be as unencumbered and spontaneous as possible. The construction of the toy itself should not present a barrier.

Fund-raising. You may choose to schedule one or more special events to raise money needed for establishing a toy collection or adding large pieces of equipment. Such events increase public awareness of your center and the services it provides. (If your center, because of its location, draws children entirely from one workplace, general community advertising is not necessary. Such work-related locations are increasing in numbers as employers recognize the need for promoting family consistency and offering parents the opportunity to spend time with their children in the middle of the day.)

Suggestions for fund-raising events that might benefit your program are listed in Figures 3–5 and 3–6. Group special events allow teachers and parents to mingle and socialize while raising money. Some other activities listed require less involvement by large numbers of parents, an advantage if your center has difficulty eliciting parent participation.

Some centers promote contributions through annual donations or from a phantom fair or tea party (no event really takes place, but tickets are sold as though a real event were happening). Others celebrate a special holiday by having children or adults bring gifts of toys or other small necessary equipment for the school to keep. This could easily be combined with a party.

ORGANIZING TOY STORAGE AND THE PLAY ENVIRONMENT

Create a plan for toy storage, just as you did for organizing the purchase of toys in the first place. In general, the methods you use will give children guidelines for helping them to keep their own personal spaces in order and to appropriately control their environment.

Figure 3–5 FUND-RAISING SALES TO BE ORGANIZED THROUGH PARENT GROUP OR BOARD

1. Garage sale, rummage sale, or flea market. This project has no overhead. Unsold valuable items can be marketed later through consignment at thrift shops.

2. Recycling. (Gather and sell aluminum, glass, paper, etc.)

3. Children's clothing exchange.

4. Auction of objects and/or professional services.

5. Bake sale in public location, on election day or other public gathering.

6. Toy and/or book sale. Use a specific toy distributor, such as Discovery Toys, or a local store willing to bring merchandise to your location and share the proceeds. Or arrange a special sale event, perhaps with an author or book authority at the store with parents, staff, and the public invited.

7. Sell items that can be easily distributed by parents, e.g., flower bulbs to beautify the area, seeds or plants, greeting cards, magazines, or light bulbs. Or you may raffle valuable donated or purchased items.

Figure 3–6 GROUP EVENTS TO RAISE FUNDS FOR
PURCHASE OF PLAY EQUIPMENT

1. Covered-dish supper followed by entertainment

2. Performance by children

3. Show put on by parents and teachers

4. Professional lecture by staff member, parent, or guest

5. Short course or adult study group on problems shared by parents

6. Dinner dance, restaurant luncheon, or brunch

7. Wine-and-cheese party

8. Gourmet dinner in elegant house

9. "Secret gardens" or house tours

10. Fair

11. Group discount for special events (easy to organize), e.g., sporting event, theater night, boat ride, ice skating, circus, or movie night

ORGANIZING A PLAN

Neatness. Provide uncluttered storage space. Help the youngsters learn to place toys neatly back in their special spots. Encourage them to carry and stack efficiently, and to finish cleanup quickly and pleasantly. As they begin to develop habits of orderliness, they will be encouraged to carry over into adulthood attitudes and behaviors that will foster efficient, well-organized work habits and daily living skills. Roommates, spouses, and employers often prefer a neat person rather than an untidy or disorganized one. Your example in the very earliest days of both helping them to store their personal belongings and for caring for your own possessions will help set the stage for an organized adult.

Of course, we are not promoting compulsive, fastidious, neat-as-a-pin order that interferes with the freedom of the play experience or that inhibits an adult from living happily with another person. However, we suggest that it is a good rule of thumb to encourage children to put everything back in its place when play is finished.

It is especially important for rooms to look relatively straightened up when it is time to go home. If everybody helps with the cleanup, whether they were involved at a specific play area or not, children will choose activities without being inhibited by cleanup restrictions and will learn to cooperate and share responsibilities.

One practice that promotes orderly care of personal space is a separate cubby for each child, with her name or picture of her choice proudly displayed.

She knows this is her very own spot to safely store her belongings. In many preschools, this cubby and the area around it also provide a space she can go to if she needs time out.

In your storage areas, keep some toys temporarily put away so that they will seem novel when presented later, especially to young children. Seasonal toys lend themselves well to this plan.

Many preschool settings keep large or out-of-season toys and equipment in closets or atop high storage units. If your storage is limited, try suspending equipment in a mesh hammock high above a play area. Be sure it is accessible to adults by stepstool or rope pulley.

Cleanup. Use toy cleanup to help develop time concepts. Putting toys away also helps a developing toddler or preschooler structure her time so that one activity has an ending, a noticeable conclusion, before she begins the next activity. This approach helps prevent the scattered, poorly goal-directed approach to time that characterizes some adults' lives.

Containers. Store toys and their small parts carefully. Organized storage can help prevent the frustration for the child of trying to carry out a play plan when pieces or whole toys are lost. Toys with numerous parts should be stored so that all their pieces are together, preferably in their original containers that show clear labeling of the contents. If no container is provided with the toy, create one. See-through plastic containers let children see the contents. Or try shoe-boxes stacked with the contents labeled neatly on the end in words or pictures cut out or drawn by the children so that they can "read" them. You could make it easier for little hands to carry and store medium-sized toy pieces by putting them in buckets made of clean, gallon milk-carton bottoms with rope handles.

Containers for small parts and pieces can help teach not only organizational skills but also how to classify by color, size, shape, or purpose, a necessary skill for math and reading readiness. Such categorization is useful in helping children learn the discriminating features and common characteristics of the vast array of objects with which they come in contact. Here are some examples: Small family figures may rest in one large drawer, while farm animals are located in another, and unused dollhouse furniture is located in still another. Jigsaw puzzle boards (each with all the pieces intact) may be stacked up neatly on one shelf or in a puzzle rack, while coloring books, blank paper, and boxed crayons may be together in one plastic box or another. Tonka® trucks and cars for the outdoors may be lined up together in one part of the closet, while jump ropes and balls may be in another.

Shelves. Use shelves rather than a toy box. Toy boxes tend to be a dumping ground for miscellaneous toys. They prevent the child from observing that there is a plan for storage. If cost is a major consideration, be creative. Use wood planks to create low shelves on a sturdy base of bricks or cinderblocks. Or buy unpainted or secondhand shelves. Acquire cardboard boxes that are discarded by business owners. These can be laid on their sides so that open edges face out into the room, providing two levels of shelf space for lightweight toys. Boxes used by photocopy and printing businesses to transport paper are at least moderately strong and come in uniform sizes.

Play locations. Design special play areas for specific activities. The size of each area depends upon the total space available and the priorities for use. The following are a few suggestions that children seem to enjoy:

1. An art room or paint corner with easels permanently set up and storage for large paper, jugs of liquid tempera, pastels, colored pencils and crayons, clay, Play Doh®, stencils, and other art materials. A water/sand table should also be available. Tables and chairs and a sink nearby for cleanup would allow this area to be used at another time for snacks or meals.

2. A dramatic or imaginative play area with a small table and chairs, play sink, stove, refrigerator, telephone, sweeper, broom, pewter dishes, pots and pans, drawers, dolls, doll beds and clothes, and stuffed toys. This section or one next to it should include a box of costumes and a large shatterproof mirror.

3. A wooden-block area should have the many various sizes and shapes clearly marked on the shelves for easy storage. Floor space should be large and open enough for creating "architectural masterpieces." You may want to place blocks near other imaginative play areas so that toys can be used together.

4. Other construction toys with small pieces could be housed in a separate spot. Legos®, Lincoln Logs®, Mega Bloks®, and other manipulatives, all in separate boxes, should be kept near open floor space and/or tables and chairs for working.

5. A music area could provide a piano or guitar, rhythm band instruments, a record player, records, tape recorder, and tapes.

6. Puzzle tables and racks contain form puzzles for the younger children, and/or interlocking wooden puzzles for the older ones.

7. Story-telling and reading time can be comfortable on a rug with books available on a nearby rack. Book covers should be visible for easy selection at children's eye level. Single-story books (rather than anthologies) will be light enough for little folks to manage. In this popular gathering place, when children are independently looking at books, they may enjoy the comfort of pillows; beanbag chairs; cuddly, soft sitting places; or small chairs with fuzzy covers fitted over the backs. Such pleasant sensory experiences may prolong the time children spend looking at books.

8. A pet corner, a bird feeder outside the window, and a fish tank are always fascinating. The budding little zoologists also enjoy visiting rabbits, puppies, or kittens.

9. A quiet place for resting is essential and should have nesting cots or small individual rugs that are stored until needed, as well as blankets and perhaps even a few personal "blankies."

10. For the toddlers and older infants, small play environments made of plastic, wood, or plastic-covered foam can provide slides, doorways, stairs, bolsters, and ramps.

11. Enclosed outdoor play space could include a paved area for tricycles, wagons, and other riding toys; a place for climbing, sliding, and swinging equipment; another for a large covered sandbox; and possibly one for a gently inclined ramp for four-wheeled scooters and/or easy movement of equipment to and from covered storage nearby.

ORDERING TOYS

You may wish to look at the catalogs of the companies listed below for ideas to supplement your toy-purchasing plan. Most of these catalogs are represented at least once among the toys that appear in the toy charts in this book. Other selections for the toy charts were made from national chains and from individually owned toy stores.

ABC School Supply, Inc.
6500 Peachtree Industrial Blvd.
P.O. Box 4750
Norcross, GA 30091

Animal Town
P.O. Box 2002
Santa Barbara, CA 93120

Bear Creek Company
Sugar Pine Road
Medford, OR 97501

Childcraft Education Corp.
20 Kilmer Road
Edison, NJ 08818

Community Playthings
33 Loring Drive
Framingham, MA 01710

Discovery Toys
2530 Arnold Drive
Suite 400
Martinez, CA 94553

Educational and Fun, Ltd.
228 Lancaster Avenue
Frazer, PA 19355

Fisher-Price Catalog
Dept. IPL
636 Girard Ave.
East Aurora, CA 14052

Growing Child Playthings
22 N. 2nd St.
P.O. Box 101
Lafayette, IN 47902

Holcomb's Educational Materials
3205 Harvard Ave.
Cleveland, OH 44105

Johnson & Johnson Baby
Products Co.
Childs Development Division
Grandview Road
Skillman, NJ 08558

Kaplan School Supply Corp.
1310 Lewisville-Clemons Road
Lewisville, NC 27023

Kiddicraft
International Playthings, Inc.
151 Forest Street
Montclair, NJ 07042

Lakeshore Curriculum Materials, Co.
2695 E. Dominguez Street
P.O. Box 6261
Carson, CA 90749

Toys To Grow On
P.O. Box 17
Long Beach, CA 90801

4

INFANT DEVELOPMENT, TOYS, AND ACTIVITIES: BIRTH TO ONE YEAR

Figure 4–1 is an overview of the maxi-milestones most children achieve during infancy. It is divided into the eight aspects of growth and development we presented in earlier chapters so that you can visualize the whole picture, like a completed jigsaw puzzle.

Figure 4–1 MAXI-MILESTONES OF THE INFANT

AWARENESS OF SENSATIONS	BALANCE AND BIG MOVEMENTS	DEXTERITY AND HAND/EYE COORDINATION	VISION
Stops crying when picked up or rocked Visually recognizes parents Turns head to sound Accurately gets thumb into mouth Tolerates solid food Enjoys being bounced rhythmically	Rolls over Sits Crawls Stands Walks around while holding on	Grasps automatically Glances at objects in his hand Carries objects to mouth for exploring Transfers objects from one hand to the other Plays with feet Plays pat-a-cake Holds small objects with thumb opposite fingertips	Visually attracted to front view of faces Follows movement with eyes, even past middle of the body Both eyes together follow object moving in close to nose and away to arm's length Looks after an object that falls Pats pictures named in book

The milestones in the columns are progressive and occur in sequence from top to bottom as the child grows older. The activities listed in the columns overlap considerably, and the eight aspects all occur at the same time, although at different rates.

Figure 4–1 Continued

SPACE/TIME AWARENESS	PERSONALITY/ SOCIALIZATION	LANGUAGE	IMAGINATION/ CREATIVITY
Plays with hands and discovers his feet	Bonding developing with parents; beginning of basic trust	Attends to sounds and voices	Imitates facial expressions
Approximates accurate distance judgment for grasping near objects	Smiles responsively	Coos; later babbles	Pretends to drink from empty cup
Realizes there is a connection between string and attached toy, and pulls string	Responds differently to familiar people versus strangers	Makes razzing, "raspberry" sounds	Imitates bye-bye and baby-so-big
Recognizes danger of falling from heights	Hugs stuffed animals	Makes double syllable sounds: "ma-ma," "da-da," "pa-pa"	Bounces to music
Plays peek-a-boo and searches for lost toy (i.e., understands "out-of-sight" concept)	Plays alone with toys for brief periods	Gestures, points to communicate	
	Hands toy to adult, but expects it to be returned	Says first word	

Take time to study Figure 4–1 before proceeding. It shows the central core of the developmental information in the rest of this chapter, and will be an important scenario for you to keep in mind as you select toys for your center or guide children's play. Each puzzle piece in the figure is an important stepping stone preparing the way for the milestones that follow.

At the beginning of this chapter, we will take the puzzle apart and detail each of the columns individually. Following the discussion of each column will be "How to Help" suggestions for promoting growth in that aspect of development. You will notice that a few suggestions are repeated to remind you that they apply to more than one developmental aspect. At the end of the chapter is a toy chart listing examples of good toys and the aspects of development they stimulate.

AWARENESS OF SENSATIONS

Every bit of a baby's environment is potentially a growth experience. The baby is very much aware of sensations, first in a general sense and later with more discriminative understanding. As he learns to sort out sensations, he learns about himself and the world around him. He is continually using his senses for discovery.

We want to stimulate this active little bundle of sensory receptors who can already see, hear, taste, smell, feel, and touch, and knows when he has moved or been moved. But we want to stimulate in ways that help him learn. We do not want to overstimulate him by bombarding him with too many sensations all at once so that he does not have a chance to differentiate them. (Remember how exhausted you felt after a day at the fair with noise and music and lights and carnival rides and cotton candy?) We want to encourage the baby's recognition of particular sensations—lots of them, but modulated and tempered so that he can enjoy and learn from them.

Mini- and Maxi-Milestones of Sensory Awareness

Touch. You can see that the newborn likes your touches, pats, and hugs by the way he nuzzles his little face into your neck or calms down if he has been crying. He learns to love the feel of his bath. If he is too stimulated, he may turn his face away from you with a frown or pull away. His intense stares, smiles, and coos will tell you how much he is enjoying your touch.

As the first year progresses, some babies show that they seek and enjoy touch experiences. They will love the textured "feely" toys and take pleasure in fuzzy teddy bears. Other babies will not be huggers, and they will not stay on your lap after their bottle or explore the feel of your hair and clothing as some babies do. The difference between cuddly and uncuddly babies will often be maintained throughout the early years of life and sometimes even into adulthood.

Movement through Space. A baby shows you he is aware of being moved by startling or awakening if his bed is jarred abruptly. Or he may stop his crying and even smile when rocked in your arms or his coach. As the months pass, some parents may report to you that their babies respond differently to the movement of a car ride by calming or falling asleep. The older baby can tell you by his giggles and squeals when he is enjoying being held or tossed above your head or bounced on your knee.

All these movement experiences stimulate the vestibular system. This system receives, sorts, and transmits information about the head's movement through space and how the body should respond to it.

Touch, Taste, and Smell. Even a tiny baby can tell the difference between hot and cold, sweet and sour, or salty and bitter. He discriminates smells, too, and sometimes responds to strong foul smells by crying. He will quickly show you he knows if his food is at a temperature he's not used to or if it has a very new flavor.

Long before his first birthday, each baby in the infant room will show you clearly his preference from among the baby foods you offer him. For some new foods, one smell or one feel of a new lumpy food will be enough to tell him he wants no part of it!

Vision. Baby is fascinated by watching moving objects, and this motivates him to repeat play experiences that provide such an interesting sensory experience. As he gets older, you will observe that he recognizes the staff, his parents, and family members as soon as he sees them.

Hearing. Baby likes quiet sounds, voices, and music, and startles or cries at sudden loud noises. Soon you will see that he begins to turn his head to look in the direction of interesting sounds. The sound of another baby crying may set off a response of tears from many of the older members of the infant group.

Position/Movement of Body Parts. Baby loves to investigate his hands. He uses them to bring objects to his mouth by making an accurate position judgment. He begins to recognize how to repeat his arm and leg movements so that they stimulate into action the toys above his play space. He may even inch along the floor so that he can approach a favorite toy. You will notice when he first learns to judge his arm and finger movements well enough to get his thumb into his mouth on purpose. Some older babies love to bounce to music.

A fairly young baby demonstrates an alertness to new sensations by stopping what he is doing. As he gets older, he responds instead by excitedly moving his arms and legs.

Touch and Taste. Baby's mouthing of objects continues for many months. His mouth, lips, and tongue are his most discriminating areas for tactually exploring the size, shape, and texture of things. Later his hands and other skin surfaces of his body will learn to help with this exploring. Mouthing of toys also helps in two ways. It coordinates the mouth with the hands in preparation for the coordination of eyes with hands that will develop later, and it stimulates the gums, tongue, and the inside of the mouth in preparation for teething and for the mouth control necessary for chewing and talking.

When solid food is first presented, some babies have difficulty getting used to both the texture and the taste of it, but as he approaches his first birthday, you will see that he has learned to tolerate even lumpy foods.

The nurturing touch and handling adults provide help foster baby's general rate of development. By the time he is one, this growing and developing little miracle can incorporate and integrate sensations from dozens of sources at once, and he uses them for new learning.

 How to Help Develop Awareness of Sensations

- Dance with the babies, holding them in a horizontal position. Also stimulate babies by jiggling them up and down and sideways when they are upright. Even an occasional brief upside-down swish through the air is good vestibular stimulation for children who are not aversive to it. Be *sure* the head is supported during this stimulating movement through space.

- When they are awake, try letting babies rock themselves in a small hammock or a bouncing chair designed for infants. These motions provide vestibular stimulation and awareness of movement and may even have a calming effect.

- If you have an inconsolable infant in your nursery, try the Sleep Tight® device that attaches to the crib and simulates the vibration and sound of a moving car. It is available from Sleep Tight®, 5613 Mueller Road, St. Charles, MD 63301 (phone 1-800-662-6542). Parents have also soothed colicky babies with the tape-recorded sounds of a hair blower, fan, running water, and vacuum cleaner.

• During feeding time, holding and cuddling babies helps them feel comfortable with touch. Talk and sing to them. Your soft, pleasant voice grabs their attention and helps them learn about sounds. Your full face, with its contours, movements, and familiarity, captures their gaze and visual interest. The flavor, texture, and warmth of the milk provides delectable taste, smell, and touch sensations.

• Have some carpeting on the floor of the babies' room so that their hands, knees, and bodies will feel interesting textures as they crawl and move around on and off an area rug.

• If your center uses a wading pool or a water-play basin, trickle water on each baby's skin. Sprinkle him with a watering can or a plastic bottle with a spray or squirt top. (Avoid the face.) This pleasurable touch sensation helps acquaint a child with his body and can be the beginning of learning to enjoy showers later on.

• As babies get older, they can use bathtub toys to pour water on themselves and may begin to tolerate splashing or pouring water on their own faces. Water toys help them learn to discriminate the feel of wet and dry, warm and cool, light (empty) and heavy (filled).

• Wash the babies' faces gently after meals. The face is very sensitive to touch and especially to water on it unexpectedly.

• Try these tips during diapering, particularly with the less cuddly children if they will tolerate it. Emphasize firm rubdowns with a textured washcloth or oil or lotion. Apply firm, steady pressure briefly to arms, legs, back, and tummy to increase awareness of the body, and help babies enjoy this quieting, comforting touch. This deep pressure stimulates the touch/response system. Finish up with a light touch using powder, cornstarch, a gentle cloth, or fingertips.

• The babies' frequent choice of teething rings for play shows you they automatically recognize the importance of mouthing. Have plenty of teething rings, rattles, and other safe objects (firm and big enough not to be chewed or swallowed) available for chewing. Wash them often. Be cautious about using pacifiers all the time since they reduce the opportunity for both hand/mouth coordination and a variety of touch experiences. (See Chapter 3 for new questions about the safety of certain chemicals in soft vinyls and rubber in toys.)

• Provide mobiles, rattles, crib toys, stuffed animals, and manipulative toys with sounds, movement, color, and textures. But do not put out too many toys at once. For new sensory stimulation, exchange them every two or three weeks with others stored in the closet.

- Play games that involve bouncing babies on your knee or foot, or swinging them high into the air *as long as they are enjoying it.* Try "Ride a Cock Horse" or "This Is the Way the Gentleman Rides." These movements encourage vestibular stimulation and sensory awareness of motion. They help develop balance, muscle coordination, and muscle tone. If a baby seems fearful, decrease the extent of the movement or try it at another time. If he remains fearful a second or third time, it is important to discontinue the game.

BALANCE AND BIG MOVEMENTS

The newborn will learn more new movement skills in his first year than in any other year of his life. From being physically helpless, restricted to lying on his back or tummy, this amazing little creature will learn to maintain an erect position, able to balance on two feet. In the process, he will follow a sequence of prewired, reflexive responses that supply the basis for the postural muscle strength and tone he needs. They will help him learn to hold his head up, get onto his hands and knees, rotate into sitting and standing positions, and protect himself from falling. He will make lots of mistakes along the way. Eventually his approach, whether cautious or adventurous, will evolve into a realistic confidence in each new balance skill. This allows him to also try other coordination efforts in each position—reaching, propelling himself, and using two hands to play with toys.

Different generalizations have been applied to the way babies refine control of their movements. Many full-term babies seem to develop new movement capabilities in the area of the head first, then in the trunk and arms, and finally in the legs. This sequence is called "head-to-toe" or "cephalocaudad." In addition, movement control often appears to occur near the center of the body (proximal) before the hands are well controlled (a more distal part of the body). The more intricate dexterity can develop independently of the proximal stabilizing influence. However, the big movement capability that baby works so hard to perfect during the first year can help position the body to use the small movement skill to its greatest advantage.

Mini- and Maxi-Milestones of Balance and Big Movements

Baby's first major big-movement accomplishment will be holding his head up without support—first when he is held upright, then when he is prone (in a tummy position), and finally when he is being pulled from a supine (on his back) to a sitting position. On his belly, he learns to hold his head stable to look all around while resting his trunk weight on his forearms and later on his straightened arms. He begins to tolerate a little sideways leaning of his shoulders in these positions, using one hand to balance himself as he reaches forward or sideways to grab an enticing toy placed within his reach.

Meanwhile, he pushes himself over onto his back and learns to roll back again onto his tummy. He is learning to coordinate the muscles that can curl him up into a ball (flexion) with those that allow him to lie out straight and flat (extension). In time, he will use his new rotation skill to assist with getting himself into a sitting position. But first he learns to maintain a sitting position only when placed there by an adult. The stabilizing ability and the new shoulder movements he has learned on his tummy, as well as his strong head control, help him know how to maintain sitting. Finally, he carefully coordinates these stabilizing abilities with the trunk rotation necessary to get into a sitting position independently. How grown up he is beginning to look!

Baby probably has begun to propel himself by this time. He inches forward on his tummy or crawls on his hands and knees to reach toys across the room. Initially if the arms are more coordinated, baby's inching forward attempts might result in backward movement. Sometimes he may just rock back and forth on his hands and knees for a while, helping his arms, legs, and head learn to function independently of each other for more accurate control. Eventually he crawls with movements of one arm coordinated with movements of the opposite leg. This helps coordinate the two sides of his body for working together. It is a precursor of the smooth walk he will have as a school-age child and adult, with one arm swinging forward with each step of the opposite foot.

As baby's balance, weight shifting, and coordination skills continue to increase, he will be ready to sit on the floor without using his hands for support. His back will be straighter and his legs will be more extended than they were when he first learned to sit. Finally, he will pull himself into a standing position. Automatic protective arm movements emerge at this age to help him catch himself as he falls, but they do not prevent all the bumps and bruises that accompany these balance experiments. He often coordinates his two legs and his weight-shifting abilities for sideways cruising while holding on before he figures out how to coordinate his arms with his legs for sitting back down safely. Now this upright little person looks ready to use his big-movement skills to seek out new learning experiences—and he finds quite a bit of mischief along the way!

How to Help Develop Balance and Big Movements

- Allow babies freedom to move their heads themselves, but provide head support as needed until they can achieve it independently. As the neck becomes stronger, use toys to encourage looking forward and sideways from a prone (tummy-lying) position.

- Playing with hands and feet, and putting them in the mouth helps each baby begin to develop an awareness of his own body—where it begins and ends, what the parts of the body are, and how the parts relate to each other. Encourage this play in babies by (1) handing them toys, (2) putting applesauce or other tasty food on their hands, (3) putting brightly colored booties on their feet, or (4) making ankle rattles of loose elastic and jingle bells sewn on firmly with heavy thread.

- Suspend toys above babies in their cribs and playpens to encourage full arm and leg movements for reaching. (Remove these for safety when babies learn to sit or pull up on them.) Striking and swiping at suspended toys help develop awareness of the body, too.

- Provide plenty of time on the floor for exploration without the restrictions of cribs, playpen sides, or baby seats. Babies need to learn to move unencumbered and to try out every imaginable new body position and movement skill. For this reason, we also recommend avoiding the use of walkers, or at least limiting their use to very short periods. Let those little reflexes and balancing reactions develop unhindered so they can more efficiently prepare the infant for walking.

- As babies achieve new balance skills—for example, leaning on their forearms from a tummy position, or sitting, kneeling, or standing— use hand-held toys to help them learn to play while balancing (a difficult task at first). After they have learned to be stable in the new position, put the toys at a little distance—or even further—to motivate them to move around in the new balance position and gain even more skill and confidence.

- Place toys within reach but at arm's length to encourage full arm movements for reaching. Put some toys off to the side so that babies will be encouraged to turn their bodies in different ways. This turning (rotation) and increased flexibility prepare the way for crawling and getting themselves into sitting and standing positions.

- Put push-toys in front of novice crawlers to encourage forward movement. Eventually they will learn that they can support and move their bodies while pushing on their toys at the same time.

- Put toys on low tables or chairs if you have babies trying to master how to cruise around holding onto furniture or how to walk short distances independently. This encourages them to travel to reach the toys.

- If a baby is one of those early walkers who decides to be up on his feet before he has really had time to learn about playing on his hands and knees or in an independent sitting position, try these playthings to reintroduce the fun of playing on the floor: soft blocks, a 10- or 12-inch ball, play centers to crawl through, chairs and tables to crawl under. The crawling stage should not be bypassed.

DEXTERITY AND HAND/EYE COORDINATION

In one short year, the little newborn with random arm movements and automatic grasp will evolve into a competent and purposeful manipulator of small objects. To accomplish this, he will develop the interaction of the intricate hand muscles for accurate dexterity along with increasingly accurate eye control and arm movements. The resulting coordination of eyes and hands will form a basis of fine-motor skills that baby can use for play and feeding and for exploring his nearby environment.

Mini- and Maxi- Milestones of Hand/Eye Coordination

The newborn infant's awareness of deep pressure and touch as objects are placed in his palm sets off an automatic grasp reflex response. Most adults melt at the feel of the little hand curling around their index finger, and this exchange of touch sensations between infant and adult fosters the attachment between them. Baby also looks at visually attractive things and in a few weeks begins to watch and play with his hands. An interesting reflex exists at this stage for a short time. It is called the "asymmetrical tonic neck reflex." It automatically extends his arm out straight as he turns his head so that the hand is at just the right position to be seen in focus by the young baby's eyes. The other arm and leg bend a little at the elbow and knee. That is why it is called asymmetrical. This reflex occurs in contrast to the frequently symmetrical movements he makes with both hands flailing or reaching fairly equally at the same time.

Next the baby learns to look back and forth between an object and his hand, contemplating and "reading" the distance with his eyes but unable to connect his waving hand to the desired object. With delight, he eventually learns to bridge this gap and begins to explore and manipulate playthings with his hands, grasping at will and no longer accidentally. This may follow a period of scratching at an object by raking his fingers back and forth on the table or mat near it. This raking helps baby get more touch information about his finger movements, and he begins to differentiate the fingers from each other. He reaches for a toy now with increasing accuracy, visually guiding the hand to its target. He grasps the toy in his palm (palmar grasp), brings it to his mouth for manipulative exploration by the tongue and lips, and may bang it on the table or play surface for the fun of listening to its noise.

As baby learns to bring his two hands together in play, he becomes intrigued. He watches this new venture intently as he passes toys right in front of him from one hand to the other. This is the beginning of purposefully coordinating one side of the body with the other in independent, less symmetrical, or reflex-based movements. Soon baby begins to realize he can let go on purpose with one hand as the other grasps a toy. In no time at all he has figured out, to everyone else's despair, that he can drop a small object over the side of the playpen or high chair on purpose. He practices this newfound skill dozens of times, reveling in the attention it brings. Just remember how much he is learning about voluntary grasp and release as you pick up the toy for the umpteenth time.

More accurate manipulation follows, and he holds objects between his thumb and fingertips (pincer grasp), no longer in his palm. He holds a toy in each hand, often banging the two together, and has learned to reach across the midline of his body to pick things up. He loves to poke a finger into tiny spaces now, and this helps him learn to differentiate individual finger movements. Along with his newly developed dexterity comes enough eye- and arm-movement coordination so that he can accurately feed himself a firm vanilla cookie and even little Cheerios®.

 ### How to Help Develop Dexterity and Hand/Eye Coordination

- Provide plenty of colorful, attractive, and cheerfully noisy toys to be held in infants' hands and carried to their mouths. (Be sure the toys are large enough not to block the windpipe.) In time, this mouth and hand exploring prepares the way for the older babies' eyes to do such exploring *without* touching or feeling objects. This also helps babies learn accuracy in coordinating their hands with their eyes, and helps set the stage for prewriting skills that will develop later.

- Encourage babies to strike and swipe at the visually stimulating toys suspended above them. This helps them learn to measure the distance of their arm movements and to coordinate the accuracy of their visually directed hand movements.

- For older infants, provide toys that entice them to poke fingers into small safe places. This helps them learn to move each finger separately, and it increases their dexterity.

- Provide older babies with small toys (not small enough to be eaten) to hold in the tips of their fingers, especially between the thumb and index fingertip (pincer grasp). For occasional learning experiences, borrow from the toddler area small wooden people figures or empty wooden spools. Supervise carefully.

- When babies can tolerate chunky foods safely and comfortably without choking, encourage them to use this new pincer grasp to feed themselves small pieces of arrowroot cookies, crackers, and cereals. Later try slivers of fruits and cooked vegetables. This highly motivating activity also promotes hand/eye coordination skills.

VISION

Learning to use his sense of vision is a grand challenge for baby and involves far more than seeing. Before sight can become useful, baby must learn to actively search for and look at things. In addition, he must learn to compare what he sees with past experience so that he can understand the meaning of what he has seen.

Baby can see better at birth than doctors used to think he could, but he has almost no past experience for making comparisons. He also has wobbly head control that is not always helpful for directing his eyes to specific targets. By the time he is on his feet, he has learned not only to find interesting things to look at but also to remember what they look like even when they are not visible. Upon seeing a familiar toy, this process occurs: Baby imagines what it feels like, how it tastes (since he has probably mouthed it before during play), the sound it makes when shaken or dropped, how to get through space to reach it, and who in the room might be most likely to grab it away from him. This is the essence of vision—this comprehension of many senses working together to imagine or visualize something—and it is far broader than sight.

Mini- and Maxi-Milestones of Vision

The infant carefully watches the environment before he has enough motor coordination to purposefully interact with it. This intense looking lays the groundwork for the more complete learning that occurs as he later begins to touch, mouth, and physically manipulate things in his world. At first when he visually focuses on an object, his other movements decrease, and you can tell that he is concentrating. Only months later, as his coordination improves, do we notice a change in how he reacts to new visual stimuli—when an object catches his attention, frantic arm or leg movements occur. This action increases the likelihood of touching and learning from that environmental object.

Visual and motor skills interact during the first year to promote development of the child as a whole in other ways. Reflex-type reactions stimulated by sight help the head automatically bring itself back into a vertical position when he is tipped at an angle. These "optical-righting" reactions help baby adjust posture and muscle tone so that very early balance skills can develop. They also help baby consistently orient to being right side up, with vertical space as a point of reference from which to develop other concepts of spatial awareness. This righting reaction plus increasingly effective coordination of head and neck movements help baby purposefully turn his head to position his gaze where he wants it.

Even the newborn infant is selectively attentive. He perceives movement right away and also likes to look at novel things. He soon learns to distinguish tiny stripes from a plain surface. He becomes especially attracted to patterns that resemble a face, even if the "face" is upside-down or turned on its side. It is no wonder. Consider how much he relies on human adults for his very survival, and how many different views he sees of the faces so important to him.

Simple designs and facial representations that are contoured are more attractive to the infant than are flat surfaces. He also likes colorful things and strong visual contrasts like black and white. Bull's-eye designs catch his attention. As he begins a few months later to observe the distinctive features that differentiate between geometric shapes, three-dimensional representations are again easier for him to distinguish than are flat ones.

The infant begins to visually distinguish that objects can be near or far and also can be of different sizes. However, he cannot initially combine the two pieces of information to recognize that the appearance of size is related to the distance of the object.

He particularly notices things that move, and within a few months of his birth he learns to follow the arc of an object moving in front of him all the way from one side across the middle (midline) to the other side of him. The two eyes begin to work more cooperatively together for sighting by this time. Later in the first year, baby learns to follow an object that moves in close to his nose and then away to arm's length. By that time, his depth perception, operating very primitively earlier in his awareness of contours, becomes a little more astute. He begins to understand the danger of falling off elevated surfaces.

Baby's comprehension of the meaning of things he looks at continues to increase. In the early months, he squeals and waves his arms with delight when he sees his bottle or a favorite person. Later he figures out where to look for toys he drops and searches for toys he watches being hidden. His interest in books increases from just loving your attention and body warmth as you turn the pages with him on your lap to actually patting the pictures that represent familiar objects. By the time he sees his own birthday cake and candles for the first time, the *sight* excites him because he has developed the *vision* to comprehend the flavor and texture, the sound of the cheerful birthday song, and the air of anticipation of others at his family party, even though he doesn't yet understand birthdays.

 ## How to Help Develop Vision

- Your face is one of the most fascinating things for the tiny babies to view, so move around slowly while talking soothingly, and encourage babies' eyes to follow your face wherever it goes.

- Provide rattles, mobiles, and other playthings with face designs to catch babies' attention. Also use bull's-eye and geometric designs, and color contrasts (especially black and white).

- Hang visually stimulating toys above babies' heads for viewing when they are lying on their backs. Also put toys at the corners and sides of the cribs or playpens to encourage babies on their tummies to pick up their heads and chests and look all around.

- Hang near babies' play space a variety of small, colorful objects that move and make sounds to attract their attention. This encourages them to follow moving things with their eyes, to coordinate their two eyes together, and to use their eye muscles to focus on things near and far. Suspended play gyms or rattles move well as babies kick or hit them.

- Place toys primarily toward the babies' right at first since babies tend to glance most often in that direction.

- Try these fascinating-looking things that move even without babies' help: windup mobiles, tropical fish in a tank, and canaries. On a windy day or near a fan, hang Christmas tinsel or plastic streamers out of reach.

- Avoid a visual jumble in the play space. Some babies have difficulty sorting out visual stimuli and may be confused by fancy sheets and decorated bumper pads as well as a large assortment of toys. Encourage careful visual discrimination by keeping the environment visually simple—not barren, just uncluttered.

- As a baby begins to develop better and better head control in all positions, place attractive-looking and interesting-sounding toys he wishes to obtain where they will encourage him to look at a distance. This eye contact with novel toys will encourage him to roll toward an object, reach farther than he has before, scoot, creep, crawl, and, of course, eventually get up on his feet to move toward his favorite playthings.

- Introduce babies individually to picture books long before their first birthdays. One picture per page is best at first. Hold these potential little prereaders comfortingly on your lap as you turn the pages for them, repeating over and over the words that label the simple objects pictured on each page.

PEEK-A-BOO

SPACE/TIME AWARENESS

The newborn infant apparently is barely able to distinguish between his own body and the surrounding environment. He has no sense of time and sequencing or location of things in relation to himself or to others. His movements result from automatic reflex reactions, and his crying and smiling usually occur because of stimuli from inside his own body. By the end of the first year, he realizes his bottle will come *after* the solid food, the toy across the room can be reached by moving his body *closer* to it, and his favorite roly-poly ball will move and jingle *as a result of* his hitting it. He grasps the idea that he is a physically separate entity, and his actions and behaviors make a difference in how the people and objects around him respond.

Mini- and Maxi-Milestones of Space/Time Awareness

The automatic, spontaneous actions that dominate the newborn baby's behavior give him little information about space and time characteristics. In short order, however, you will notice an innate curiosity that encourages baby to repeat actions that bring him pleasure. He likes the *feel* of sucking his thumb, so he bends his elbow to bring his hand to his mouth. He likes the *sound* of his overhead toy rattling or jingling, so he straightens his elbow to allow his hand to reach it. He likes the *look* of his fingers wiggling and moving, so he stares at them repeatedly. Later he even touches and plays with his feet and begins to purposefully bring his two hands together to feel each other.

In these ways, baby first learns to measure space and distance. The awareness of sensation that motivates him to interact with his environment helps him learn where his own body ends and the world around him begins. It also helps him recognize where one part of his body is in relation to another. This developing body awareness serves as a basis of measurement for spatial characteristics of other things.

When he notices that his movements and behaviors result in sensations he enjoys—sounds and sights and textures and delicious tastes—he begins to form a hazy notion of cause/effect relationships which, eventually, will form the basis for logical decisions. Also his cause/effect observations help him notice the sequence in which certain things usually occur. This forms a basis for later understanding of time.

At an early age the infant learns the special form of distance perception involved in recognizing a cliff—a noticeable change in the elevation of the surface under him. He discriminates this depth awareness around the time he learns to crawl and he begins to grasp the concept that going past the edge of the "cliff" (the side of his dressing table or top of a flight of stairs) could be harmful because he might fall. It is fascinating to observe that the cause/effect understanding of this spatial concept develops right at the time baby is becoming more mobile and, therefore, more able to injure himself. Of course, he cannot be trusted fully to avoid falling off of heights before a year, and barriers are still necessary near stairways. However, his caution is developing as spatial and cause/effect awareness matures.

Baby usually learns to figure out where his toy went when he dropped it before he develops enough spatial awareness to realize that some objects have a reverse side—an interesting front and back ready to be explored.

At an early age, baby begins to learn the fun of hide-and-seek games. He loves to search for a favorite toy he watches you hide, or one peeking out from an obvious hiding spot. Later he learns to search in a few nearby easy spots when he is not sure which one contains the toy you hid there. Peek-a-boo games are fun for baby at this time, and he still thinks if he covers his eyes you can't see him.

Hide-and-seek and peekaboo games demonstrate more advanced time and space concepts. Another new game baby plays proudly and enthusiastically by this time is baby-so-big, which shows off his new understanding that he has size and occupies a certain amount of space.

 How to Help Develop Space/Time Awareness

- Infants learn about space first from their own bodies. Encourage them to play with their own hands and feet. "This Little Piggy" and other opportunities for lightly touching or squeezing fingers and toes serve this purpose well. Occasionally place babies in their cribs with feet touching the footboard to increase awareness of the lower half of the body. Give them firm rubdowns after water play, including hands and feet.

- Rotate the toys you suspend above the babies in cribs and playpens, changing them from one child to another every week or two to maintain their interest. This expands the opportunities each child has for variety in measuring and later estimating the space between himself and the distant objects.

- Give babies toys that squeak, jingle, or move when touched so that they are sure to notice the effect their movements have had on them. This helps babies learn "before" and "after" time concepts (*long* before they understand those words) and cause/effect relationships.

- When babies are very young, begin to call their attention to their bottles, baby food jars, or other eating supplies at a distance. This helps them begin to connect what they see with the taste that will soon follow. It also promotes using vision to predict and anticipate a coming event.

- If the babies' normal and healthy desire to drop toys over the sides of the playpens or high chairs is irritating to you, tie toys to the sides of the furniture with *short* pieces of soft yarn. Eventually the babies will learn to retrieve the toys for themselves by pulling the yarn. (Avoid longer pieces in which babies could become entangled.) Also try suction toys that the babies are not so likely to drop.

PERSONALITY/SOCIALIZATION

How will that soft, wiggly, wrinkled little bundle in the hospital nursery ever develop into an independent adult, able to find his place as a contributing member of society, interacting comfortably with others in the give-and-take of the grown-up world? To achieve this, he will need to develop a capacity for warmth and cooperation in social relationships and to organize himself to master tasks and solve problems.

The all-important first year will provide the foundation for the skills and confidence needed to succeed in this gigantic task. The influence of the environment and his genetic personality traits will combine to help him move toward this goal in a unique way, different from any other child you have ever known.

Mini- and Maxi-Milestones of Personality/Socialization

The newborn infant is like a little social bud—its petals closed so that the beauty of the personality that lies inside is delicately obscured. At first, it receives and absorbs the nurturing offered in a dependent, inwardly focused way. The newborn earnestly sucks in nourishment for emotional development as well as for physical growth.

The automatic searching for soft, available food sources and the nuzzling and grasping that are at first automatic help to endear him to his caretakers. This helps bring the response of love and affection as well as the physical care that this dependent infant requires for survival.

Affection strengthens as smile responses, watching, and other purposeful movements begin to develop, and chuckling and cooing emerge. The infant and caretaker woo each other, and their lives unite in an overlapping, mutually gratifying relationship. This loving attachment helps provide the confidence baby needs to try new experiences. He reacts to your facial expressions with responses of his own. His face may show interest, fear, distress, anger, sadness, surprise, or love.

Baby's personality, whether placid, irritable, or curious, will become evident very early. It will both influence and be influenced by the personalities of others around him. Here are some examples: Baby cries, and other babies in the room may start to cry. Or you pick up baby on a day of tension and anxiety, and baby is irritable or rigid. Or baby smiles and you smile back and remember the day hasn't been so bad. Or an older youngster introduces a toy hide-and-seek game that delights baby, who tugs at her later in the day with the toy expectantly in hand.

When the caretaker's responses are consistent and dependable, the young baby begins to develop a basic trust in his world and the people in it. If his needs are met comfortably and predictably, he feels safe, and this safety gives him confidence to explore and learn.

As the learning proceeds, baby begins to make individual choices about which goals he wants to achieve and how. He will not need to be pushed to be curious. Curiosity is natural. Forcing learning at your schedule would only make him fearful.

As his movements become even less automatic and more purposefully directed toward locomotion and achieving goals, he begins to think motorically. He begins to plan his actions and learn about himself. Other sense discriminations are becoming more accurate, too. He shows strong preferences for his favorite rattle or objections to his least favorite vegetable, sometimes with a loud voice or vehement gestures. He may become worried about strangers—to the despair of the occasionally visiting grandparent.

Through his play, he tries hard to satisfy his ravenous curiosity by exploring himself and the small world that immediately surrounds him. He exercises some control and begins to take the lead in purposefully doing things that bring him pleasure. He repeats movements of his own body that result in interesting feelings, sounds, and visual stimuli. As big movements emerge, he plays by moving through his space to touch and manipulate more distant toys. Sometimes he watches and carefully observes people and events around him. He remains the center of his own play behavior.

By the time he is one year old, he is beginning to have a sense of his own body and of his influence on his immediate world. He knows he is attached to other people and things in his environment, yet separate from them. He recognizes and trusts familiar staff and knows he can do things on purpose to influence their actions. He knows some of his behaviors that delight them or make them angry. He is just beginning to learn the art of charming others on purpose.

 How to Help Develop Personality/Socialization

- Give babies lots of cuddling and attention when they are awake to help them adjust to their new environment. Play with babies often. Feeding and dressing are not enough. The interaction with you is a *must* that is just as important as meeting the babies' physical needs.

Work out a schedule with other staff members so that you can have time to play with each baby individually every day.

- Keep in mind all the sensory inputs recommended in the sensory awareness section of this chapter. They help the babies feel accepted and loved and safe. These feelings, in turn, provide a basis for emotional stability and positive self-esteem in later years.

- Follow the lead of each baby's individual emotional rhythm. Allow an emotional attachment to develop like a dance in which you and baby establish a unique synchrony with each other. Talk, sing, pause, smile, wait. Rock and touch as you and baby react lovingly to each other's responses. As the babies grow older, provide responsive play supervision.

- Naturally babies will be irritable at times. If irritability does not subside in a reasonable length of time, consider other factors than the obvious problems of hunger, fatigue, soiled diapers, or a need to burp or change position. Remember that a baby cannot tell you how he feels about other sensory experiences. Maybe he feels too warm or cold—look for flushed or blanched skin or for drops of perspiration, and adjust clothing layers appropriately. Maybe his environment is too noisy for him or too quiet—try singing, playing quiet background music, turning off the record player, or temporarily moving him to a different room. Maybe the surface he is lying on is too unsteady or too still—try rocking or changing him to a firmer surface. Maybe the room is too light or too dark—try a dim background light. Maybe he feels too isolated—try an oil rubdown all over or placing his crib closer to activities so that he can see and hear.

- Babies love the warmth and closeness of being held comfortably on your lap while listening to your familiar voice. As the first birthday approaches, begin reading picture books to them so that they will learn you value books and the information they contain.

- Talk to dolls and stuffed animals with soft murmuring words. Pretend to rock the toys to sleep. Babies will mimic your actions.

- Once reasonable behavioral limits have been established and you are certain a baby is capable of understanding and obeying the limits, be firm and stick to your established guidelines. For example, do not allow tearing books, hurting children, or leaving the safe environment. Avoid inconsistency so that babies will not be confused.

- Praise babies for behavior you want them to repeat. Ignore undesirable behavior unless it is dangerous to themselves or others. Avoid physical punishment. Firmly and quietly removing a baby from an unsafe or forbidden activity is better than using a loud voice or angry hand. Better yet, try distracting a baby by presenting a more desirable activity.

LANGUAGE

The plaintive cries of the newborn infant tug at the heartstrings of the adults in his world. Without realizing it, this infant is communicating his needs to his caretakers by using his voice, facial expressions, and sometimes frantic gestures. He understands only vaguely that the responding verbalizations and actions from adults around him help relieve his distress.

It is hard to believe that someday he will be able to organize the sounds he makes into intelligible words and sentences that relate information and describe his feelings. He will also be able to understand the needs of those around him and to think logically and make inferences.

In baby's first short year, he will begin to learn that language is a symbolic representation of all the concrete sensations and abstract concepts he has begun to assimilate. The words he recognizes will be sound symbols representing for him the sum of all the touch, sound, sight, movement, and other sensations he understands on a particular subject. He will recognize that the word "bottle" means that curved container with the soft top that makes him feel full and contented when he sucks on it. In time, he will understand that the word "milk" represents the good-tasting liquid inside.

Mini- and Maxi-Milestones of Language

Baby's ability to express himself develops rapidly. The cries heard in the hospital nursery clearly signify a need. This undifferentiated crying is a reflexive communication response. In a few weeks, he learns to make happier sounds like chuckling, cooing, and babbling. He is initially surprised to recognize his own voice, but in a few months begins to copy his own sounds and those of others.

His vocal attempts are grossly inaccurate at first, but that does not discourage this determined little striver. He makes repeated attempts to perfect the accuracy of his vocal sounds. Razzing sounds and finger-playing with his lips help him develop control of his mouth. Eventually he learns to repeat syllables, and his family helps him attach the sounds to family members—"da-da," "ma-ma." He begins to use sounds and simple gestures on purpose to get attention or a particular response.

Learning to speak is only one portion of developing language skill. He is also learning to listen with rapt attention. At first, he is delighted with the rattling and jingling of his favorite toys, and he turns his head to find new sounds and voices. He may recognize the sound of his parents' voices. Later he carefully watches nearby speakers, and in time he learns to understand many words and meaningful gestures. He learns to tell by your intonation whether you are angry, afraid, feeling in a hurry, or enchanted with him.

By the end of baby's first year, he will have begun to understand simple greetings, verbal labels, and instructions. His jargon resembles the rhythmic patterns and melodic sounds of real speech, which paves the way for full-scale verbal communication in the future. He may even have learned that all-important first word. His choice of earliest words will not be random, but he will let you know some of the ideas that seem the most significant to him—family or staff members' names, "bye," and "car," for example.

 How to Help Develop Language

- Talk and coo with even the youngest babies. They will listen with interest to the gentle quality and changing pitch of your sound. Listening is an essential part of language development, and your responses to their initiated sounds have an impact on their language development.

- Speak slowly in a warm, soft voice. Don't verbally pounce on babies in a loud voice as you approach, but give them a chance to adjust to your presence. The words aren't nearly as important to the young babies as the tone.

- Use eye contact. Look directly in a baby's eyes to let him know your soothing sounds are intended directly for him.

- Provide toys that make sounds to enhance listening skills and sound discrimination—windup musical toys, rattles, and squeaky toys, for example. Musical toys attract babies' attention and get them to tune in to the pretty sounds.

- Make sure there are periods of quiet, too. They will soon tune out if they hear a familiar sound continuously. These quiet times also inspire them to experiment with their own voice sounds or focus their attention on feeling or looking at things.

- Use each baby's name, along with terms of endearment, to get his attention when you play with him so that he will soon learn to recognize the sound of his own name.

- Imitate early sounds babies make accidentally, and encourage them to repeat the sounds on purpose.

- When a baby has learned a new sound or word and has repeated it many times, encourage him to add on a sound or syllable that changes it just a little. Eventually "mmmmm" can change to "mah," and "mah" can change to "ma-ma."

- Respond to cute vocalizations with interest so that babies can see that making sounds is rewarded by your attention. Of course, this must be tempered to prevent their becoming overly demanding.

- When you notice that a baby has understood what you have said or a gesture you have made, let him know you noticed: such as, "Thank you for giving me the doll," or "Good boy, you stopped splashing me with your bathwater." Remember to congratulate the baby for understanding language as well as for saying it.

- Do not anticipate the older babies' every need. Allow and encourage them to express their needs, initially with gestures and later with words.

- Encourage older babies to help you "read" from their books, whether they are sitting on your lap or independently looking at the cloth or cardboard books provided for their use. The resulting babbling or jargon is likely to follow the intonational pattern of your reading. Choose some books that describe animal sounds. Babies love to hear you read "moo," "meow," "bowwow," and so on, and will learn to repeat the sounds back to you.

SO BIG

IMAGINATION/CREATIVITY

The newborn infant feels himself almost indistinguishable from his environment. His very limited experience and immature nervous system do not provide a sensory and intellectual basis for experiencing full-fledged creative thinking. However, even in the first year, each child makes a unique contribution to the small portion of society immediately influenced by his presence and begins to develop the groundwork for developing an imagination. Imitation and early problem-solving are first steps and require sensory memories of all the areas mentioned earlier in this chapter.

Mini- and Maxi-Milestones of Imagination/Creativity

Baby begins at an early age to demonstrate that he is developing not only automatic, reflex-based movement skills but also purposeful movements that he can use creatively for fun and exploration. He sees a toy and figures out how to get to it. He learns early to initiate social contact by smiling or cooing at just the right time to win someone's attention. Do these require a primitive imagination? Are these forerunners of early creativity?

Toward the second half of the first year, baby begins to demonstrate the performing skill of imitation. He first imitates movements he can see himself perform since the visual information helps improve his accuracy. He begins to match his body movements or vocal sounds to those of familiar gestures or sounds made by someone else. At first, his efforts are inaccurate, but as his motor skills for mouth and body control develop, accuracy increases. He learns to clap in imitation and babble back the familiar sounds you make. He shows baby-so-big, plays peek-a-boo, and waves bye-bye, often looking at his hands to verify that they are doing the right thing. Earliest words are his attempts at a direct copy of words he has heard repeatedly.

Baby's imitations become more and more refined. He imitates the motions to pat-a-cake first, then mimics the singsong quality of your voice before he can repeat words of the nursery song. He copies "kissy-kissy" with relatives and staff long before he learns the socially appropriate time to initiate throwing a kiss good-bye.

We recognize when he begins to combine his newly acquired motor skills with his ability to visualize and recall past events in a new creative game: pretending. He pretends to drink from a cup and knows how to respond when you laughingly pretend to take his bottle or favorite toy from his hands. (No teasing. Be sure baby is smiling or laughing in response. If not, stop the game or change your behavior so that he knows you are pretending.)

His early affectionate hugs with a new teddy bear are an imitation of your hugs. He has already acquired enough imaginative skill to show that the new bear is handled differently from his favorite blanket, which may seem almost an attachment to his own self. He knows that, while hugs can be applied to an inanimate bear, they are not appropriate for furniture, toy trucks, or even rattles decorated with a face design. How could he make such discriminations without some glimmer of imagination and creativity?

How to Help Develop Imagination/Creativity

- Play music near the babies' play space—either recorded or live. Show them that you are interested in listening to it. Your example is important to them. Avoid overstimulating their environment continually or loudly.

- Encourage affectionate gestures they can copy by pretending to kiss, rock, or even feed a soft washable doll or stuffed animal.

- If a baby begins to sway and bounce rhythmically to music, show interest and gently encourage this big-movement response.

- Read to older babies the books with large animal pictures. Animal sounds that you make for them and that you encourage them to make as you read help to foster imitation.

- Use toys creatively during your play with babies after they have had ample time to try them out for themselves. Provide a model of imaginative play but without removing initiative from the babies.

TOY CHART

In the chart on the next pages are examples of good toys. They are divided into ten categories that are listed alphabetically. Toys in each category are presented approximately developmentally. All the toys provide learning experiences and, therefore, are educational. The most important aspects of child development that can be stimulated by each toy are marked in columns on the right. The reasons for some marks may not be immediately obvious, and they should encourage you to notice wider possibilities the toys offer. Toys mentioned in the text are not necessarily repeated in the chart.

The toys listed show examples of the attributes a particular type of toy should have. If you experience difficulty finding the toy listed, there will generally be toys of similar quality in catalogs or on the toy-store shelf that will accomplish the same goals.

EXAMPLES OF TOYS FOR THE INFANT: BIRTH TO ONE YEAR	Awareness of Sensation	Balance and Big Movements	Dexterity and Hand/Eye Coord.	Vision	Space/Time Awareness	Personality/ Socialization	Language	Imagination/ Creativity
ARTS AND CRAFTS Not generally recommended for infants.								
BIG EQUIPMENT *Sassy® Cradle Bouncer.* Washable contour cover on spring frame supports whole body while bouncing. Limit time to allow play on tummy.	●	●						
Safety Mirror. Childcraft®. 12″ × 48″ acrylic nonbreakable mirror, hardwood frame, mounts vertically in play area, horizontally in crib.		●		●		●	●	●
Toybars™. Century Original™. Free-standing activity center 20″ × 20″ with 9 toy clips and 2 plastic toys. Other toys can be attached.	●	●	●	●				
Busy Center. Today's Kids™. Plastic floor enclosure, 8 play areas, small train runs on top edge, tiny slide and steps, 2 big holes to peek into. Shape sorter, and xylophone on side. For infants that are crawling and older.	●	●	●	●	●	●	●	
Bye-Bye Baby Buggy. Angeles. Wagon set up with car seats, holds 4–6 babies safely for walks.	●			●		●	●	
BOOKS *Baby Animals.* Stahlwood. Small, plastic, washable, with one picture on each page.				●		●	●	●
Baby's First Cloth Book. Random House. Washable, nontoxic, large pictures labeled "The cow says moo," etc. For toddlers, too.				●		●	●	●
Dressing. Friends. Playing. Helen Oxenbury. Simon & Schuster. Small board books, one picture on each page.				●		●	●	●
Very First Books. Rosemary Wells Dial Books for Young Readers. Brightly colored, cardboard, about Max. Clear pictures, simple language.				●		●	●	●
CONSTRUCTION *Cloth Cubes.* Toys to Grow On®. Bells inside 8 brightly designed, washable, squeezable, stackable, chewable blocks.	●	●	●	●	●			
Large Soft Tactile Blocks. ABC School Supply Inc. 6 soft, nontoxic 3½″ square blocks.	●	●	●		●			
Stack 'n Store Nesting Cubes. Litte Tikes®. Brightly colored pictures on sides.		●	●	●	●			

EXAMPLES OF TOYS FOR THE INFANT: BIRTH TO ONE YEAR	Awareness of Sensation	Balance and Big Movements	Dexterity and Hand/Eye Coord.	Vision	Space/Time Awareness	Personality/ Socialization	Language	Imagination/ Creativity
Bunny Building Set. Fisher-Price®. 5½″ soft, plastic bunnies that are easy to connect.	●	●	●	●	●			
Giant Rock-a-Stack®. Fisher-Price®. 8 colorful, graduated plastic donuts (teether) on detachable base for late infancy and up.	●	●	●	●	●			
GAMES *Peek-a-Boo Baby.* Fisher-Price®. Puppet for adult to hold. Soft washable cloth with rattle squeaker. Holds independently after 1.	●		●	●	●	●	●	●
Play Mirror. Kiddicraft®. Safe, flexible mirror, holes for fingers to poke. Peek-a-boo.	●		●	●	●	●	●	●
Soft and Nice Big Ball. Chicco. Washable, smooth-textured fabric, rattle sound. Make up a game.	●	●	●			●	●	
Puzzle Post. Johnson & Johnson. 8 stacking circle, square, triangle shapes for sorting, rolling, nesting. Fit post in any order.		●	●	●	●	●	●	
IMITATIVE PLAYTHINGS *Perfect Image™ Baby Mirror.* K.B. Enterprises. 12″ × 16″ acrylic, plastic, unbreakable, for crib, play area.		●		●	●	●	●	●
Baby's First Soft Doll. Chicco. Washable, squeezable doll.	●		●			●	●	●
Baby Soft Touch Teach and Play Baby. AmToy®. Activity doll with mirror, dial, music, rattle, squeaker. Attaches to crib.	●		●	●	●	●	●	●
Crib Friend. Fisher-Price®. Washable doll with rattle in feet, squeaker in body.	●		●		●	●	●	●
Security Bunny. Fisher-Price®. Washable, squeezable, fluffy material, permanently sewn eyes. Older baby can use it as hand puppet.	●		●			●	●	●
Food Carrier. Truck. Little Tikes®. Wide stable toys to push on wheels, load with toys.		●	●	●	●		●	●
Busy Choo-Choo®. Playskool® Baby. Push-along colorful train with 7 activities.	●	●	●		●		●	●
MANIPULATIVE *Wrist Jingles®.* Playskool® Baby. Washable. Fastens on wrist or ankle. Rattling sound.	●	●	●		●			

EXAMPLES OF TOYS FOR THE INFANT: BIRTH TO ONE YEAR	Awareness of Sensation	Balance and Big Movements	Dexterity and Hand/Eye Coord.	Vision	Space/Time Awareness	Personality/ Socialization	Language	Imagination/ Creativity
Cradle Play. Kiddicraft®. Mobile that spins, swings, rattles as baby swipes, reaches, tries to grab. Remove when baby can pull to sit.	●	●	●		●			
FischerForm Cot Toy Rod. Fischer American. Heavy red plastic rod that attaches to crib, table, chair. Holds versatile FischerForm mobiles. Rotates out of the way when desired. Adjustable.								
Infant Stim-Mobile®. Wimmer-Ferguson Child Products. 6 washable vinyl black-and-white vertical and horizontal geometric designs, faces. Baby learns wriggling makes it move.	●	●		●	●			
Crib Activity Arch. Johnson & Johnson. Use adjustable arch for 5 months. Detachable toys can be used until 1 yr. Combines mobile and crib gym. Spinners, rattles, paddles, teether.	●	●	●	●	●			
Grab-Me Animals. Gund®. Washable, soft, rattling animals with hand hold.	●		●					
Red Rings. Johnson & Johnson. Soft plastic teethers to hold with feet, too. Bell sound.	●	●	●					
Little Hand and Foot Teether. Chicco. Bright, soft, lightly scented vinyl.	●		●					
Flower Rattle. Fisher-Price®. Mirror on one side, face with eyes that move on other side.			●	●				●
Touch 'ems Clutch Ball™. Playskool® Baby. 5 different textured handles on soft ball to grab. Bell inside.	●	●	●	●				
Tracking Tube. Johnson & Johnson. Squeezable bulbs that squeak and jingle on ends of clear plastic cylinder. Disk inside appears and disappears as toy is tilted.	●		●	●	●			
Grababall. Chicco. Lightly scented vinyl ball. Indentations for fingers to grab. Makes noise.	●		●		●			
Flip Fingers. Kiddicraft®. Nontoxic, colored plastic spinners, also teether.	●		●					
Original Busy Box®. Playskool®. 10 sight, sound, touch activities.	●		●	●	●		●	
Peek 'n Play. Playskool®. Soft, plastic inflatable cylinder with window, bells inside.	●	●		●				

EXAMPLES OF TOYS FOR THE INFANT: BIRTH TO ONE YEAR	Awareness of Sensation	Balance and Big Movements	Dexterity and Hand/Eye Coord.	Vision	Space/Time Awareness	Personality/ Socialization	Language	Imagination/ Creativity
Geoffrey® Bop & See. Largo®. Weighted bottom, see-through window, inflatable bounce-back toy.	●	●		●				
Spinning Butterfly. Fisher-Price®. Butterfly and small pebbles spin inside clear plastic ball atop rubber suction stand for high chair.		●	●	●				
Stand-Up Man. Johnson & Johnson. Toy stands up when hand grip is pulled, falls down when baby lets go.			●	●	●			
Wee Animal™. Playskool® Baby. Small plastic animal with hand grip, rolls on wheels, rattles.		●	●	●	●		●	●
Hedgehogs. Linco. Soft, washable, squeezable, textured vinyl animals. Squeak, cute faces.	●		●		●			
Learning Curve™. Panosh Place. Washable, textured ball pulls apart, fits back together, 5 toys in 1.	●	●	●	●	●			
Baby Links™. Playskool®. 5 brightly colored C-shaped links. Put together, pull apart, teether.		●	●	●	●			
Snap-Lock® Animals or *Beads.* Fisher-Price ®. Colorful plastic pieces, pull apart. Toddlers can snap them together again.		●	●	●	●			
MUSICAL/LISTENING *Rock a Bye Timmy.* Dakin™. Plush bear with sounds of mother's pulse and fluid motion that baby heard before birth. Soothing for crying newborn. 9-volt battery and sound unit removable when washing bear.	●							
Dancing Animals Music Box Mobile™. Fisher-Price®. Windup, 4 soft animals revolve while music plays. Shapes clearly visible from baby's view.	●	●		●	●		●	
Disney Musical Busy Box®. Playskool®. 10 musical activities attach to crib, play area.	●	●	●		●		●	
Lullaby Rainbow®. Tomy®. Attach musical arch to crib. Rainbow face travels across arch with eyes moving and spinning balloon attached.				●			●	
Musical stuffed animals. Eden®, Gund®,. etc. Soft, windup to play music, shake to rattle.	●	●				●	●	●
Chime Ball. Fisher-Price®. Clear, roly-poly ball. Rocking animals move inside. Floats.	●		●	●			●	

EXAMPLES OF TOYS FOR THE INFANT: BIRTH TO ONE YEAR	Awareness of Sensation	Balance and Big Movements	Dexterity and Hand/Eye Coord.	Vision	Space/Time Awareness	Personality/ Socialization	Language	Imagination/ Creativity
Baby Can Too. Melody House Recordings. Songs: "PeekaBoo," "Pat-a-Cake," etc.		●				●	●	
Infantasia™. V.I.E.W. Video. Animated colors, animals, shapes, sounds, songs, rhythms, music.		●		●		●	●	●
RIDING *Baby Safe Rocking Horse.* Toys To Grow On®. Wooden horse. Detachable back support, armrest. No-tip ride for oldest infants, toddlers.	●	●						
WATER PLAY *Terry Thums Pony.* Gund®. Terry cloth. Good tactile toy for washing while playing.	●					●		
Flutter Ball®. Playskool®. Clear plastic ball with large moving butterfly inside. Floats.	●	●	●					
Water Mates. Kiddicraft®. Clear ball. Self-righting duck and small pieces float inside ball.	●	●	●					
Balls in a Bowl. Johnson & Johnson. Clear container holds water. 3 small balls spin inside.	●	●	●		●			

5

TODDLER DEVELOPMENT, TOYS, AND ACTIVITIES: ONE TO THREE YEARS

Figure 5–1 is an overview of the maxi-milestones most children achieve during the toddler years. Like the figure at the beginning of Chapter 4 on the infant, it is divided into the eight aspects of growth and development we have selected for presentation in this book. The figure will help you visualize a whole picture of the toddler years, like a completed jigsaw puzzle.

Figure 5–1 MAXI-MILESTONES OF THE TODDLER

AWARENESS OF SENSATIONS	BALANCE AND BIG MOVEMENTS	DEXTERITY AND HAND/EYE COORDINATION	VISION
Insists on "blankie" often	Walks	Scribbles	Recognizes named body parts and familiar objects in pictures
Enjoys range of foods but expresses preference	Uses push-pull toys	Eats with utensils	
	Squats/stoops	Inserts things, letting go accurately	Begins copying simple two to four block designs
Loves sand and water play	Runs	Stacks a few blocks	
	Jumps	Strings large beads	Completes familiar formboard puzzles without trial and error
Dislikes visit to doctor because of previous injections	Up and down stairs standing	Pulls apart/puts together large pop beads	
Rocks on toys and chairs			Matches colors
Can identify familiar items by feel			

The milestones in the columns are progressive and occur approximately in sequence from top to bottom as the child grows older. The activities listed in the columns overlap considerably, and the eight aspects are all occurring at the same time, although at different rates.

Figure 5–1 Continued

SPACE/TIME AWARENESS	PERSONALITY/ SOCIALIZATION	LANGUAGE	IMAGINATION/ CREATIVITY
Repeatedly fills and dumps containers	Fluctuating need for dependence/ independence	Action response to commands	Copies pat-a-cake and blowing kiss
Reaches toy by pulling surface it rests on	Solitary or onlooker play	Uses phrases and gestures	Colors randomly on blank paper
Requests help activating toys that respond. Realizes cause/ effect relationship	Likes social approval	Overgeneralizes word meanings	Pretends, using object to represent (block for car)
Automatically rotates familiar formboard puzzle piece to fit	Says "no" often, sometimes even when means "yes"	Telegraphic speech	Begins dress-up play
Begins to grasp "big" and "little"	Parallel play	Understandable pronunciation	Plays trucks, house, tea party
			Sings

Take time to review Figure 5–1 carefully before you continue reading. It concisely depicts the heart of the developmental information presented in the rest of this chapter, and may help you understand children better as you select toys for your center or guide children's play. Each puzzle piece in the figure is an important stepping stone preparing the way for the milestones that follow.

Following Figure 5–1, we will take the puzzle apart and detail each of the columns individually, just as we did for the infant in Chapter 4. Following the discussion of each column will be "How to Help" suggestions for promoting growth in that aspect of development for the toddler. At the end of the chapter is a toy chart listing examples of good toys and the aspects of development they stimulate for toddlers.

AWARENESS OF SENSATIONS

The one- to three-year-old shows an increasing ability to seek her own sensory stimulation. Her new big-movement mobility allows considerably more sensory exploration than that experienced by the infant. Her increased language comprehension and emerging verbal skills allow her to understand more meaningfully the sensory information and to request the sensory input she desires. Gone are the days when she waits and hopes someone will respond to her tears or coos with a rocking movement of her carriage or a soothing pat or a drink of juice.

Mini- and Maxi-Milestones of Sensory Awareness

The toddler receives touch and pressure input through the soles of her feet as well as through her legs and hands as she walks or plays on her hands and knees or climbs on a wide variety of textured surfaces.

The toddler remembers dangerous and pleasurable sensations. She avoids hot and prickly objects she has experienced before and learns to be appropriately cautious around stairs. She may show a consistent attraction to cold ice cream cones, sand warmed by the sun, the movement of riding in a car, and a favorite, beloved "blankie." Her food likes and dislikes may be very clear at this age because of strong taste or texture preferences.

Her movements and touch experiences greatly enhance the learning process. They also provide sensations that help her integrate and coordinate knowledge. The sensory input enhances her understanding of visual information and awareness of time and space, and her use of language. The curving of her fingers around a ball helps her understand the visual and language concept of roundness. The big arm movements of a circular scribble further develop this awareness, which will help form the basis for her understanding of circles. Similarly, she learns the *feel* of squareness from carrying her jack-in-the-box and from building with her blocks. Her body sensations as she crawls or toddles to destinations across the room help her learn about space and about the length of time it takes to get there. In addition, she is sensing the sequence of objects she passes along the way. It isn't necessary to teach the toddler these concepts purposefully since she will form them unconsciously as she plays. When she is older, she will want to acquire the language skills necessary to express these sensory experiences.

The toddler has the motor skill necessary to make rocking chairs and hobbyhorses go. The rocking provides sensory stimulation to the brain's vestibular system. This system helps interpret the head's position and movement through space and gives information to the body's muscles about how to respond. Many children require more than average stimulation to this vestibular apparatus of the nervous system and spend time rocking or banging their heads in their cribs.

By her third birthday, the toddler has learned to confidently and aggressively grab ahold of her sensory world. She moves through space with her head in a variety of topsy-turvy positions, muscles responding adroitly to the vestibular stimulation. She can slither off a couch headfirst to retrieve a toy without stopping to think how to do it. She processes new sensory information rapidly, automatically integrating touch and movement impressions while talking, listening, and visually checking out her environment.

During play, she scuffs the toes and knees of her clothing as she chooses to ignore the warning roughness of the cement sidewalk or blacktop play surface. The scuffs on her clothing show that she has the ability to place such obvious tactile information into the background of her awareness because it suits her purpose in the play environment. She can also choose to bring sensory information to the forefront of her attention if it will benefit her. She can accurately recognize the sound of her brother's voice and the sight of her own toy car in the array of other children's cars. She can feel the difference between her furry teddy bear and her soft, floppy stuffed doggie even in the dark. She has the ability to judge through her muscle and joint sensations (kinesthesia) which jungle gym she is not skillful enough to climb safely. She stands by, watching in awe, as her older playmates achieve the very top of the highest bar.

It is clear that the three-year-old can switch from gross, general sensory awareness to fine, careful discrimination at will. She uses this so-called foreground/background capability to selectively attend to the sensations that have the most survival or pleasure value at the moment. She displays this human characteristic well. Unfortunately, her choice of an important sensation that requires her attention may differ markedly from the choice of her little friends or of the staff!

 ### How to Help Develop Awareness of Sensations

- Provide plenty of opportunity and encouragement for children to experience novel textures and pleasurable movements in the toys and play surfaces and big equipment they experience. These provide a sensory basis for building knowledge through the toddler years.

- Use recorded music to help establish a pleasant sensory atmosphere. Try soothing music to quiet the overly active or fearful child, happily stimulating music to pep up the quiet, lethargic child. Be sure the music is not overstimulating, and carefully monitor whether or not it is contributing to the positive effects you want.

- Wear light fragrances. Not only will you smell good and feel good, but toddlers will associate the fragrance with you.

- Allow carefully supervised playtime for toddlers to enjoy the comforting, soothing sensation of water play in a basin or water/sand table. In a wading pool, encourage big arm movements and kicking.

- Select water toys that can sprinkle, float, splash, pour, or fill. Terry cloth bath toys' slightly rough texture promotes touch awareness. Even two plastic cups stimulate a variety of sensory play experiences, including weight discrimination. Commercial bath toys that do cute tricks encourage fine-motor pouring activities and hold visual attention.

- Let each toddler get used to the potentially scary tactile sensation of water on her face in the pool by allowing her to splash when you are appropriately dressed, or to pour water on her head with a bucket.

- After water play, wrap toddlers in big floppy towels and dry them with short, brisk, firm movements. They will enjoy the deep pressure on their muscles from the massage and the nice feeling of the towel on their skin. These sensations will make them more aware of the size, shape, and feel of their bodies. After this pleasurable rubdown, smooth baby lotion onto their skin for more touch input. Finish with light strokes and a hug.

- Drying and massage must be done very carefully so that there is no parental misunderstanding or possibility for abuse. Many parents are concerned and often instruct their children not to allow touching. When that is the case, discuss your activities and sensory awareness goals with the parents, and always get their permission before beginning.

- Use tactile words like "warm," "soft," "cuddly," "smooth," and "rough" so that toddlers associate these sensations with words and actions. Quiet times provide a perfect opportunity to sing these words in a song you make up.

- Buy toys that provide sensory stimulation such as colorful push-along trains that whistle and toot, or soft clutch balls with indentations that squeak. Children will learn about "feel" and sounds, and how much pressure is needed to move or manipulate the toy.

- Provide textured blocks to add touch information to the kinesthetic and manipulative experience of playing with blocks.

- For the toddlers who don't mind, vary the texture of sleeping surfaces to increase sensory input. Try flannel crib sheets or huge terry cloth beach towels on the cot for a change.

- If a toddler is a head-banger on the mattress or other supporting surface for prolonged periods (this is usually particularly evident just before she falls asleep), be sure the surface is well padded. Provide this child with extra opportunities for vestibular stimulation through movement activities. That may be the sensory experience she is seeking. Try swings, rocking horses, rocking chairs, and swinging her around or tossing her up in the air.

- Discontinue the swinging or tossing activities right away if she seems fearful or uncomfortable. Instead try introducing activities with more gentle movements.

- If you twirl a toddler around in space, *be sure* to hold her under the arms, not by the elbows or hands as you swing her. You might injure her tender shoulder joints. For the same reason, don't pick her up by her upraised hands or elbows.

- If a toddler is comfortable with this kind of movement, she may love being held upside-down and swung gently back and forth. Hold her firmly at the hips or waist, not by the legs, to prevent injury to hip joints.

- Corrugated paper rubbed with fingers, crayon, or dowel and cellophane for crinkling and stuffing offer interesting textures.

BALANCE AND BIG MOVEMENTS

The cautious, tentative steps that characterize the new walker gradually give way to the confident, fluid movements of the three-year-old. This older toddler can run and jump and turn efficiently while manipulating toys in her hands and holding a running conversation. She has acquired enough big-movement skills to do plenty of exploring and roaming and can perch comfortably atop a variety of movable playthings.

Mini- and Maxi-Milestones of Balance and Big Movements

The position of the hands of the novice walker provides information about how comfortable she is with this complex motor task. The precarious balance skills of those first few independent steps are accompanied by the fairly rigid, "high-guard" position of the hands near or above the shoulders. Meanwhile, her feet make their halting efforts wide apart. The trunk lurches and sways side to side as she waddles, the whole body turning in the direction of each step. As walking competency increases, the hand position moves. Instead of near the shoulders, her hands are held near the waist or below and often swing freely at her sides. By the time she has been walking for a couple of years, the inflexible positioning of the hands gives way. Instead she maintains a smooth, rhythmic arm movement that alternates reciprocally with the opposite leg movement. Her reciprocal crawling movements of the infant years helped prepare her for this coordinated walking pattern.

In the early days of walking, falls occur often, and recovery is quick. As upright skills are being perfected, they require full concentration. Newly emerging language competencies are put on hold for a few minutes until a more stable sitting or hands-and-knees position is assumed temporarily. The rambling jargon or words that accompany her play suddenly become quiet when she tries a few independent steps. Earlier balance skills are practiced often during the first months of walking. The new toddler can be seen rehearsing her sitting or kneeling balance on chairs, low tables, and laps with equal aplomb. Short-wheeled riding toys are propelled, gingerly at first, with her feet on the floor. In a few months, she begins to manage the big spring-suspended horses.

The discovery that she can climb out of a crib or playpen delights the toddler but brings some degree of distress to the staff!

As her confidence increases and her repertoire of movement skills grows, she creeps up a staircase and inches her way cautiously down backward. Some children go through a phase of sitting on each step on the way up or down. Later they venture to try, and eventually succeed at, walking up and down the stairs without help.

Big movements of the toddler generally become more fluid and smooth-looking as balance and coordination improve. The development of new automatic reflexes and the lessening of the influence of ones that are no longer needed allow more advanced balance accomplishments. By the toddler years, the youngster's shoulders and arms, hips, and legs are automatically making adjustments to compensate for changes in head position, terrain, and angle of the supporting surface underfoot. Some of this automatic activity is stimulated by the continually developing vestibular system. This system gives the muscles information about head position and how to make corresponding appropriate muscle responses to maintain balance.

The toddler's immature nerves are continuing their work of carrying instructions telling the muscles what to do. Her coordination will be enhanced as her nerves go through a maturing process called "myelination." This is a process in which a sheath or covering automatically grows around the nerves, allowing them to function more efficiently.

Watch the new walker as she picks up her ball or dropped stuffed animals from the floor. Her occasional careful stoop requires slow, considered movements. At first, it seems to be a long way down there! Yet something happens as the months and years go by. The older toddler can easily switch from reaching overhead to retrieve a toy from the highest shelf to squatting down to push her cars and trains around on the floor. The "something" that has happened includes the reflex and myelination changes that allow more advanced big-movement skills. In addition, she has gained confidence from each successful attempt at jumping off and over small things, and running with good stops, starts, and turns. This confidence helps the three-year-old to dare try more and more complex movements in play. She experiments and finds out that she can walk backward or with her eyes shut without stumbling. She even tries the tricky new accomplishment of kicking a ball without toppling over. But notice how her arms again fly up near the shoulders as she adjusts her weight to balance on the nonkicking foot.

Her interest in the games of pointing to and naming body parts on herself and others also helps build her confidence. It helps her recognize that her body is a useful tool for implementing her creative and playful thoughts. The upright balance skills and coordination efforts of the energetic three-year-old are a joy to watch. She demonstrates good trunk flexibility and an ability to plan new movements to maneuver through tricky new places. She clearly shows an integration of many parts of the body together into a unified whole of ewriggling, bouncing, swaying, climbing, exuberant movement.

How to Help Develop Balance and Big Movements

- Push-toys are good for new and still unsteady walkers. A toy corn popper, a sweeper, a bubble-blowing lawnmower, or a push chimer gives some support and holds their attention as they practice walking.

- Pull-toys are more of a challenge since toddlers don't get any help for balancing. Pull-toys help them learn to change directions, stop, go, and motorically control the toy on their own. When trunk rotation is good, they can turn around and watch the toy as they pull it along in back of them.

- If they are sitting on the floor, it is easy and good practice for toddlers to roll and catch a large ball between their legs. They enjoy coordinating the two hands together for throwing the ball in the air, even though they can't catch it.

- Help the child avoid W-sitting on the floor with her feet outside her legs and buttocks. Instead, encourage sitting with ankles crossed (tailor fashion), or with feet straight forward, or with both feet to one side of her thighs.

- When handing a toddler a toy, occasionally try placing it to her left or right side rather than always directly in front of her at her middle. This will encourage her to rotate her trunk, bend, reach, and cross her midline with her arms and hands.

- Toddlers with good balance are ready to try low rocking toys that do not support the back. Make available small rocking puppies or horses with handles to be held firmly and a rocking ledge on which to rest the feet. Then children will feel secure as they move back and forth, stimulating balance and the upright position while rocking.

- Riding-toys to sit on and move with their feet also stimulate balance and postural adjustments since the little drivers must shift their weight as they move the toy along. Small animal and vehicle designs are available. A tiny indoor/outdoor four-wheeled bike that has no pedals makes her feel particularly grown up. Be sure the riding toys move easily, are well balanced, and have comfortable seats. These toys not only improve strength and endurance, but they also coordinate the hands with the legs by requiring intricate steering combined with the leg power necessary for propelling. The more advanced skill of pedaling is not required.

- Be sure you have enough riding-toys. They are very popular with toddlers and will be in great demand.

- A very small three-wheeled bike is also available and comes with pedals. Children can move it with their feet even before they have learned to pedal. It takes coordination to pedal and steer, but most youngsters begin to get the idea by the time they are three.

- The toddler years are not too early for a pool or water big-movement program if it is available for your facility to use. Start slowly; don't rush any child to keep up with other youngsters, and *always* put safety first. Make sure you have written parental permission for this activity! It is also important to have a trained swimming and/or physical education instructor. Some centers combine swimming with simple gym activities.

- A folding, collapsible tunnel is a safe yet adventurous toy. It's a little scary to some children at first, but most learn to love crawling through. It gives lots of practice on the hands and knees. To help a reticent little one, crawl through with her if you can fit, or peek in at the opposite end to give encouragement.

- A small indoor/outdoor climb and slide toy is fun for toddlers not yet ready to tackle the big kids' climbing equipment. They are challenged to use skills of crawling through, climbing up and sliding down, and can feel quite proud of their big-movement accomplishments!

- Sit'n Spin® is a sturdy toy that children can play with for years. It provides important vestibular stimulation, as well as bilateral coordination of the arms, and motor planning for changing directions. Children love turning slowly at first, and faster as arm movements improve. Many become expert at changing directions speedily.

- Foam wedges and cylinders are fun to crawl over and around. Make an obstacle course of some of your equipment and see what these daring youngsters will dream up.

- Teeter-totters and rocking boats allow youngsters to sit together and share the balance and vestibular experience.

- Seesaws go much higher and need careful supervision. Explain the rules carefully, and prevent hard bouncing or getting off the bottom seat so that the top youngster falls.

- Gymnastic balls of varying sizes can create exciting and challenging balance and coordination experiences. Hold a toddler firmly as she sits or lies on her stomach or back adjusting her posture to stay on top. If a ball is small enough, a child can try sitting on it herself or leaning over it to touch the floor with her hands and feet.

DEXTERITY AND HAND/EYE COORDINATION

Baby polishes off a piece of her first birthday cake with a shower of crumbs and icing on face, clothing, and floor. At this time, even her handling of cookies and hotdog slices often switches from intricate, careful fingertip grasp with accurate reach and hand/mouth coordination back to palmar squeeze and sticky cheeks. For the one-year-old, fine-finger intricacy and accuracy seem at times to be too much trouble.

By age three, she will have learned to manage a spoon and fork fairly efficiently as well as to show an elementary skill in manipulating small playthings. Even a crayon will be a toy of choice for the three-year-old whose hand/eye coordination is developing well. However, she may have difficulty predicting in advance the outcome of her sweeping crayon movements.

Mini- and Maxi-Milestones of Dexterity and Hand/Eye Coordination

The newly developed pincer grasp that allows a one-year-old to hold Cheerios® between her index fingertip and thumb requires careful concentration and high motivation. This grasp is often at its most accurate when she is picking up tiny items of food.

She also takes pleasure in picking up small toys in her fingertips and in allowing her eyes to guide her hands toward moderate-sized openings in containers. There she inserts the small pieces carefully, listening with delight as they clatter to the bottom. She often shakes the container, reinforcing what fun it is to play the game. The filling and dumping sequence is repeated over and over again as she masters fitting objects into increasingly smaller holes. She also learns to fit dowels into holes in wooden blocks and easy-grip pegs into pegboards.

The voluntary release (or letting go) of objects into these small openings is a refinement of her previous skill of purposefully dropping toys over the side of her crib or high chair. A further refinement in the timing of this voluntary release occurs gradually as she learns to roll a ball, then cast a toy aside when angry or when she is tired of it. Finally, she learns to throw a ball accurately to an older child standing ready to receive it a few feet away.

The young toddler often uses her two hands together symmetrically (for example, in clapping and in "baby-so-big"). In such bilaterally symmetrical actions, both sides of the body are working together doing the same thing at the same time. The toddler spontaneously begins to seek out such actions in more resistive activities that require more strength. She pushes a wooden wagon full of blocks and dolls and pulls apart plastic pop beads, using all the strength her little arms can muster. As she is learning to do resistive activities that are bilaterally symmetrical, she is also learning to coordinate her hands in less symmetrical movements, although at first without resistance. She can wind an easy jack-in-the-box while holding it with the other hand.

Resistive activity increases strength of the upper trunk and shoulder muscles. This helps provide a stable hub near the center of her body and, in some cases, allows the forearms and fingers to function more efficiently. You yourself know that a difficult hand/eye maneuver like threading a needle or tying an angler's fly sometimes requires stabilizing the elbows on a table or against the sides of your body.

Here is another example of the important relationship between big-movement competency and hand/eye coordination. If a youngster does not have erect trunk balance in a sitting position by the toddler years, she may frequently use her hands for support and balance. This will interfere with and delay use of the hands for practicing fine-manipulative activities.

As hand coordination for pincer grasp and bilateral activities improves, several notable changes evolve. These include improvement in (1) fine coordination, (2) separation in the function of the fingers and of the two sides of the body, and (3) wrist control. The first of these changes, improvement in fine-hand coordination, is characterized by increased strength and intricacy, and more accurate integration with her eye movements. It is also accompanied by greater integration of function with the other hand. For example, she learns to put together the pop beads she has been pulling apart for months, carefully inserting the small knob that fits tightly into the bead's tiny hole. She can, with effort, coordinate a complex manipulation that is as difficult as putting a string of beads or a long play necklace into a tight container, easing the unwieldy parts slowly into place.

The second change, separation (or "dissociation") of the fingers from each other, helps this intricacy develop. The fingers no longer work only in a total grasp. Instead, they work separately to turn and explore small objects. This is a further refinement of the dissociation observed when the younger baby was fascinated by poking her fingers into tiny openings and holes.

The hands also begin to function more separately, one helping the other to achieve a goal. The toddler begins to string wooden beads successfully, switching hands often to achieve success as one hand holds the bead and the other carefully inserts the string. She hammers wooden pegs with one hand while holding the toy being pounded with the other hand. She stacks up blocks in a tower, sometimes stabilizing the lower blocks with one hand while the other adds blocks on top. She removes the wrapper from a lollipop with intricately dissociated fingers while the other hand holds the stick.

A third advance that occurs as the young child's grasp improves is the development of more mature wrist rotation. This palms-up, palms-down movement allows for a flexibility of the hand movement previously impossible. How eagerly she reaches for an ice cream cone with her palm turned sideways instead of downward! She may reach up for a toy with arms outstretched and palms upward. These wrist rotations are automatic and allow her to succeed when she later manipulates screw-and-bolt toys, unscrews nesting barrels, and turns doorknobs. They allow her to open peanut butter jars or to eat her Jell-O® without dumping it as her spoon turns on the way to her mouth. They allow her to drink from a cup one-handed and with a dry bib.

The hand/eye coordination of the three-year-old has come a long way toward helping her establish her independence. In the reading corner, she can turn her own book pages one at a time. At the lunch table, she can handle her own drink, eat her hamburger while keeping her face clean, and use utensils to eat her dessert without spilling. She can carefully scribble or make little circles at the coloring table, holding her crayon awkwardly in her fingertips. It is hard to believe this capable little youngster was a babe-in-arms just three short years ago!

 How to Help Develop Dexterity and Hand/Eye Coordination

NOTE: Be especially certain that tiny, nonedible objects like mothballs, marbles, and rodent repellent nuggets are stored well beyond the reach of a toddler's inquisitive pincer grasp. Also beware of tiny toy pieces.

- Activity boards attached to the sides of cribs can be borrowed from infant play areas occasionally for play on the floor of the toddler area.

- Provide plenty of hand-sized manipulative toys for practice with pincer grasp and finger opposition—"inch" cubes, small wooden or plastic figures, large beads, and so on.

- Blocks come in all sizes, shapes, and textures. Your assortment can provide a variety of different sensory, manipulative, and hand/eye coordination experiences while children pile and stack, push and carry them. More advanced shapes like arches and cylinders may be of more interest to the older toddler and the preschooler.

- Blocks that interlock or snap so that they won't fall down or come apart easily help eliminate frustration for young builders. Try giving the novice builder a few blocks at a time at first so that she can make her building discoveries without being overwhelmed by too many.

- A wagon filled with blocks is a pull-toy that can be used at first for piling the blocks inside. Later, when hand/eye coordination improves, toddlers can fit the blocks in one layer.

- Provide a variety of stack toys, blocks with holes that fit on dowels, and jumbo stringing beads to encourage the hands and eyes to coordinate.

- If a toddler becomes tired of just taking apart Snap-Lock® Beads and is showing frustration with trying to snap them together, provide a little help. At first, hold and stabilize one bead while helping her fit and push another one to attach it. Later help her hold both beads herself at the same time. This independence will maintain her interest in the toy for longer periods.

- To encourage forearm rotating, provide toys like screws and bolts that also fit together but in addition require pushing, turning, and twisting the pieces at the same time.

- For maximum benefit, store toys with small pieces carefully so that the pieces do not become lost or broken.

- Hand/eye coordination toys that fit together sequentially and pop apart when a lever is pressed (like a Humpty-Dumpty effect) add the extra dimension of cause/effect awareness to the fine-coordination challenge. Avoid frustrating young toddlers with this more advanced construction toy.

- A cobbler's bench is fun for banging and hammering while developing accuracy, arm strength, and color recognition. Some also have parts that screw on and off. Toddlers' understanding of cause/effect relationships is enhanced as they watch the pegs disappear, then turn the toy over and notice the dowels have gone through to the opposite side.

- Nesting/stacking blocks that fit inside of each other become even more of a hand/eye coordination challenge when toddlers try building a stable tower with them.

- Large wooden beads can provide hours of enjoyable hand/eye coordination for older toddlers. For extra laces, buy shoelaces with long tips, or make a firm point on the end of a piece of yarn by wrapping masking tape around it or dipping it in nail polish. For variety or extra beads, save empty spools from thread since they have nice big holes, too. How delighted toddlers will be to wear the resulting necklace or to give it to you to wear for a little while.

- Toddlers will love the fun of using large crayons, washable markers, chalk, and even finger paints and tempera colors for coordinating eyes with hands. Provide large plain sheets of paper, and let them have a free hand for random scribbling. Provide strict guidelines (given pleasantly, of course) for keeping colors on the paper and not on the walls!

- When a child is showing more control in her use of coloring implements, introduce a coloring book with a single drawing on each page and made with few lines, like one giant baseball or ice cream cone. See if she is ready to approximate coloring within lines. She may not be wonderful at it yet, but you can tell if she has the idea.

- Pouring water from one toy to another is a good hand/eye coordination activity. If no tub or sink is available at your center, you might set up children at a table with lots of newspapers and a basin partially filled with water. For a real dexterity challenge, let them try filling individual spaces in an ice-cube tray, each with a different color!

- On a warm summer day, try this fascinating outdoor water activity using plastic squeeze bottles. Let children squirt water toward targets—a large bucket or a floating duck or a chalk line on the cement or blacktop. In the winter, try this in the snow using colored water. Be sure to point out targets or lines in the snow to aim toward. While the squeezing is good for dexterity, the aiming creates more of a hand/eye coordination game.

- A little time for relaxed water play after a messy art project provides a wonderful opportunity to get children's hands and faces clean before they go home.

VISION

By her first birthday, the toddler's visual scanning and observational skills are more efficient. They supplement mouthing as a way of gaining information about objects in her environment. Now she carefully studies herself in the mirror, offering the baby a toy sometimes, and delighting in its movement and smiles. She can accurately look for and find partially hidden toys. She also looks carefully at pictures in her books rather than just glancing pleasurably at them, mouthing the corners of the durable pages, waving the book, and casting it aside. She watches actions on TV with interest, sometimes using her body to imitate movements. However, she usually has little awareness of the storyline. This selective looking skill combines with her increased memory ability. This allows the toddler to make visual interpretations and decisions way beyond the simple visual skills she had during the infant years.

The toddler's visual acuity has not yet reached the level of 20/20 vision she will achieve later. She must stand closer than an average adult in order to see objects clearly. Nevertheless, many new looking skills are developing. She learns to point to familiar objects you name in her picture book and can correctly select a simple shape to fit in the wooden formboard puzzles she has tried before. By age three, she can even match blocks by color, although her visual memory and language skills are not yet advanced enough for her to name the colors.

Mini- and Maxi-Milestones of Vision

Compared to the baby under age one, the toddler shows clear evidence of more advanced visual perception (the ability to make sense out of what she sees by associating it with things she has experienced before). As an infant, she had learned to perceive that her bottle was a special source of pleasure. The sight of it initiated a sense memory of taste, relief from hunger, warmth, and cuddling.

By the time she has reached the early toddler years, this perceptive tot's ability to analyze distinctive features has become more refined. She can perceive increasingly more specific information. Now from an array of objects she can choose crackers, Cheerios®, and a cup of juice as treats to reach for enthusiastically when she is hungry. But her enthusiasm for them is limited. If she uses a bottle to go to sleep, *that* is what she would pick instead if given the array to choose from at naptime. Her improved visual perceptual skills help her choose the goodies she loves best.

Her increasing awareness of differences in distinctive features is also evident in her use of toys. She recognizes the implications of these differences for play and will notice a simple hindrance that will prevent the play from working smoothly. By the toddler years, she would not even try to fit a solid round hockey puck onto a dowel used for stacking plastic donut rings, even when it is mixed in with other rings. But she might try one of the preschoolers' quoits.

Initially the toddler notices differences among similar things when the colors are different or the designs on them vary considerably. Only later does she learn to notice differences in shapes of things well enough to match them. She usually notices and can match circle- and cross-shape similarities before she can match square or triangular shapes. She learns to show you toys that match simple pictures in her books. By age three, she can match most familiar geometric shapes to their pictures although she cannot name them. She can even "read" pictures well enough to know the familiar actions they represent (boy running, girl laughing).

In addition, the toddler can synthesize individual features together into a unified whole. If she sees a corner of her familiar winter hat peeking out from a pile of mufflers, she knows the corner is part of the whole and can find her hat if you ask her to. She also knows if you get her hat out of her cubby that it is part of another unified concept and means she will probably be going home with her folks or outdoors for an adventure. Her analysis of the perceptual features of the hat will assuredly make it clear to her that it is her hat and not her diaper or teddy bear.

Soon after the first birthday, she begins to recognize when a toy is hiding under a flat or cloth surface because the surface is displaced. She grins when she realizes the lump under her blanket is probably her missing cuddly doll. This suggests a visual memory of the construction or shape of the doll. It also reminds us that visually guided behavior is becoming more advanced. The toddler will reach for the hidden doll only after first making a visual judgment deducing where it is hidden.

The toddler's progress along the path of visually perceiving more and more different types of information has just begun. Her skills still need to be further refined. She will still pick up a harmful mothball and eat it because it looks like a tasty morsel. She will not be able to complete interlocking jigsaw puzzles yet, although she can complete lots of familiar geometric formboards by age three.

The toddler's visual perceptual skill gradually becomes less centered on herself. She slowly matures beyond concentrating her attention exclusively on one obvious visual cue at a time. Then she begins to visually analyze a whole display. On the wall where the creative masterpieces of her class are displayed, she may notice whether one of the pictures has been taken from its place. She might even know whose it is if it had particularly unusual characteristics.

Her perceptual skill matures slowly, and she still makes mistakes in her primitive attempts to visually organize her world. She might call all small animals "bowwow" or all men with horn-rimmed glasses "Unca' Bob." This shows she is likely to try forming a whole concept based on particular details.

By age three, the toddler's visual memory is well developed enough that she can find the toy truck she hid purposefully a few hours earlier. (Of course, she will not recall the location of the many items she has cast aside un-consciously during play when her attention has been drawn to a new toy or activity.) She can remember the covers of her favorite books well enough to find the one she wants you to read. And she can sometimes amaze you by selecting a specific tape, record, or videocassette she loves by using a private, secret decoding method (visual memory).

  How to Help Develop Vision

- Try putting yourself in a child's place. Think of what the world looks like from her eye level and from her limited visual experience. Her seemingly irrational fears or irritations may make more sense to you. An approaching new adult looms bigger and more frightening than she might look to you. Crowds at the school Family Day look more confusing from a knee-high view.

- One particularly scary or unfamiliar view for many toddlers is a big man with a white fluffy beard and red suit and hat. Even though the man may have a pleasant ho-ho-ho laugh, he is such a novel sight that many toddlers scream or cling rather than allow themselves to be placed on his soft, ample lap. To make matters worse, usually this scary creature is first encountered up close in a confusing, unfamiliar mall environment or at a noisy Christmas party at your center. Toddlers' perceptions come from their point of view, which is very different from yours. Respect their accompanying emotions, and don't rush into things before they are ready.

- Read to toddlers often, encouraging them to point to the pictures as you read about them. This is an opportunity to help them notice visual details. But don't be tempted to turn a pleasurable story hour into a perception lesson! Keep the warm, cuddly, social language experience primary.

- Encourage toddlers to make finer and finer visual discriminations of the distinctive features of toys and other objects. For example, notice when a toddler has grasped the idea of stacking plastic donut rings on their plastic post, a fine-hand/eye coordination activity for the just-over-one youngster. Don't be tempted to get involved too soon. First, give her a chance to practice happily for a few months. Then, if the toy she usually selects has a straight post, bring out a stacking toy with a pyramid-shaped post. Or, if her usual choice is already pyramid-shaped, help her notice how to stack the rings so that the shapes are graduated in sequence from big to small. Start with two rings, the largest and the smallest. Congratulate her when she gets both to fit. Later try three, then four. She probably won't be able to stack all the rings in order until she approaches the preschool years.

- Don't expect a rapid jump in children's perceptions. They will gradually build on each other over time. That is the reason we suggest using the biggest and smallest donut rings first. They are the most perceptually different. Later, when you add another size, pick one that is the most perceptually different from the other two. The goal is to assure success. Only months later could toddlers be expected to graduate all the rings correctly. When you are encouraging children to notice increasingly more refined perceptual differences, grade up the task slowly.

- Shape-sorting boxes with cutout shapes in them are commercially available in both simple designs for the one-year-old and in more complicated designs for the older child. They are also easy to make. Cover an empty two-pound coffee can with Con-Tact® paper; cut out two or three shapes in the plastic top; then put the top back on as the lid. You might trace the end of an empty spool for the circle, a small block to make the square, and a small empty matchbox to make the rectangle. As children ease the items in through their matching holes, a hearty shake of the can gives novice sorters a cheerful sound reward for their success.

- Build a three- or four-piece simple model of multicolored blocks or other construction toys for a toddler to copy. Then suggest that she make one for you to copy, or that she repeat a model she just made. This simple "copy mine" or "copy your own" activity with the older toddler enhances visual perception. She will pay more attention to the color arrangement than to the shapes of the pieces initially.

- Toys that travel along the floor with a cheerful noise or whirling pretty colors attract toddlers' visual attention. They encourage good watching skills, ocular control, and convergence/divergence of the two eyes. Try simple windup, friction, or battery-operated toys. This is one purpose these noncreative toys can serve.

- Show toddlers how to blow either bubbles through a wand or a feather off your hand. These attractive, slow-moving objects are fun for young toddlers to follow with their eyes, which helps to refine smooth visual tracking.

- To make inexpensive soap bubbles, mix detergent or Ivory Snow® and water. A few drops of glycerine will make the bubbles heavier and stronger.

- Sorting objects by color provides an entertaining and educational play activity for older toddlers. Try jelly beans or pegboard pegs on different days for sorting because they will be the same except for the color characteristic. "Let's put all of this color in this cup and that color in that one." They cannot yet respond to "Give me the red one," or "What color is this?" Remind toddlers not to put small plastic pieces into their mouths.

- Mention any color matching that you notice in the small world around the toddlers. "Look, your shirt is the same color as mine," or "I see that your new sneakers match Jason's pants."

- Blocks and beads can be sorted by color *or* by shape *or* by size. Remember that toddlers will not be able to sort or select by two or three features at the same time. Try "Let's put all this shape in this bucket," not "Let's line up all the small, square green beads on this table."

- Cleanup time offers an excellent opportunity for encouraging toddlers to notice visual perceptual differences by sorting. Mark storage boxes or large coffee cans (covered with plain Con-Tact® paper) with a single shape. Help one small group of toddlers to put away all the round beads in one container. Other youngsters can put all the square ones in another container or all the triangular-shaped ones in another.

- With your help, youngsters can enjoy learning to put blocks away by matching their shapes to the shapes you have drawn on the storage shelves or block boxes.

- If a jigsaw puzzle of several pieces is too complex for a toddler to complete by herself, try removing just one piece at a time to see if she can figure out how to put it back in. Later try removing two pieces from separate points in the puzzle (the head, the foot). When she can put those in, try three pieces, and so on. New puzzles present the greatest spatial and perceptual challenge when children are permitted to solve them by themselves.

- Beware of puzzles having busy designs that will distract a toddler from paying attention to the shapes of the pieces.

- By the late toddler years, the adult in a car pool or pickup bus can begin to play car games that encourage visual scanning of the environment. It may help to keep youngsters interested, their visual attention directed, and the noise volume down. "Matthew, can you see the school bus (or airplane)?" "Joyce, can you point to the picture of the lady on the billboard?" Take turns so that they can use their developing language skills to name and describe objects they see when scanning the roadside. Help them select particular items from a confusing visual background.

SPACE/TIME AWARENESS

The infant months have laid a firm foundation for developing spatial awareness. The variety of sensations she experienced earlier helps the toddler begin to be aware of and understand the concept of space. Some researchers emphasize the role of visual experiences in developing this awareness, others the role of touch or movement through space. Jean Piaget, the Swiss cognitive psychologist and famous child-development expert, concluded that an understanding of speed, movement, and time forms an important basis for spatial concepts.

By the time the toddler is approaching her third birthday, she can match shapes in some very familiar toys she has used often. She also has a clearer understanding of the cause/effect relationship between the way her movements and behavior change the actions of her toys and the people around her. This is a time concept that helps her understand "before" and "after" relationships. The toddler is slowly becoming a little expert at anticipating how to solve a problem without having a period of trial and error. Jean Piaget calls this "representation."

Mini- and Maxi-Milestones of Space/Time Awareness

Early impressions of space are very disorganized. Shapes are not rigid but seem to change often. Teacher's face looks different as she comes closer or turns to the right or left. A young toddler does not yet understand the view *she* sees in relation to the view from another position in space. Her tears, when she watches her parent walk down the street after leaving her with you on one of her first days in your center, may partially be a reflection of this confusion. It may scare her that her parent seems to grow smaller as she moves farther away.

It becomes clear that the toddler understands distant toys can be reached by walking toward them. She also knows she can pull an attached string or blanket that a toy is resting on until it comes closer. She learns she can poke a stick or long handle around a toy to draw it near. These examples show that she knows some kind of movement through space must occur first before she can have her toy. We can see that baby is demonstrating an emerging understanding of cause/effect relationships and of space/time awareness.

Amazingly, the toddler also instinctively understands the natural force of gravity well enough to tug on a short string attached to a toy that fell down out of sight. This saves you a lot of bending over and brings the youngster a feeling of accomplishment.

Filling and dumping become favorite pastimes for the very young toddler. By putting little blocks into a bucket and dumping them out again, over and over, she is demonstrating that she has begun to notice the interrelationship of the size of things. As this spatial concept matures through practice and cognitive development, her ability to select and fill accurately increases markedly. In a few months, she learns to put together nesting toys of just a few parts, a refinement of the spatial concepts learned through filling and dumping.

She loves toys that do something when she activates them, for example, a toy that "talks" when she pulls the string. If she does not have the motor coordination to make it work, then she is likely to hand it to you to turn on. Her imploring look or gesture clearly indicates her understanding of cause and effect. One of the young toddler's favorite cause/effect "toys" is a light switch, which mysteriously causes a bright room to become dark or vice versa. The trick of having toddler "blow" out the light doesn't last long. This bright little observer soon comes to realize that the light switch does the magic! Then she may reach past your shoulder on many a trip to the bathroom to try to flip on the light switch herself.

The toddler demonstrates an increasingly accurate awareness of the space her body occupies. Her understanding of the spatial relationship of furniture and objects around her is also growing. She begins to learn not to bump her head when she reaches under the table to pick up something. She reaches accurately without overshooting or undershooting her hand as it approaches the object to be picked up. By age three, she can inch her way through fairly narrow places with appropriate twisting and turning of her body to make herself fit. These are indicators of the integration of spatial awareness with the motor planning of big- and small-movement skills.

The toddler also shows an awareness and memory for familiar spatial qualities of nearby space. If a member of her group is missing from his seat at the lunch table, the toddler may ask, "Cheryl gone?" If the furniture in her room at the center has been completely rearranged to make room for a meeting the night before, her quizzical look will alert you that she has spotted the changes. If her ball rolls behind the big, fat teddy bear, she watches for it to come out the other side. She may even reach for a toy behind herself without looking because she remembers it's there.

She gradually observes simple interrelationships of the spatial qualities of her toys. She learns that a particular block or puzzle piece will fit into one matching, small empty space. Eventually she notices that upside-down puzzle pieces can be rotated to match shaped openings that are right-side up. Only later does she comprehend that several puzzle pieces together fit into the space of some wooden puzzle openings.

In the early toddler years, she still does not always distinguish among the spatial characteristics of squares, circles, and triangles, and she certainly cannot draw them differently. She may, however, learn to match particular geometric shapes in familiar form puzzles or designs on other toys. At first, she cannot generalize that awareness. She is not likely to notice the relationship between those particular squares, circles, triangles, and similar shapes in a new toy she is playing with until it has been pointed out. It may take awhile for her to learn to match, in this brand new toy, shapes or designs that she had already learned to match in the old one.

Looking at and matching forms and designs develops before a spatial awareness of size emerges. Size awareness comes slowly. Formboard and matching play skills develop, and the filling, dumping, and nesting mentioned earlier continue. They produce a visual and manipulative groundwork for beginning to discriminate gross size differences. By the late toddler years, the labeling of "big" and "little" comes in as a language manifestation of the spatial concepts that she has grasped.

She is also showing clear indications of emerging time awareness. In infancy, her internal clock made her acutely aware of the approach of mealtime or bedtime—and often her behavior let you know it, loud and clear! But now she doesn't just cry as she had earlier, showing she feels a generalized discomfort. By the late toddler years, she can tell you the next meal will be lunch, not breakfast. She knows that after lunch it will be rest time. During her afternoon play, she also knows when it's approaching time for cleanup, or for Daddy to come and pick her up.

The older toddler begins to be more aware of the shape of *structures* she builds with blocks or sand. They become less random *piles* and take on purposeful shapes. She begins to notice the relationship of blocks to each other and can copy the position of a couple of blocks you put together. Then she learns to copy three or more. By the late toddler years, this curious little investigator has figured out how to build a block tower that looks different from a house, or a sand castle that looks different from the moat around it.

Her buildings may not look like the more polished architecture of her six- or eight-year-old counterpart, but they show that her constructional play feels like fun to her for some new reasons. She used to love to build just because she liked the feel of the blocks or sand or water, or because of the mastery she felt from seeing the blocks or sand respond to being pushed around. Now, however, you can see that real spatial concepts are emerging.

 How to Help Develop Space/Time Awareness

- Occupy toddlers with interesting activities as their parents leave during their early days at the center. Avoid having them watch parents walk down a long corridor or a long way down the street before they are out of sight.

- Provide plenty of containers as well as objects to be dropped inside. Be sure the small objects will fit easily but are too big to be eaten. Try using buckets, kitchen pans, wide-mouthed plastic bottles into which can be dropped clothespins, spools, film-mailing tins, and small blocks.

- During water play, provide plastic containers so that toddlers begin to observe how much water fills the space inside, and which container can be dumped into another without overflowing.

- Make sure toddlers have a variety of cause/effect toys, for example, push- or pull-toys that make interesting sounds or movements as they walk, a jack-in-the-box, a simple-to-operate spinning top, other friction or battery-operated toys that respond to simple pressure, or toys that talk when the strings are pulled. Children will notice the "before" and "after" sequence and will learn to modify their own actions to produce the result they want.

- Provide a variety of shape-sorting and formboard toys. In time, they will notice not only which pieces fit into the shaped holes but also the idea that turning a piece around or upside down will allow it to fit in its hole.

- When a toddler is doing a new form puzzle, allow her time to figure it out. Do not be tempted to demonstrate the answer. Repeating a puzzle you have shown her how to do gives her far less spatial information than completing it independently the first time!

- If a toddler has tried a new wooden puzzle without success and seems frustrated, try this trick. For puzzles that have several pieces, each of which fits into its own opening, cover half the openings so that the toddler has fewer spatial choices to make. If the openings include an apple, a pear, a banana, and an orange, and the toddler is having trouble, try covering the banana and orange and see if she can solve the two remaining ones.

- Provide blocks and other construction toys for piling and building. Express interest in the results of these spatial learning activities. Ask the toddlers to tell you about their structures without making any suggestions about size, shape, or accuracy. Wood-colored blocks particularly encourage attention to spatial features rather than color during building activities.

- Movement-through-space experiences for the toddler and her toys are grand learning opportunities. A toy car running down an incline and a dropping ball teach her about gravity. A ride on your shoulders or a climb to the top of a sliding board ladder teach her about height. (Be sure to take safety precautions so that a fall won't injure or scare her.) Crawling through a toy tunnel, climbing through a play environment, and maneuvering a ride'em horse through a maze of toys and furniture will help, too. They create an awareness of the size of her body and the spatial characteristics of riding toys and playroom furniture. Be sure all toddlers have access to these kinds of experiences.

- Use spatial words when playing with the toddlers—*big, in, on, under, out of, away from*—even though they may not be ready to use these words themselves yet.

PERSONALITY/SOCIALIZATION

The docile, cute one-year-old who needs her parents' or caretaker's approval suddenly seems to acquire a mind of her own sometime during the next year as she strives to establish more independence. Soon the novelty of those first charming words is forgotten as the determined toddler begins to use her newly acquired verbal abilities to express strong personal opinions—sometimes in opposition to her authority figures.

By age three, some of her negative behaviors have subsided, and she has begun to learn to delay gratification—she can wait for a cookie or a TV program or attention from an adult. This shows that she is advancing in her understanding of the passage of time and cause/effect relationships. Although she is still the center of her world, the three-year-old can initiate social contacts. She is beginning to identify with others.

Mini- and Maxi-Milestones of Personality/Socialization

Separation and Independence. By the age of one, the toddler has acquired a basic trust and sense of security if she has had consistency, physical comfort, and nurturing in her upbringing, and her needs have been met. Now she is beginning to develop an awareness that she is a separate being. It is natural for her to begin to realize she is different from her world and the people around her, not just an attachment or an extension of them. Then she dares to branch out toward more independence and eventually a greater autonomy. She begins to break the umbilical cord of dependency she experienced toward her parents in the early months. The development of an independent sense of self, both emotionally and intellectually, helps her begin to understand her special role and place in the world. It also encourages her to recognize that she can do things for herself—and smart adults allow this bid for independence to mature happily. You can watch with delight when she tries by herself to turn the pages of the picture book being read to her and when she refuses to stay in your lap as much as she used to. Soon she will not need to hold your hand as she climbs up the stairs or walks with you to the playground.

However, that newly independent toddler will not be outgrowing any time soon her need for consistent and loving adults available in her life. Indeed, the new emotional separateness she experiences is far from complete. While she likes trying out the idea of being independent, it is so new that she is somewhat afraid of the separation. Tears may flow when Mommy or Daddy leaves her. Small arms may wrap around her familiar caretaker's neck when a stranger approaches or she is taken to a new environment. Her strong attachment to her blanket or favorite stuffed toy provides another example of her continuing dependence and sense of insecurity. Just try separating a toddler from her special "blankie" at bedtime! She will let you know when she needs security or feels tired or just wants to hold your hand. Let her set the pace. She will seesaw between dependence and independence for a long time.

Inconsistency. She will show other signs of inconsistency that make life with a toddler a frustrating challenge. She may change her mind often as she tries with difficulty to identify and meet her needs. You may not enjoy the toddler's unexpected outbursts or her energetic spurt of movement that causes another child's block tower to fall. But think of the frustration the toddler herself will be experiencing! She is dealing with the separation/dependency conflict. In addition, her rapidly expanding big-movement skills encourage her to explore new play adventures. But competencies are not perfected and they lack judgment, so spills and bruises occur often. Also her brand new language skills are certainly not complete enough to express her feelings or make a complex request.

Her inconsistency and ambivalence are particularly apparent in the area of potty training. A toddler may enthusiastically say that she wants to wear "panties," not diapers, and go to the potty like her big sister. Yet her sensory awareness and fine-motor coordination for those small sphincter muscles may be inadequate. Some researchers believe that her social ambivalence (holding on and possessing versus letting go, as well as independence versus dependence) is a major contributing factor to the delay some children show in completing the toilet training process.

Egocentricity and Autonomy. As the realization dawns on the toddler that she is a separate being, not attached to her environment, she takes delight in the notion that perhaps she is the center of her little universe, like a beaming small sun attracting things to orbit around her. This egocentric view of the world is normal for her age and helps to explain her surprise and frustration when things don't go her way. She also begins to think of herself as autonomous—so independent that she can handle life's every challenge by herself. She is again surprised and frustrated when she cannot. When you understand the conflicts and inevitable frustrations that are whirling around in this little tyke's head, you realize she has a lot of hard social lessons to learn in a short time.

No wonder the "terrible two's" arrive with a vengeance, and the vehement "No" becomes a part of her everyday speech. Although she may resist your behavioral boundary-setting, she needs your consistent structure to help her develop. She needs to learn habits and a daily living schedule that will help make her life predictable and socially comfortable. This provides a solid basis for seeking out new adventures and play experiences. She may not like the arrival of her naptime like clockwork every afternoon or the apple slice she receives for a snack after playtime instead of a lollipop. She may even give vent to a loud "No." But these rules keep her healthy and rested. Once they are established, she learns to rely on their consistency and may show resistance or confusion if changes in the routine occur. In fact, she may even seem almost ritualistic in adhering to rules she has accepted.

Feelings and Behavior. A toddler shows a new array of feelings—not just the feelings of resistance and frustration expressed in her "No." Now that she is past the infant stage of fairly simple demanding/satisfied behavior, you may gradually realize that her emotions have become more complex. You may even notice jealousy when you pay attention to another child. She expresses her emotions rather expansively in generalized terms, and they are often accompanied by big-movement representational expressions such as clapping and dancing. She is even beginning to recognize more accurately that feelings affect your own behavior. She begins to "read" you and to adjust her behavior to your emotional cues even without words or explanations from you. You may hear from her, "You tired?" "You happy?" "You mad at me?"

Toddlers vary in their behavior just as babies do—but even more so. The relative importance of heredity and environmental factors has often been debated by the experts. You may also have strong opinions on the subject. Regardless of the cause, differences do exist. By the toddler years, personality and disposition will clearly differentiate the children. Each one will use toys differently. The opportunity for individual choice and the difference in children's dispositions will affect development. A placid toddler's timetable may be different from an active child's. The quieter youngster may be advanced in trying out new social skills like the give-and-take of rolling a ball back and forth with you. She may, however, be taking her time getting acquainted with the world through big-movement exploration. Nearly all babies will catch up a little later in the areas where they temporarily lag behind.

Not only do toddlers display differences in basic temperament, but each toddler's behavior is also influenced by whether she is rested or fatigued, hungry or satisfied. Behavior also varies with the environment and the attitude of the people most important to her. She may seem almost like a different child in her own quiet living room when compared to the same child at her busy day-care center—expecially on the day before a state inspection committee's visit, when the stress level may be high. Your ability to stay calm in a crisis or when she is already very anxious or upset will help her retain a feeling of security.

Play with Toys. The toddler loves to play with and explore toys, practicing and experimenting with them over and over. By the middle toddler years, she will probably begin to make believe with her toys and will generalize behavior and information learned in one context to new toys or even nontoys. A large stick becomes a broom or horse, or a small one a stirring spoon. A block becomes a cookie for dolly or a hat for teddy bear, perhaps accompanied by her own cascade of giggles as the clever toddler acknowledges to herself the fictitious nature of the play experience. She is not yet capable of expanding such brief encounters into extended imaginative play with a story line.

Play with People. The toddler's play with other toddlers is separate and alone. At first, she may be an onlooker, observing other children as they play and occasionally chatting briefly with them. She has little interest in what they are actually playing. She has no sense of belonging or being part of a group of friends. She may even think of other toddlers as objects to be explored. The exploree may not love the idea! Interactions in the earliest toddler years may include hugging or touching—even hitting or biting—but never cooperative exchanging or sharing of playthings. This does not represent selfishness but an incomplete understanding of ownership.

In time, the developing toddler begins to play independently beside or near other children with similar toys. She may seem almost unaware that another child is there. This is called parallel play. It is a normal stage of development, and it is not reasonable to expect a child to share toys happily at this age. Her firm "Mine" reminds you that it is a good idea to have plenty of toys for each child when toddlers are together.

The toddler particularly likes to play with older siblings and very familiar adults such as parents and most familiar teachers. Such an adult can be the young child's best friend and also her favorite plaything—animate, responsive, and loving. The interaction of your-turn my-turn games makes her feel that she is important and cared about. In the earliest toddler years, she can take turns with a simple hide-and-seek game with a teacher or older child. She has object permanence now and understands that the person or object hiding hasn't disappeared for good. She will also enjoy the shared interaction of showing you a favorite toy. This social use of objects suggests the toddler has an internal representation of that object. That is, she has some understanding and appreciation of its function. When object representation in a symbolic system appears in the form of naming things and pictures, then she will want to share that with you, too.

Her attempts to get across ideas to you and others in her play environment help to further stimulate the innate biological language capacity that is unfolding. She will use more language to name things when interacting with someone than when she is alone. Interactive play with people using more complex toys and language will develop later.

You and other important older friends play a major role in her social development. Imitation of such significant role models becomes a vital part of the older toddler's experience. She pays closer attention to you than you might suspect, picking up and copying your actions, speech, and emotional responses, sometimes to an uncanny degree. You will begin to see that some of her favorite play experiences are simulation activities—pushing a toy lawn mower around the play yard, sweeping or vacuuming with a stick or toy appliance, scolding dolls with your exact words.

Because the child is still quite dependent on you, she may not always resist it if you interfere inappropriately in her playtime. Examples of such inappropriate interference include suggesting uses for toys before a child has had time to discover their possibilities and demonstrating uses that are too hard for her to accomplish.

Independent Play. The toddler also needs play experiences separate from you. If the toddler toys for your center are selected carefully, they can help increase each child's self-confidence and sense of power. Toys that have been chosen correctly may prevent the frustration and conflict children feel in other aspects of their lives from occurring at playtime, too. A toddler enjoys playtime most when her toys do not require adult help for them to be fun. Then playtime can be a time she can feel truly independent and in control of her environment.

She will love toys that give satisfaction without strict limits for success— for example, small wagons that can be filled with toys and pulled easily to any location, low rocking horses she can mount by herself, and crayons with large, blank pieces of paper. Not recommended are complex mechanical or construction toys that won't work without minute, intricate winding or fitting together. These are beyond the capability of immature little fingers. Signs of frustration, perhaps even escalating to aggression or tears, may result from their attempts.

The toddler's new independence is also enhanced when she can make her own selections from among available playthings. Keep the number of choices reasonable to avoid overload (overstimulation). Additional toy surprises can always be brought out from higher shelves or closed cabinets at an opportune moment. Keep available toys where they can be reached by the children with few restrictions. The act of making choices of toys provides positive decision-making opportunities now that help prepare for the decision-making process in the future. This practice will help establish good work habits in the early years. These habits will serve a child well when she enters school and will also help prepare her for adulthood.

Encourage toddlers to help you put toys away at the end of playtime. Even though it is not a natural tendency for children to clean up, a happy, playful time of providing at least a little assistance, in harmony with a caretaker, will further enhance independence and responsibility. You will want her to learn that the work of cleanup time can be pleasantly rewarding.

By the third birthday, a toddler's newly acquired language skills allow a new level of self-expression. This contributes to her emotional growth and ability to communicate meaningfully with others. Her new listening-comprehension ability helps her focus her attention, thereby increasing the amount of information she can take in. This helps her succeed during interactions with others.

She feels more comfortable now about her individuality and much less anxious about separation. If her needs have been met through these difficult toddler years, she will have gained confidence and understanding about her place both in the tightly knit society that is her family and in the familiar small group she sees daily. By age three, she has become an engaging little citizen. She is beginning to have a good idea of the consequences of disobeying the simplest social standards. Her smile of appreciation shows that she understands what praise is. She may be old enough to tolerate attending a birthday party—or having one—provided the activities there are not overstimulating and the number of guests is limited. She is well on the way to becoming a charming new member of the preschool society.

 How to Help Develop Personality/Socialization

Play

- Toddlers will need lots of time to play alone. Encourage them to use their own inner resources to entertain themselves with toys or other playthings of their choosing. Make yourself quietly available nearby. They will know they can call on you when needed. If necessary, you can occasionally redirect a child whose frustration with a toy escalates out of control.

- Toddlers will also benefit from their exposure to other children, although sharing toys and playing together may often require your intervention. Allow a few minutes for toddlers to try to work out a compromise on their own, but stop their interactions short of tantrums or hitting.

- Play with toddlers sometimes. Follow their lead in choosing and playing with toys that most appeal to them. Use terms like "Aren't we having fun?" or "Let's have fun building with the blocks." This helps create a positive feeling about play when more than one person is involved and helps pave the way for socialization through play with other children.

- Allow time for a toddler to figure out and succeed with new toys or those that require manipulation like wooden insert puzzles.

- Wait for trial and error or practice, and the learning that comes from processing information about toys at her own pace. You might provide verbal encouragement to keep trying. If necessary, occasionally provide the *little* touch of help that allows her to achieve success herself. Particularly respect the methodical, analytical thinker, who needs more time to comprehend her toys. If she feels pressured to provide fast answers, it could take away the fun and reduce her interest in the toy. For any toddler, premature intervention by an adult can reduce her tolerance for frustration and foster a demanding, quick-fix attitude. As toys become familiar and spontaneous new uses of a toy become sparse, that may be a cue for you to gently expand how it is used.

- Take notice if a very high level of frustration develops often in a toddler's play with certain toys. Though they may be good toys that will be fun and foster development at an older age, they may be too hard for a child of this age. Without fuss or embarrassment to the unsuccessful child, move the toys to the preschoolers' room or store them high enough to be out of reach to toddlers.

- Hold dolls or stuffed animals closely in your arms and rock, love, and pet them. Toddlers will imitate you and learn how to gently love and care for their "babies" as they hold and move them.

- Bring common household items to your center to provide inexpensive play experiences for toddlers. For example, sturdy pots and pans or plastic containers are great for pounding, filling, and dumping. Wooden spoons are fine for banging and "cooking."

- Avoid the temptation to *play* with toddlers by instructing them in reading signs in the building and outside. The exception to this is the child who spontaneously begins asking questions about advertising logos or other frequently encountered words in the environment. We do not recommend drilling very young children in reading signs or words in books. Instead, we suggest using the time to let their natural curiosity develop. Prodding and pushing can sometimes create a feeling of stress or pressure. This can take its toll in reduced interest in academic or intellectual activities and take away a child's joy in learning. Often children pushed into reading at an early age read about as well as other schoolchildren by second or third grade anyhow. It is more important for toddlers to learn by discovery than by prodding.

- Use books often. Look at pictures with young toddlers while cuddling them warmly, or encourage them to look at the pictures independently. Do not allow ripping of pages. Older toddlers may enjoy sitting quietly in a comfortable circle or alone next to you while listening to your reading a very few short, simple stories—over and over again.

- Try having a lunch or tea party with older toddlers to reinforce mealtime social skills and to encourage pretend play. Use doll dishes and doll guests to encourage politeness, manners, awareness of social cues, thank you, please, use of a napkin, and so on.

- Provide opportunities for toddlers to play and interact with preschoolers in addition to other toddlers. This stimulates language and social development by providing older role models.

- Try to maintain long-term staff commitments at your center with little staff turnover so that the children in your care will experience consistency of personnel taking care of them.

Behavior Management

- A loving attitude that reaches out to children helps teach them how to love and reach out to others. Sprinkle your conversation with lots of affectionate words.

- You can learn a lot by observing how toddlers treat their dolls and stuffed toys. They give cues that tell you what message they are receiving from you or their parents about expressing love. If they are curt, harsh, or punitive toward them, listen to your own words in the future as you speak to them or correct their behavior. Are you using words and behavior you would want them to repeat to their friends or stuffed animals?

- One part of providing a loving environment for toddlers includes setting clear limits—gently but firmly. When resistance or naughty behavior occurs, first identify whether the youngster has understood the guidelines. Did she know crayons are for drawing on paper, not walls? If not, state the guidelines clearly and calmly in a quiet voice. Be sure the guidelines or expectations are reasonable. Perhaps the toddlers are showing you that crayons should not be stored within reach. Keep them in view, but let her ask you for them when she wants a turn so that you can direct her to the art corner or to an appropriate writing surface. If there is a specific time set aside for using crayons or for painting, tell her you are all going to wait so that everyone will have a chance to color together. Once the guidelines are understood, stick to them so that she will know you mean what you say. This gives her a sense of security while she is also learning the rules of social behavior. When she complies with the guidelines in the future, be sure you let her know how pleased you are with her good behavior.

- Remember that praise and a feeling of satisfaction about an experience go a long way to encourage a toddler to repeat the behavior that just preceded it. ("Good girl, you are being quiet while Michael is resting" or "Good boy, you put your blocks away in the box.") Avoid verbalizing praise to a child for everything she does. That reduces the impact and effectiveness of praise for those accomplishments that really deserve it. A smile or pat may be enough.

- Scolding or other disciplinary measures let a toddler know you did not like her behavior. "Don't you ever do that again," however, does not suggest alternatives to help her behave more acceptably next time. If she experiences scolding or punishing words or actions very often, she will habituate to them—that is, she will come to expect such reactions from you, and they will have little effect on improving her behavior. (In the same way, she has habituated to the noise of the furnace, or the squeezing on her foot of her tied shoelaces. They do not change her behavior positively. But if given the chance, she would rather play far from the furnace and in stocking feet.) Use praise for a more positive effect.

- Respond to pleasantly expressed, reasonable requests promptly and happily when you are available. However, be firm about refusing to acknowledge repeated requests for attention or objects that are unreasonable.

- Ignore whining and nagging to prevent children from developing such language as a habit. Children often learn to whine because they think it is the only way they can get an adult to listen. When a toddler needs your attention and you cannot respond immediately, tell her you will come just as soon as possible. Then ignore further nagging. Be sure to stick to your word. Give her attention when you finish what you are doing, along with a pleasant word of praise for her good waiting behavior.

- Try to ignore inappropriate behavior (like nagging or angrily stamping her foot), especially if you are busy talking or making a telephone call. If the toddler is ignored, in the future she will not use such behavior to get your attention and manipulate your reactions.

- Prevent inappropriate behavior from providing some other secondary reward. Instead, substitute a more desirable activity. (If, for example, she is throwing toys one after the other down the stairs and is rewarded by hearing their cheerful clatter on the way down, move her to another room and redirect her attention to throwing beanbags into a wastebasket.)

- Striking or roughly shaking children **really** is harmful and unacceptable discipline and will provide a model of using violent measures to solve problems instead of thinking through a creative solution.

- Do not be alarmed if a toddler uses tears to express anger, pain, frustration, fear of separation, or sadness. Although crying may be distressing, recognize that the tears represent important feelings she cannot express verbally. Watch for body language or hesitant words through the tears that give clues to the cause of the crying. Then understandingly state the child's apparent emotion calmly in clear short sentences. "I see that you are sad because your dolly broke," or "You look angry. You wish you didn't have to stop playing now, don't you?"

- Recognize that an occasional temper tantrum is inevitable. Sometimes toddlers experience intense frustration because they lack the ability to express their anger in words or to argue logically. They may feel their only recourse is to lie down on the floor, screaming or kicking. If a tantrum should occur, focus on the feelings of the child and try these suggestions:

  1. Move her a few feet to another spot, or to a quiet corner so that she knows you are in control of the situation.

  2. Prevent the child's physical movements from hitting you. Children should not feel that they can hit adults to gain power.

  3. In a calm, quiet voice, briefly mention why the child cannot have her way, then proceed with your planned activities.

  4. Do not give in to the child's demand, or her inappropriate requests will become more frequent and more demanding. Don't be tempted to bribe her to shorten the noisy emotional event.

  5. Be loving but firm and consistent. Remember that this youngster is only two years old and depends on you to retain your adult behavior and help her through this crisis. Some specialists suggest she will calm down faster if one of the teachers hugs the child throughout the entire time she is crying or screaming.

- Try to avoid head-on confrontation. Provide an enticing toy as a distraction if a child is approaching the frustration point in her play or repeatedly handles a forbidden object.

- Suggest to the toddler choices of socially acceptable ways of expressing her needs. This will help her learn to control her own behavior and to have a preliminary understanding of bargaining and compromise.

- Humor may be helpful to prevent behavior from getting out of hand, but avoid poking fun at a toddler.

- Keep your own emotional life stable and comfortable if possible. Your feelings affect toddlers, even if you try to curtail their negative effects. Reduce stresses that overchallenge your life and produce anxiety that clouds the environment.

- Your attitude toward achievements will greatly influence the children's feelings about themselves and the development of their personalities. Allow them to feel proud of each new accomplishment without pushing them on to something new before they are ready. Take delight in their achievements, but strongly avoid giving the impression that your affection is dependent on them.

- Do not be overly solicitous to children's needs or inappropriately worried about health or rigid obedience. Their reaction to your anxiety will show that they understand the effect of their behavior on you, an obvious but undesirable cause/effect response mastered by toddlers. Your frequent question "Are you all right?" when a child is happily playing quietly may cause her to wonder if she *is* all right. "Be careful you don't fall off the hobbyhorse" over and over will make a child anxious that she is not capable of riding it. When a big production is made about every scratch or fall encountered during playtime, the children may feel it necessary to complain loudly about any little bump or bruise.

- Try to maintain a reasonably consistent schedule for the toddlers. Be consistent without being rigid. An occasional change of schedule allows for spontaneity.

- When changes in the routine are expected, let the toddlers know in advance so that they can begin to adjust themselves in preparation for accepting the change calmly. Use very short explanations, for example, "Today we will be going to story hour at the library," or "After your lunch, the zookeeper will be bringing animals to visit."

- Let toddlers help make choices, for example, between two games you are thinking of playing or which record to hear. This adds to their self-confidence and good feelings about themselves.

Potty Training, Sensory Awareness, and Toys

- If potty training does not proceed smoothly and cooperatively, you may wish to use a toy, book, or recorded music in the bathroom to encourage toddlers to stay on the potty longer. Be sure these do not distract or confuse children about the real purpose for being there.

- Remember that sensory awareness plays an important role in toilet training. A toddler may not be able to clearly discriminate her sensation of needing to urinate or have a bowel movement from her feelings of hunger, tight clothes, or pressure on her bottom when she is sitting down. Running water in the sink may provide a sensory clue and help stimulate a physical response.

- Other children may strongly dislike the pressure of the toilet seat on their bottoms. In fact, an indented ring may be apparent on their skin for several minutes after they leave the seat. A few fascinating play activities while they are seated might help these tactile-sensitive children forget their discomfort.

- Sometimes a child fears the sensation of sitting up high with her feet dangling in space if the toilet is not small. She may feel precariously balanced. In that case, a box underfoot or a small climbing stool in front of the toilet is preferred. Even better would be on-the-floor potty chairs. If none are available, you can reduce the size of the full-sized toilet seat hole with a flat, plastic insert. This insert ring will travel better than a potty chair if you are taking the children out for the day.

- Schedule time before activities, lunch, rest, or going home to have the children use the potty. Keep small washbasins with soap and towel-holders close by. Make sure youngsters know they can also go to the potty anytime they feel sensory cues announcing the need.

LANGUAGE

Those precious first words, which become indelibly imprinted in the memories of parents, are soon accompanied by other words and phrases, often mispronounced, that help you realize the primary things that capture the young child's attention. Her readiness for expressing interests and needs in real words encourages adoring caretakers gently and persuasively to prod and coax each new word by example.

The toddler soon learns to use her words purposefully for more and more complex communication of information, eventually learning to relate fascinating events of the day. Astute adults shift their responses to that of listener rather than prodder, although their listening also encourages the new talker to express herself. They nod and smile silently with rapt attention as they listen to the three-year-old's personal news events reported in fairly complete sentences. During the toddler years, a real language explosion has taken place!

Mini- and Maxi-Milestones of Language

The majority of first words so lovingly recorded in baby books around the world are nouns that give a verbal label to an important person, object, or event in baby's immediate experience. The youngster is developing the concept of *naming*. She is unconsciously discovering that these sounds called *words* are symbolic representations of *things*, and that their use makes communication with other people much easier. She is no longer tied to cries, coos, babbles, and smiles as a way of expressing herself to other important people in her life.

Many early words involve activity (for example, the word "plane" for a toddler whose parent travels a lot, or the common early word "bye-bye"). Others represent commands and are used to report a need and to gain a response from someone ("bottle," "ball," "more").

Earliest words are frequently accompanied by overstated gestures, perhaps made in great excitement. During the middle toddler years, the gestures may include pulling on your clothes or your hand to show you something. Later, pointing will occur to give reference to events or objects being mentioned. Unfortunately, this occurs without an awareness of the frequent social inappropriateness of such pointing.

During this period of early talking in words, the alert youngster also demonstrates that she comprehends language she cannot yet verbalize. For example, she makes an action response to requests by others (such as retrieving a toy or waving bye-bye on command). Within a few months, she can point on request to many named staff members, familiar objects, and some youngsters in her nursery group. She begins to show she comprehends prepositions of location like "in," "under," and "on." Later she shows that she understands opposites like "come-go" and "run-stop." Listening to stories is a grand treat for the toddler, and she requests the same ones over and over.

As she is listening to you and comprehending your messages, she is subconsciously focusing on both your words and your body language—how your face looks and your body moves, as well as the tone of your voice. She is learning to focus her attention on your words and nonverbal behavior, then to process the information she is hearing so that it has meaning for her.

Although the toddler's understanding outstrips her capacity for talking, her speaking skills are developing, too. Short sentences begin to occur, and around the second birthday she learns that all-too-familiar word "no." She uses it often, to the distraction of most adults. With her loud "no" she may be so determined to assert her independence that she says "no" even when she means "yes." Other overgeneralizations occur (like extending the meaning of such words as "doggie" or "cow" to all four-legged animals). In addition, she may use original applications of grammatical rules she is trying to understand. For example, overregularization of verb endings may create words like "comed" or "goed" or "breaked." Her development of an understanding for the structure of language will include many of these applications that are inaccuracies ("Me no like beans" or "Me blowed candles"). However, they will be logical mistakes, not random errors, and you can hear that she is beginning to catch on to the idea of how to generate language so that it communicates more and more complex thoughts.

One interesting pattern that emerges during the toddler years is telegraphic speech. This early form of talking resembles the sentence structure you would use for sending a telegram, omitting nonessential pieces of linguistic information. One teacher calls it "caveman talk." It presents the deep structure or essential elements of speech that give the most meaning, primarily nouns and verbs, and sometimes adjectives. At the same time, it eliminates the additional less informative functional components used by adults to create the familiar surface structure of speech we are accustomed to hearing (Mommy is coming soon = "Mommy come" or "Mommy soon." Here comes Mary = "Mary come").

The child's telegraphic speech reduces not only the number of words but also the number of sound units that convey meaning. For example, -*ing* and -*s* endings may be eliminated. *Un*- as a prefix may be dropped. Each of the minimal sound units of speech is called a "morpheme." (*Phil rolled the balls* = six morphemes.) While morphemes include phonetic (sound) information, they more importantly are used to define the structure and grammatical meaning of speech. Morphemes give information about not only the sound of speech but also the form of speech.

8 MORPHEMES

Initially, a toddler probably will have trouble matching her plurals ("We's playing" or "My doll fall") or her tenses (for example, describing a *past* event "Bow-wow jump in bathtub" or a *future* event ("Me play Grandma's"). Notice that by age three these mistakes are beginning to occur less frequently.

Major cues that help the developing little orator listen and communicate more effectively include speech melody, sound patterns, and inflection. Certain words in adults' sentences that receive the less heavy inflection are often the very words omitted from the toddler's speech. They include prepositions, auxiliary verbs, articles like "the" or "an," and adverbs. This consistent neglect of the words automatically de-emphasized by adults clearly highlights the importance to the very young child of the sound, intonation, and rhythm of your talking. You are providing an important model that the youngster copies closely as she practices her early words, phrases, and sentences.

As the third birthday approaches, pronunciation is erratic and often incorrect. However, the toddler can make herself understood even by people who do not know her well. She experiments with a wide variety of vocabulary words and uses several hundred in her speech. She begins to label the haphazard scribbles and circular shapes her small fingers are learning to create. By doing this, she is announcing that she intends the markings to represent symbolically real things in her small realm of experience. This new skill reminds us of her earlier unconscious realization that *words* are also symbols for *things*.

By three, the toddler sometimes surprises the adults around her with grown-up comprehension of some concepts she is not yet able to express. Teachers realize they have to be careful about talking in front of a youngster about the delayed arrival of her parents (if that will bring tears) or the injection she will receive at the doctor's office the next day. Yet teachers are glad her developing comprehension may promote excellent behavior during a medical emergency for another child, when she musters her most cooperative behavior to help others get through the crisis. The developing little conversationalist is also learning to be an effective listener.

 How to Help Develop Language

- Initially accept gestures as a way of asking for something or explaining a feeling or event but substitute the correct word as you respond. In response to a young toddler's pointing, say, "Ball. Here's the ball you wanted." In response to tugging say, "I see you want me to look at your doll."

- Let children know you have understood their verbal messages to you by giving feedback. Provide the paintbrush they asked for, if it is appropriate. Restate their abbreviated, disjointed, or poorly articulated sentences so that they know you understood them. ("Thank you for telling me about your new baby.") This feedback tells children how the language ought to sound and lets the novice speaker know you understood her.

- Be careful how you make direct corrections of mispronunciations and grammar, and never laugh at toddlers' errors. Avoid inhibiting their development of speech. Also, do not repeat the new talkers' language errors since they will be modeling their own language after yours. Copying you and trying to both please you and communicate ideas to you will be a primary encouragement for learning to speak.

- Talk to toddlers in a natural, conversational voice with short, easy-to-understand phrases, using simple words with the most obvious meanings. Often these are nouns with clear, concise definitions. Use topics and speech content that make it easy for children to both recognize the words and associate them with their meanings. This policy helps children not only communicate about the topics at hand but also learn about the structure of language itself.

- Help children learn to listen and respond to each other. This stimulates both language development and social interactions.

- Encourage even young toddlers to use the correct word when asking for something. Do not respond to constant whining or tugging at your clothing in place of verbal requests you know they can say in words. If you respond to whining or nagging, you will be encouraging this common but unappealing means of communication.

- When you are listening to toddlers speaking to you, give your undivided attention. This lets them know you value their words and thoughts, and encourages words rather than the nagging just mentioned. It also provides an early lesson in paying attention and listening. Toddlers need to recognize that their bodies must be ready to listen (eyes focused on speaker, hands usually still), and their minds need to be focused and receptive (not thinking about something else).

- Do not be tempted to repeat directions often. First, say a child's name and wait until she responds by giving you her visual as well as her auditory attention. Then say the instruction once and wait for her to comply. Speak slowly, be certain that she hears you, and keep your sentences short. Be patient and allow time for the toddler to process your words and act on them. Do not keep repeating, or toddlers will soon learn they don't have to listen the first few times.

- Avoid curse words and harsh language or you will later hear them repeated by toddlers. Would you feel comfortable about scolding or disciplining children for using language they learned from you?

- Encourage each toddler to point to the parts of her body as you name them. When she can do that very well, try having her name facial features or appropriate parts of the body that you point to (this is considerably more difficult). Knowing body parts encourages the toddler's awareness of the location of and relationship between portions of her body, a significant help in motor planning big movements.

- Use stuffed animals or puppets to encourage youngsters to discover and name things they see and touch. This may help increase their vocabularies and pay attention to the structure of language.

- Use concrete language first, then add a brief comment about the concept along with it. "Don't touch the hot pot; you will get burned." He cannot understand a longer explanation, and it would only confuse him.

- Use action words if you are playing with or watching children play. "Are you *rocking* your doll to sleep?" "Isn't it fun to *roll* the ball?" "Can you *crawl* through the tunnel?"

- Continue using those spatial words mentioned earlier in this chapter. Your correct use of the words initially helps her grasp the concepts. Later she will be ready to say those words herself. Use phrases like "Here comes the *big* ball," "Let's walk *away from* the swings," "Roll the ball *under* the table (or *on* the table)," "Can I help you get *into* the wagon (or *out* of the wagon)?"

- Use sensory activities like playing with water, sand, clay, Play Doh®, and mud to stimulate language. Children love to talk about how these textures feel, and their use can stimulate awareness of body parts.

- Use movement songs often to encourage motor planning, rhythm, and vestibular stimulation while at the same time increasing language skills and auditory memory. Examples are "Ride a Cock Horse," "Ring around the Rosy," and "Rockabye Baby."

- Make up new songs, with or without movement, by putting personalized words (including her name) to songs or rhymes. Try, for example: "I love Julie, yes I do, she's my sweetheart through and through" and so on (to the tune of "I love coffee, I love tea"). Make sure you give each child a turn with her name in the song. Encourage all the toddlers to join in.

- Repetitive songs delight toddlers and stimulate sound discrimination, speech production, and auditory memory. Songs like "Row, Row, Row Your Boat" or "Three Blind Mice" help her feel a sense of accomplishment because she can master some of the words so easily. Also try the animal sounds in "Old MacDonald." The whole class can give a rousing rendition of "E–I–E–I–O!"

- Read to the toddlers often. Keep an intimate sound to your voice and use inflection appropriate to the story rather than a stilted "lecture/reading" voice. In the early toddler years, large single-picture books promote the idea that everything has a name. Talk about the pictures. Later graduate to books with more complex pictures and an increasing number of words on each page.

IMAGINATION/CREATIVITY

The developing toddler has begun to acquire considerable awareness and competency for carrying out purposeful efforts. She has a sensorimotor basis for imagining movement, sounds, and play experiences she has not tried before. Her new successes are no longer accidents as they often were in her infant years. She is reinforced in her efforts by the pleasure she feels in trying out brand new play experiences. She also loves the smiles, applause, and hugs she receives as she imitates and later originates simple songs, rhythmic movements, block structures, pictures, and pretend behaviors.

By age three, this creative little mini-performer is beginning to grasp the scope of possibilities inherent in the play equipment and accessible indoor or outdoor objects that surround her. With encouragement, her imagination can soar to new heights of experimentation and trial and error. She is well on her way to combining actions and objects in representational play that helps her clarify and refine ideas, feelings, and experiences.

Of Special Interest

Evidence of creative abilities often emerges early. It should not be overlooked in the excitement of documenting the toddler's more commonly reported maxi-milestones such as first steps, talking in sentences, or riding a tricycle. Some adults recall outstanding block-building skills in the early years of children who later became architects. Parents of one adult artist recall that, by his first birthday, he could put together a twenty-six-piece jigsaw puzzle!

Another mother reported that her child could construct exceptionally intricate and complex block structures, even copying advanced designs from the instruction sheet during the toddler years. He later exhibited severe reading and handwriting problems that required his attending a variety of schools for the learning disabled. In time, he achieved early entry into art school. By age twenty-one, his innate creative talent was exhibited by his professional glassblowing, through which the three-dimensional forms he created earned him local and expanding renown.

One toddler with no particular talent in the visual arts could, by fifteen months, carry a tune while other family members harmonized with her. She had a penchant for movement, climbing and running before her first birthday. She bounced and swayed rhythmically to music so often that, for her birthday, her grandparents appropriately gave her a music box with dancing, swirling figures on top. This toddler was always alert to the feelings of those around her. Her calm, quiet disposition turned to tears and anxiety if others in the family were experiencing stress, time pressures, confusion, or grief. It is not surprising to learn that by age twenty-five, this child was earning her living as a New York City actress, singer, and dancer.

A toddler may not grow up to pursue a vocation in the arts, but a lifelong appreciation of such endeavors may begin in the toddler years. Young children who feel noticed, supported, and encouraged in their creative efforts learn to value this aspect of human development.

Mini- and Maxi-Milestones of Imagination/Creativity

Blowing a kiss, waving bye-bye, and playing pat-a-cake are part of the standard imitation repertoire of the just-past-one-year-old. They represent efforts by the young toddler to respond purposefully to actions other people clearly are modeling for her to copy. They are actions the toddler can see herself performing. Another example is rolling a ball back that has been rolled to her.

In addition, the alert toddler begins to notice and mimic other more subtle behaviors of those around her. She particularly copies people's behaviors that are directly related to herself—like feeding herself and making faces at someone. She may also adjust the urgency, pitch, and rhythm of her vocal sounds to imitate her caretakers' voices, in addition to copying their words and, later, phrases. She may begin to copy certain gestures or body language without realizing it, although initially she may not be adept at it.

A toddler is likely to show interest in just scribbling on paper with a crayon, using zigzags and circular scribbles. Later she begins to pretend her action is a replication of what she has noticed others doing. In time, she even learns to imitate your drawn straight lines or circular strokes and to repeat her own oval shapes. She enjoys noticing the marks this creative activity makes and the feeling of the accompanying sweeping arm movements. At first, she won't pay much attention to the color or the symbolic meaning of what the lines are. Imagining a meaning for them will come later. Then her accidental or purposeful circle may be labeled "head" or "ball."

The toddler finds more and more ways to expand the imitation of movements and sounds and sights that surround her. She begins to bring her own wishes and feelings into the action. The resulting pretend play that surfaces in the toddler years will show that imagination is beginning to smolder and will soon burst forth in bright spurts of action, sound, and color.

Imitations will expand beyond using herself to pretend (like pretending to sleep or to eat an imaginary cookie). She will learn to use other objects. At first, she uses them passively by pretending a doll is eating or a stuffed puppy is sleeping. The toddler is using such a toy as an agent or symbolic representation of a real object in her world. As pretend play grows, she will begin to substitute a less representational toy agent, such as a block for a car. At first, this substitute agent will play a passive role. Soon these meaningful substitutions crop up actively time and time again in the imaginative toddler's play day. You will see her "drink" from an empty nesting barrel, sweep with a small tree branch, or help her dolly feed herself with a craft stick (like a Popsicle® stick). Later she may copy the noise of her visiting uncle's motorcycle while "revving up the engine" by turning the handles of her tricycle or hobbyhorse. Domestic mimicry of common household chores will become popular with the older toddler, and soon she will begin to enjoy simple dress-ups using the contents of the costume box or makeshift toy beads.

As cognitive skills increase, it becomes apparent that this emerging little creative artist and performer can imitate models that are not visible at the moment. That is, she can reconstruct memories and pretend that something she has previously observed is happening again now.

The emergence of creative impulses will begin to move beyond simple mimicry or even pretending of familiar remembered routines. Many toddlers know what to do with their bodies while rhythmical music is playing, although they may never have seen anyone dance before. They will know what to do with a paintbrush and tempera colors, though they may never have watched anyone paint before. A toddler will intuitively know how to turn stuffed animals and dolls into imaginary people. She may pretend she has an invisible friend with her, though no one has ever demonstrated this innovative idea to her. She will build block structures that just feel right and are not necessarily imitations or copies of structures she has seen before.

She will love the stories you read to her and will begin telling stories of her own. At first, she just tells news about her immediate experiences. Then she retells special events that happened a few days before. She speaks in unique phrases with original applications of grammatical rules, and says "the darndest things" that make you wonder where she is getting such ideas. Actually, she is getting the ideas from deep inside her, where the source of her imagination glows. This source will be ready to burn brightly when fanned steadily by a nurturing environment. The resulting warm coals of imagination form the basis for kindling new ideas and creative expressions in the teen years and adulthood.

Your smiles, laughter, and clapping for her original antics or artwork will spur her to repeat or expand her accomplishments. After all, the toddler takes unremitting delight in being the center of attention. Wise adults strike a balance between fanning the flames of creativity and overpraising inappropriate attention-seeking behaviors of a potential show-off.

When a child responds rhythmically and enthusiastically to music, you can smile with her and share her joy. But if she frequently exaggerates her dancing *because* she observes that others are watching her, we suggest you turn your attention elsewhere. Take notice of what your praise is encouraging. Do her creative actions seem to be motivated by internal, subjective feelings of joy and self-expression or by the external purpose of getting someone's attention? Appropriate expressions of creative feelings and imaginative thoughts give toddlers confidence. They lay the groundwork for expanding these expressions in the formative preschool years ahead.

 ## How to Help Develop Imagination/Creativity

- Stimulate curiosity during this new stage of development. Encourage pretending, exploratory play, and creative expression. Listen with interest when a child expresses new ideas or wants to show you her latest work of art or new construction.

- To promote the most creativity and use of imagination by toddlers, avoid making suggestions about *how* to play with a toy unless they have already had a lengthy period to investigate it. Instead let the exploring little scientists do their own experimenting and figuring out with their toys about cause/effect relationships and what is satisfying. Watch the children. If given enough freedom, they may come up with novel approaches for using the toys that are beyond your wildest imagination.

- Encourage toddlers to imitate your speech and also sounds in the environment (like a train, a fire siren, or a car motor). Imitation helps lay the groundwork for initiation of speech, and, later, use of words to create and express new ideas.

- If a toddler gains pleasure from using her body to demonstrate her appreciation of music by swaying and bouncing, or clapping and stamping, dance with her. Provide lots of opportunities for her to experience different types of music. Perhaps her parents can bring in one of her favorite records to play at the center.

- If at a young age, a child shows that she loves to listen to vocal music or to sing, hum or sing along with her or her favorite record. Help her learn the words of simple songs—or make up new ones. Tape her early creations and play them for her parents. They often miss the creative moments when they are working, and they would appreciate your thoughtfulness.

- Let toddlers sometimes experiment informally with rhythm band instruments borrowed from the preschool room—with or without an accompanying record or song. Such instruments encourage not only self-expression but also big-arm movements and timing. Tambourines, bells, and other instruments for shaking with one hand are easiest. Small cymbals and rhythm sticks involve the use of two hands doing the same action. Triangles, bongo drums, and hitting a tambourine require even more coordination as one hand hits and the other hand holds.

- For novelty, a toddler could try rubbing a long wooden spoon against rough textures like sandpaper, corrugated paper, or plastic screening. Make drums from upside-down wastebaskets, empty cans, oatmeal containers, or salt boxes. Also try a wooden spoon on the back of a pan, and remember that two pan lids make great cymbals (if you can stand the noise!). Triangles and xylophones add melody to the "music" and may keep a toddler creatively engaged for long periods. Older toddlers may be ready to try instruments in a group occasionally, marching and singing as they drum—maybe for an impromptu Fourth of July parade or another celebration.

- Give children lots of opportunities to create new things with their hands. Use a variety of construction toys. Also try large blank paper for drawing and coloring. Avoid suggesting what to build or draw, or how to do it. Whatever a child decides to make will offer a chance to think, plan, create, and feel good about herself when she finishes. If her idea doesn't work out the way she planned, she can change it, proving to herself that she can solve the problem by herself.

- Express interest in each young artist's creations and ask the creator to tell you about them. Never say, "What is it?" This suggests that either it *ought* to represent something besides itself or, if she did intend it to represent something else, her attempt was somehow unsuccessful. Make positive general comments like, "Oh, what a pretty red picture."

- Display these creations prominently and change them frequently. Point them out to family members when the children are listening, and send them home for safekeeping. Your interest will increase the children's motivation to continue creating new things. Suggest that parents save the creations for documenting gradual improvement and growth. This also helps toddlers realize their creative efforts are valued.

- Buy bright, large, washable crayons that are thick enough for little hands to grasp. Start with four to six colors and try to find crayons with a flat side so that they won't roll away. Give children a place to use them where they can scribble to their hearts' content without damaging the surface underneath if the crayon line should slip off the edge of the paper. Try newspaper, shelf paper, or an old plastic cloth if extra protection is needed. Many children like to color while lying on the floor. If they are sitting at a table, be sure their feet rest on a flat surface—on the floor or on a firm box if the table is a grown-up size. Low tables and chairs *really* are essential.

- After children have had plenty of time to experiment with crayons on their own, you might show them novel ways to color, like rubbing unwrapped crayons on their sides or coloring over different textures. You can also tape or tie several crayons side by side so that their strokes make a variety of colors with each swipe.

- Introduce finger painting and see how inventive children can be. Many will love the feel of fingers, fists, and palms in the paints—even forearms and elbows. This is one of the best mediums for very young children since they do not have to adjust to tools like paintbrushes, pencils, or markers. Watching the marks left by their moving hands and fingers helps children notice the hand/eye connection between their movements and the visual stimulus on the paper. Encourage lines and swirls, shapes and dots, and interesting use of color. Scribbles, circles, and zigzag lines may be their first masterpieces. They will manipulate colors without caring about form. You might want to try one of the recipes in Figure 5–2.

Figure 5–2 RECIPES FOR INEXPENSIVE FINGER PAINTS

1. Use flavored pudding or Jell-O® for a delicious finger-painting experience if a young toddler tends to nibble playthings. Mix the pudding-paint in a different bowl from the one you would use to serve pudding. Then she will not think she is being encouraged to smear food when she is eating at the high chair or table. When nonedible finger paints are introduced later, be sure she recognizes that they are not to be eaten.

2. Mix liquid starch with liquid tempera or show-card paint. If necessary, thicken with cornstarch.

3. To 1 quart of boiling water, add powdered color or a few drops of food coloring. Stir in 1 cup of cornstarch and 1/2 cup of Ivory Snow,® and cook briefly. (When food coloring is added to any recipe, it should be added to the liquid first to reduce staining.)

- After an adventure of trying various finger-painting experiences, wash off little hands gently, helping toddlers use words to describe how pretty the water in the sink becomes.

- Help toddlers drop tempera color onto paper, which they fold carefully to create irregularly shaped designs. Hang small versions up as holiday decorations. Not only is this creative, but paper folding is also a good dexterity activity for the older toddlers.

- Toddlers will enjoy dripping little globs of paint onto paper with a paintbrush, spoon, or straw, using a variety of colors. Then they can tilt the paper and watch the colors blend and make designs. Some children might rather use a paintbrush or dull plastic knife to mix the colors together.

- Toddlers can benefit from using Play Doh® or an equivalent homemade recipe. See Figure 5–3. (Save clay, with its firmer texture, for the preschoolers.) Encourage squeezing, shaping, indenting, and feeling. With a little imagination, older toddlers can make pretend snakes, hotdogs, pies, cakes, and cookies. Sometimes pounding, poking, and rolling doughy mixtures also helps release excess energy and frustrations.

- Although it is generally desirable for toddlers to have free selection from among available playthings, messy creative activities will be an exception. Of course, they will need adult permission and a little

Figure 5–3 RECIPES FOR SOFT, PLIABLE DOUGH

1. UNCOOKED VERSION
   2 cups flour
   3/4 cup salt
   3/4 to 1 cup colored water
     (use food coloring or powdered colors)
   1 tablespoon vegetable oil
   Mix. Knead until consistency is smooth. Keep in refrigerator.

2. COOKED VERSION
   1 cup flour   1 cup water (with a few drops of food
   1/2 cup salt   coloring added)
   2 teaspoons cream of tartar   1 tablespoon oil

Mix all ingredients and cook over medium heat until ball forms and it becomes translucent rather than milky. Knead. Store in plastic bowl in refrigerator.

help structuring the use of paints, finger paints, markers (be sure they are water soluble), crayons, and modeling doughs. Children might try testing the rules regarding approved surfaces where they may use these materials and whether or not they need a smock, even with the incentive of using old work shirts of their fathers'. If you have set up these art experiences casually, it should not provoke a confrontation before the fun. If the rules are pleasantly consistent, children can direct their energies to the creative use of the supplies themselves, not to rebelling against necessary rules.

• Let toddlers play with safe household items or toys that imitate real-life utensils and equipment so that they can mimic the activities they see at home. Provide a clean dust rag or chamois, or a brush and dustpan. The kitchen is a never-ending source of imitative playthings for imaginative play—pots and pans, wooden spoons, metal measuring cups, pretend food, and so on. Look in toy stores for small brooms, carpet sweepers, or lawnmowers (they will love the bubble-blowing ones). Toddlers will enjoy "working" along with you on cookie-making day or as you organize lunch.

• Pretend play is a perfect use for some of those new inexpensive telephones that no longer work. Remove the cords and you get new, free, imaginative toys. Or purchase toy telephones that ring or talk to keep youngsters motivated for hours of phone conversations.

- Unbreakable tea sets encourage imaginative activities with dolls, stuffed animals, and real people in creative play. At the same time, toddlers can be learning social skills and practicing fine manipulations.

- Once a toddler has learned to use objects as symbols, her pretend play can expand infinitely. Her stuffed animal can be her baby now, and her shoe can be driven around like a car. She can use an empty yogurt cup to float like a boat she has seen or fly like an airplane. It can even pick up and discharge passengers made of spools, plastic spoons, or cotton balls. Encourage by example such creative use of objects.

- Small plastic or wooden play-family sets encourage pretend situations. Sometimes they reveal surprises when you listen to a toddler use the doll figures. Does her grown-up figure use strong language and punitive words you didn't realize you were prone to use? Do her family figures act out home situations you didn't know existed? You might want to share in the play occasionally to help her pretend to relive a recent happy event, a past experience that scared her, or a coming event that she feels worried about. Follow her lead in the play, and do not be tempted to interpret heavy psychological implications. Just the act of pretending with you might help her understand that her feelings are important and acceptable. This might give her confidence for being innovative and creative in trying new activities or events in the future. You might want to share this type of news with parents at a conference or, if you think it can't wait, when you see them at pickup time.

- Sock puppets are easy to make and can inspire creative communication. Draw faces with felt-tipped markers or glue on facial features if a toddler is past the stage of pulling off and eating small, nonedible objects. The shape of the sock helps create the puppet. A long sock makes a snake or a giraffe. A short one can be a baby or a puppy.

- A sand table offers endless opportunities for creating designs just with hands or small beach tools. Drops of water poured from a watering can onto plain sand or castles they have built make interesting designs. Sand and water toys add interest. If you have a sand box outside, it will be kept cleaner (cats can't get into it either) if you have a cover that fits tightly on top when it is not in use.

- Ask parents to help expand your items for a costume collection. Keep them simple and easy for toddlers to put on. Try hats, pocketbooks, and sturdy, bulky costume jewelry. Include buckles or bows to decorate the fronts of flat-heeled pumps or Jellies®. Costumed pretend play becomes much more complex as children get older, but the opportunity of putting on "big" clothes in the toddler years increases the fun of creative play.

- Keep costumes in a large box with a safe lid or in a cardboard packing box. Some centers have an old dresser with drawers for dress-ups.

- Blocks of various shapes and sizes produce and stimulate true creative experience. They can be made into anything and have no suggested guidelines for how to build with them. Have little cars, trees, buildings, wooden animals, or doll figures available near the blocks.

- Blocks also help the new little construction engineers begin to learn basics about symmetry, balance, and size. Building toys that snap or stick together, bolt, stack, or fit can be added to the blocks to expand the fun and the learning.

- Avoid being manipulated into doing the building for toddlers. Let them use their own creativity. Train the children at an early age to know they may not throw blocks or knock down structures built by other people. These simple rules promote physical as well as creative well-being.

TOY CHART

In the chart on the next pages are examples of good toys. They are divided into ten categories that are listed alphabetically. Toys in each category are presented approximately developmentally. All the toys provide learning experiences and, therefore, are educational. The most important aspects of child development that can be stimulated by each toy are marked in columns on the right. The reasons for some marks may not be immediately obvious, and they should encourage you to notice wider possibilities the toys offer. Toys mentioned in the text are not necessarily repeated in the chart.

The toys listed show examples of the attributes a particular type of toy should have. If you experience difficulty finding the toy listed, there will generally be toys of similar quality in catalogs or on the toy-store shelf that will accomplish the same goals.

EXAMPLES OF TOYS FOR THE TODDLER: ONE TO THREE YEARS	Awareness of Sensation	Balance and Big Movements	Dexterity and Hand/Eye Coord.	Vision	Space/Time Awareness	Personality/ Socialization	Language	Imagination/ Creativity
ARTS AND CRAFTS *So-Big® Crayola®. Binney & Smith®. Jumbo Wipe Off Crayons.* Toys R Us®. *Jumbo Chalk.* Rose Art®. *Finger Paints.* Milton Bradley®. *Dry and Liquid Tempera Brushes. Felt-tipped markers.* Nontoxic.	●	●	●	●	●	●	●	●
Giant Picture Coloring Book. Karman. 48 pages with thick paper, big, simple, clear pictures.		●	●	●	●			●
Super Fun Coloring and Activity Books. P.S.I. & Associates. Large pictures with few lines to distract. Also other games.		●	●	●	●			●
Play Doh® Kenner®. Nontoxic cans of modeling material in different size sets.	●	●	●		●		●	●
BIG EQUIPMENT *Softscape.* Educational and Fun, Ltd. 11 large pieces, indoors or out, with tabs to connect ramps, squares, cylinders.	●	●				●	●	
Tot Swing. Flexible Flyer™. Plastic swing with safety strap. Attaches with safety grips to tree or gym set.	●	●			●			
Turtle Sand Box with Cover. Little Tikes®.	●	●	●			●	●	●
Jumbo Hide "N" Slide. Little Tikes®. Elephant slide, steps, place to crawl into.	●	●			●			
Nursery Gym. Community Playthings. Wooden pieces. Stairs with sides, platform, barrel (tunnel), slide, ramp.	●	●			●	●	●	
Tree House. Little Tikes®. Slide, steps, platform. Indoors/out. Preschoolers, too.	●	●			●	●	●	
Rocking Boat. Childcraft®. Turn it over, stairs. Holds 4.	●	●				●	●	
Tunnel of Fun. Geoffrey®. Folding, vinyl, ventilated 9-foot-long tunnel.	●	●		●	●			
Gymboree® Gym Tubes. Connor Toys. 3 large, colored tubes to roll, stack, crawl through.	●	●		●	●			
BOOKS *Pat the Bunny.* Dorothy Kunhardt. A Golden Book®. Sensation story book with things to feel.	●		●	●		●	●	●
Baby Farm Animals. Garth Williams. A Golden Book®.				●		●	●	●

EXAMPLES OF TOYS FOR THE TODDLER: ONE TO THREE YEARS	Awareness of Sensation	Balance and Big Movements	Dexterity and Hand/Eye Coord.	Vision	Space/Time Awareness	Personality/ Socialization	Language	Imagination/ Creativity
Where's Spot? Eric Hill. G.P. Putnam. Movable flaps that hide surprises.			●	●	●	●	●	●
Small Coated Cardboard Books. About animals, houses, people, things.				●		●	●	●
See and Say Books. Tuffy Books. 5" X 7", heavy cardboard, bright colors, clear designs about simple objects, shapes, colors, etc. 12–18, 18–24, 24–36 months.				●		●	●	●
Mother Goose. Nursery Stories. Many editions.				●		●	●	●
The Little Engine That Could. Classic story.				●		●	●	●
Good Night Moon. Margaret Wise Brown. Harper and Row. Many other sweet, simple storybooks.				●		●	●	●
Snuffy. Dick Bruna. Author of 50 wonderful young children's books. Illustrated.				●		●	●	●
The Read-Aloud Handbook. by Jim Trelease. Penguin Books. Guide listing 300 stories, by age or grade, plus reasons for reading aloud.								
CONSTRUCTION *Great Big Blocks.* Little Tikes®. Jumbo-size block set.		●	●	●	●			●
Open stock. *Wooden blocks,* many shapes. Add additional shapes as needed.		●	●	●	●			●
Star Builders. Toys To Grow On®. Unbreakable, interlocking plastic stars. 6 bright colors.		●	●	●	●			●
Creative Blocks. Fisher-Price®. Small colored blocks with 18 various shaped pieces with dowels.		●	●	●	●			●
Mega Bloks®. Preschool. Ritvik. 24 bright vinyl pieces for building, stacking, shape sorting, puppet play with characters, pull-toy.		●	●	●	●			●
Magnet Blocks. Clover Toys. Various shapes held together by magnets to make vehicles, etc.		●	●	●	●			●
Preschool Basic Building Set Duplo®. Lego®. Interlocking blocks. Add sets to it.		●	●	●	●			●
Pre-School Super Blocks. Tyco®. Interlocking pieces with wagon, with various plastic heads like dinosaurs.		●	●	●	●			●
60 Colored Wooden Blocks. Sandberg®. Various shapes that fit into wagon. Plastic wheels and pull string.		●	●	●	●			●

EXAMPLES OF TOYS FOR THE TODDLER: ONE TO THREE YEARS	Awareness of Sensation	Balance and Big Movements	Dexterity and Hand/Eye Coord.	Vision	Space/Time Awareness	Personality/ Socialization	Language	Imagination/ Creativity
Structo Cubes. Kaplan's School Supply Corp. 1⅛" pliable, plastic cubes. 6 colors.	●	●	●	●	●			●
Wee Waffle™ Blocks. Little Tikes®. 3" interlocking colored plastic pieces.		●	●	●	●			●
GAMES *Beanbags.* Variety of sizes, shapes.	●	●	●	●		●	●	
Vinyl Beach Balls. Rubber Playground Balls. 8"–12". Roll, throw.	●	●	●	●		●	●	
Activity Hoops and Holders. Holcomb's Educational Materials. Tough plastic blocks can support hoops upright for stable crawling through. Obstacle course later.	●	●			●	●	●	
IMITATIVE PLAYTHINGS *Dolls.* Soft, cuddly, washable. Vinyl is unbreakable.	●					●	●	●
Animal Sounds Barn. Fisher-Price®. Barnyard, press lever, animals make typical sounds.	●		●		●		●	●
Doll Stroller. Little Tikes®. Molded body, good balance, washable. Preschooler, too.		●					●	●
Toy Sweeper. Broom. Small Housekeeping Toys.		●					●	●
Play Family. Fisher-Price®. House, bath, utility, or nursery sets.			●				●	●
Bubble Mower®. Fisher-Price®. Blows bubbles, makes realistic sound as child pushes. Bubble solution included.		●			●		●	●
Walker Wagon. ABC School Supply Inc. Wooden, low-to-ground handle helps support new walker.		●	●		●			●
Corn Popper. Fisher-Price®. Colorful beads pop up and make noise in plastic dome when pushed by handle.		●			●			●
Melody Push Chimes. Fisher-Price®. Plays song when pushed.		●			●		●	●
Chatter Telephone. Fisher-Price®. Pull-toy, rings when dialed voice says "chatter chatter."		●	●		●		●	●
Clatterpillar. Kiddicraft®. Centipede makes noise, eyes wiggle, antennae shake as it moves.		●			●		●	●
Toddle Tots® Family Car (with little people). *Road Builder.* Little Tikes®. Small molded-plastic toys to push, pretend.		●	●		●		●	●

EXAMPLES OF TOYS FOR THE TODDLER: ONE TO THREE YEARS	Awareness of Sensation	Balance and Big Movements	Dexterity and Hand/Eye Coord.	Vision	Space/Time Awareness	Personality/ Socialization	Language	Imagination/ Creativity
Discovery Cottage™. Fisher-Price®. Roof lifts up, 12 activities, movable pieces.			●				●	●
Toy Cars. Trucks. Sturdy small friction toys without tiny pieces. Make sounds. Some wind up.	●	●	●		●		●	●
Toddler Kitchen. Fisher-Price®. 10 various play activities.			●			●	●	●
Little Fix-it™ Tool Box. Shelcore®. 6 plastic tools.			●				●	●
MANIPULATIVE *Bowl of Balls.* Walt Disney®. 3 plastic rattle balls fit inside bigger ball, Mickey Mouse characters on balls.	●	●	●	●	●			
Kiddie Links™. Fisher-Price®. 15 colored plastic links fit together 4 ways.			●	●	●			
Cobbler's Bench. Playskool®. Colored wooden dowels in small, sturdy bench push through to other side when hit with a small mallet.	●	●	●		●			
Rhythm Rollers. Johnson & Johnson. Truck with 3 attached cylinders that fit on top and stack. Makes sounds when pulled.			●	●		●	●	
Busy Poppin' Pals®. Playskool®. Sesame Street® designs. 5 knobs unlock pop-up surprises. Toys come out for play.	●		●	●	●		●	●
Build-a-Ball. Shelcore®. 9 interlocking rings on center spool to take apart, put together, and build different shapes.			●	●	●			
Busy Play Ball. Blue Box®. Bright yellow ball, with ringing telephone dial, mirror with beads. Makes clicking, squeaking sounds when different spots are pressed.			●	●	●		●	
Pound a Round. Playskool®. Spinning top. Watch balls move, stripes twirl when plunger is pushed. Stay put stand.	●	●		●	●			
Shape Sorter. Lakeshore. 3 simple shapes.			●	●	●			
Baby's First Blocks™. Fisher-Price®. 12 plastic blocks in cannister with sorting lid of 3 shapes.		●	●	●	●			
Push Push Train. Chicco. Fit train sections of brightly colored plastic with pegs on bottom into holes to assemble and tow it.		●	●		●			●

EXAMPLES OF TOYS FOR THE TODDLER: ONE TO THREE YEARS	Awareness of Sensation	Balance and Big Movements	Dexterity and Hand/Eye Coord.	Vision	Space/Time Awareness	Personality/ Socialization	Language	Imagination/ Creativity
Barrels. Chicco. 6 brightly colored nontoxic plastic barrels, screw and unscrew, fit into one another or stack.		●	●	●	●			
Twist 'n' Turn. Kiddicraft®. Aim, push, and turn pieces to screw/unscrew toy.		●	●	●	●			
Size, Shape or Animal Puzzles. Childcraft®. Insert puzzles with knobs on each piece.			●	●	●			
Place and Trace® Puzzle. Discovery Toys. 18 dinosaurs, animals, vehicles. Use puzzle for stencils, cookie cutter, lotto, color matching.	●		●	●	●			●
Stack 'n Pop Humpty Dumpty. Playskool®. 5 pieces fit together sequentially, pop apart when lever is pressed.	●		●	●	●		●	
Big-Little Peg Board Set. Lauri Enterprises™. 25 easy-grip pegs fit holes.	●		●	●	●			
Hammer Board. Ideal™. Plastic workbench, hammer 8 different shapes into correct place.		●	●	●	●			
Giant Pegboard™. Discovery Toys. 25 large, colored, plastic pegs fit into plastic pegboard, stack, sort, string pegs.		●	●	●	●			
MUSICAL/LISTENING *Musical Jack-in-the-Box.* Playskool®. Sesame Street®.		●			●		●	
Sesame Street® Musical Box TV. Fisher-Price®. Turn knobs, 2 continuous picture stories move with music. Portable.			●	●	●		●	
Busy Band. Playskool®. 10 different sounds.		●	●		●		●	
See 'N Say®. Mattel®. "The Zoo Keeper Says" has sounds of 12 different animals. "Mother Goose Says" has 12 stories and songs. Point disk, pull string, watch, and listen.			●	●	●		●	●
Xylophone. Little Tikes®. Pull-toy on wheels, has washboard on back to make other sounds.	●	●	●		●		●	
Wee Sing™. Price Stern Sloan, Inc. Tape and book of nursery rhymes, lullabies.						●	●	●
RIDING *Rocking Pony.* Fisher-Price®. Clip-clops, has padded mane.	●	●						●

EXAMPLES OF TOYS FOR THE TODDLER: ONE TO THREE YEARS	Awareness of Sensation	Balance and Big Movements	Dexterity and Hand/Eye Coord.	Vision	Space/Time Awareness	Personality/ Socialization	Language	Imagination/ Creativity
Rocking Puppy. Fisher-Price®. Low riding toy. Dowels at ears to hold. Ledge for feet, soft ears, squeaker tail.	●	●						●
Easy Ride Pony. Little Tikes®. Close to floor, turns in one movement.	●	●						●
Runaway Horse. Chicco. Moves on carpet, neighing sound. Child's weight and movement advances horse.	●	●			●		●	●
Sit 'n Scoot. Little Tikes®. Lightweight but stable, sturdy toy without pedals. Also fire engine, train, bus, etc.		●	●		●			●
Cozy Coupe Rider. Little Tikes®. Doors open, feet move it without pedals.		●	●		●			●
Tyke Bike®. Playskool®. 4-wheeled, contour seat, no pedals, steerable.		●	●		●			
Trike Bike®. Fisher-Price®. Wide, stable wheel base. Raised, adjustable seat.		●	●		●			
Wagon. Radio® Flyer. Wooden wagon with sides.	●	●			●			
Tot Sleigh. Blazon-Flexible Flyer®. High backseat rail and sides. Tow rope.	●	●						
Sit 'n Spin®. Kenner Preschool®. Sit on disk, close to ground, turn wheel in either direction.	●	●	●					
WATER PLAY (VERY CLOSE ADULT SUPERVISION REQUIRED IN POOLS)								
Wading Pool. Inflatable or polyurethane.	●	●				●	●	
Bubbles. Wand. Bubble pipe.	●			●	●		●	
Pail, Shovel and Sifter Set.	●	●	●		●		●	●
Bath Ducks. Kiddicraft®. Plastic duck-shaped cups float, link, nest, have spouts to pour.	●	●	●		●		●	
Big Bird Busy Boat. Playskool®. Floats, attaches to basin, 5 activities.	●	●	●		●		●	
Floating Family. Fisher-Price®. 3 figures to fit in and out of turtle, boat, and roly-poly pitcher.	●	●	●		●		●	
Bathtime Water Works. Johnson & Johnson. Yellow barge floats with cups, sprinkler, squirter, paddle wheels.	●	●	●		●		●	
Plastic Wash Basins. For indoor water play. *Galvinized Metal Basins.* For outdoors.	●	●	●		●	●	●	●

6

PRESCHOOLER DEVELOPMENT, TOYS, AND ACTIVITIES: THREE TO FIVE YEARS

Figure 6–1 is an overview of the maxi-milestones most children achieve when they are about three to five years old. It is divided into the eight aspects of growth and development we have been discussing in this book. It allows you to visualize the whole picture of a preschooler's development, like a completed jigsaw puzzle.

Figure 6–1 MAXI-MILESTONES OF THE PRESCHOOLER

AWARENESS OF SENSATIONS	BALANCE AND BIG MOVEMENTS	DEXTERITY AND HAND/EYE COORDINATION	VISION
Loves swings, seesaws, sliding boards Recognizes food by cooking odors Recognizes weight differences of full/ empty cartons May develop strong opinions about clothes of a certain feel	Walks/runs swinging arms alternately below waist Pedals tricycle Hops briefly Climbs jungle gym and tall sliding board Keeps moving swing going and jumps off successfully Up and down stairs, 1 foot per step	10-block tower Opens doorknob, jar Bounces/catches large ball awkwardly Catches by trapping ball with arms, later hands Cuts straight line Draws recognizable person May print name Manipulates video games with dexterity	Names colors Matches by both size/color at once Matches simple line designs and copies simplest Acquires almost 20/20 visual acuity

The milestones in the columns are progressive. They occur approximately in the sequence listed from top to bottom as the child grows older. The activities listed in the columns overlap considerably, and the eight aspects are all occurring at the same time, although at different rates.

Figure 6–1 CONTINUED

SPACE/TIME AWARENESS	PERSONALITY/ SOCIALIZATION	LANGUAGE	IMAGINATION/ CREATIVITY
Knows approximately when favorite TV show comes on Begins to recognize empty space as part of design Grasps position/ quantity concepts like more, next, and middle Understands morning, afternoon, and evening	Potty trained Associative play without division of labor Realizes own sex and that of others Cooperative, organized play emerging Acquires friends real and/or imaginary Understands and cooperates with rules for simple games	Sentences Recites nursery rhymes Tells story of recent event Intuitive thought: Comprehends simple plots of stories, TV programs Asks questions; says "why" often Converses clearly and with complex sentence structure	Tells/plays original stories based on reality or personal past experience Magical thinking Draws picture and labels it Rhythm bands, action songs Creative block play Clay, paint, markers, finger paint Creates stories beyond own experience Pretends planned sequence in group play

Review the eight column figure carefully as you have in the preceding two chapters. You can see how we have been following a pattern of expanding the milestone information on the chart throughout each age chapter. Play skills of the preschooler will be closely related to the milestones already achieved. Later milestones depend on the development of those listed earlier.

Following Figure 6–1, we will take the puzzle apart and detail each of the columns individually, just as we did in the previous chapters for the infant and the toddler. The "How to Help" suggestions that follow the discussion of each column will point to ways you can promote preschoolers' growth in that aspect of development. The toy chart at the end of the chapter lists examples of good toys and the aspect of development they stimulate.

AWARENESS OF SENSATIONS

Sensations bombard the blossoming preschooler every moment of every day. Sights and sounds flash past his sensory receptors. Smells waft from kitchen, bathroom, countryside, and city streets. Textures press on his skin. Many head positions and movements stimulate brain responses and stretch/ pressure sensations in the joints and muscles as he climbs, runs, and hangs upside down. His discrimination and memory for all these sensations allow him by school age to recognize and respond to many of the stimuli in the world around him confidently and knowledgeably.

Mini- and Maxi-Milestones of Sensory Awareness

The preschooler pays attention to sensory stimuli more selectively than he could as a toddler, appropriately picking out the ones most likely to provide useful or pleasurable information. He has long since learned how to adapt to and ignore constant sensations like the feel of clothing, the pressure of his buttocks on the play surface, the sound of clocks ticking, or a dishwasher running. They rarely distract him from noticing more novel sensations.

He sorts the information carefully now, without realizing it, and automatically relates it to memories he already has of previously experienced sensations and their meanings. These previous memories give a degree of reliability to his sensory awareness by the preschool years—he knows what snow will feel like, or hot chocolate, or sand, or a pillow, or Daddy's beard, or a soft lap. This helps to give him confidence in the predictability of his world.

Two other factors allow him to respond more puposefully to sensations than he used to: (1) His motor skills and language are more capable of reacting, and (2) he can now more carefully discriminate and pick out *what* it is he wants to respond to and *how*. After sorting out and acting on the sensory information around him, he stores it away in his expanding memory for future reference. Then he can even more effectively remember sensations in the future and respond to them.

Vestibular. The preschooler seeks out new, more daring ways to stimulate the brain's vestibular receptors, which give him sensory information about his movement and head position. The preschooler knows how to rock hard on a big spring-suspended toy horse if he wants to rock it across the uncarpeted floor— or gently if he wants to be sure it stays in one place. He is attracted to swings and seesaws and will try tall sliding boards (sometimes even headfirst). He will sometimes lie on his tummy over a swing for novelty and will hang upside-down from trees. His vestibular system will love the stimulation of this inverted head position.

Tactile. He knows which new clothes he likes the feel of and may begin to express a strong dislike of wool or clothes that are too tight at the waist, cuffs, or neckline. He can now make sense out of a "feely box" with holes in the sides or cloth over the top. By reaching his hand inside, he show a preliminary ability to find from an array of objects, one that matches the one he sees next to the box. Later he learns to reach both hands inside and find two different objects that match. Differences must be pronounced—like picking circles instead of the triangle or square in the array, or picking the piece of sandpaper instead of the satin or terry cloth. He can select the spoon instead of the pencil but will have great difficulty with such fine discriminations as picking the teaspoon from the tablespoon.

He expands his vocabulary of sensation words to include "rough" and "smooth" if they are taught to him. He is also able to learn "soft," "heavy," "sour," "loud," "warm," and color names.

Kinesthesia. He has, for some time now, used his kinesthetic (movement) awareness to help him point to his nose and mouth, even though he cannot see the target he is pointing to. Now he can do that with his eyes closed, giving no visual clues at all. He can also reach quite accurately to scratch a mosquito bite in the dark and to point out to you a new sore spot he cannot see on his elbow or on the back of his leg. He is developing a subtle awareness of muscle adjustment he must make to lift heavy versus light objects. He lifts a cardboard juice carton if he wants to know whether it is full or empty.

His energetic jumping adventures and pushing other children on swings or in wagons give strong compression to many of his joints. This in turn provides to the body proprioceptive (stimulated by the organism itself) information about joint pressure. Carrying or pulling heavy playthings and climbing outdoor equipment stretches out the joints and muscles. This also provides strong proprioceptive and kinesthetic information to his little body. These strong sensory inputs help develop the child's internal, unconscious awareness of his body positions. They also help tone up his muscles for strong, accurate movement responses. They help him plan and carry out more and more complicated actions automatically. Each successful new movement attempt provides sensory feedback that monitors his performance and applauds his effort. The feedback system gives his muscles instructions to make the minute changes necessary to assure accuracy in carrying out the plan and encourages him to plan and carry out even more complicated movements.

Smell and Taste. If is a favorite of his, he will know you are warming spaghetti sauce for lunch when he notices the aroma as he comes in from the play yard. He will peek with interest through the door to the toddler room if he smells popcorn cooking there and may announce it in a loud voice if he thinks one of the little ones has dirtied her diaper.

He probably will not notice smells that seem obvious to an adult but are less interesting to a preschooler, like the smells from the local bread bakery or the very first indications that something is wrong with the oil furnace.

Hearing and Vision. Enhanced *sound* discrimination allows the preschooler to recognize a car honk from other traffic noise, Sesame Street's® versus Mr. Roger's music, and the teacher's voice from the new helper's. *Visual* discrimination skills are improving, too, and he has a more accurate sensory awareness of similar color hues and shades, and the details of visual shapes and forms.

 How to Help Develop Awareness of Sensations

- Let each child decide how much movement experience is fun for him. Some children love—even crave—swinging, playground merry-go-rounds, carnival rides, and other rotational activities and toys as well as hanging upside-down. Other children tend to avoid these activities or enjoy them only in small doses. *Never* pressure a child into accepting movement experiences that are uncomfortable for him.

- Ask a preschooler to help you carry heavy toys from the storage shelf to the play table to provide lots of sensory input to the tendons, muscles, and joints. You might begin with one or two boxed games or a few beanbags, and eventually build up to a box of blocks, a big bag of clay, or a basket of beanbags. Be sure to consider the preschooler's size when you give him these little jobs.

- Have lots of tactilely stimulating toys and activities available for children to select. Most preschoolers will love sand, clay, finger paint, water play, mudpies, leaf rubbings, and a variety of other arts and crafts that provide considerable tactile experience. Some commercially available products that have novel sensations include Silly Putty®, Ecto Plasm™ and a Koosh® ball.

- You might keep some colored soap foam at the sink where children can enjoy the novel sensory experience, then wash it off as soon as they are ready.

- Invite a preschooler to the kitchen to help you with messy food preparation like kneading cookie dough, mixing meat loaf or making meatballs for lunch. Even the squeamish child might be motivated to help if he knows he will love the resulting food treat.

- If you have ample indoor space, try creating a large box of "feely" things for youngsters to walk in (barefooted) or jump in. If they are deep enough, children love to "swim" in them. You can use foam packaging peanuts, small chunks of foam (Do you have a foam manufacturer nearby who discards scrap?), or the small pressurized balls commercially made for the purpose (try the Educational and Fun, LTD, catalog).

- At snack time, see if the children can identify some of their favorite foods by smelling them. With their eyes closed, put some peanut butter or orange sections or cinnamon-laced apple sauce close to their noses and let them guess. Or, if they are willing to try, let children close their eyes and take a bite of a sandwich, then guess if it is jelly, egg, or tuna salad.

- Youngsters can enjoy a game of "Guess the Body Part." Spray with colored soap foam or apply a small piece of masking tape or paper tape to a child's wrist, shoulder, or hand. Have him name the part. If this seems too hard for him, it will be easier if you name a body part and have him point to where you should put the foam or tape. If, instead, having him name the body part is too easy, try the game blindfolded or with a gaily decorated paper bag on his head. The blindfolded game gives both touch and kinesthetic feedback information.

- A quiet, warm sunny afternoon is a perfect time to set up the sprinkler and allow a small group of youngsters to run in it and jump over it for an enjoyable sensory experience. If they wait to leap over the changing position of an oscillating spray, they can gain temporal and spatial information that they can coordinate with their movement response.

- Try this slippery sensory experience for another hot day: Place a large piece of oilcloth or an old, smooth plastic tablecloth on the grass. Wet it, and sprinkle it with a small amount of liquid soap. Let a few children slide around on their backs and tummies and buttocks. Follow this with a sprinkle with the hose to wash off the gooey soap. Then offer a firm rubdown in a giant terry cloth beach towel. *Monitor these water activities carefully to avoid injury* and to inhibit dangerous play behavior.

- Make sure that the children have swim clothes, shorts, towels, and an extra change of clothes. When they are getting ready to play outside with the water, it is a good time to remind them how to fold their clothes and put them away in their cubbies. When they are dressing after the fun, show them the easiest ways to put their clothes back on if they are having difficulty.

- A wonderful winter surprise might be a pretend "Day at the Beach." Have every child bring a bathing suit, towel, and suntan lotion. Be sure to wear beach clothes yourself. Set up one room or area with small, portable plastic play boxes filled with sand, another with a pool filled with water. Put beach balls and sand toys around on the floor. Some of the children might enjoy having their faces made up with washable soap crayons. This may be the messiest cleanup ever, but it will also be one of the most memorable days for you and the children. Be certain the rooms are warm enough. Allow enough time at the end of the day to let everyone get dried and dressed. Perhaps a few parents could help.

BALANCE AND BIG MOVEMENTS

The preschooler is a lovable bundle of movement and energy. He may be a youngster who bounds enthusiastically from one play space to another or one who flows quietly and easily around the playroom and nearby playground equipment. Regardless of his personality, he is a far cry from the tentative toddler of a couple of years before—waddling unsteadily through his daily play experiences. Now he climbs and jumps and squats with increasing ease. During the energetic preschool years, he will easily perfect running, pedaling, descending stairs and climbing a jungle gym.

His body's increasing ability to manage the movement demands of the play yard will give him new confidence. His expanding spatial awareness and curiosity will give an internal urging toward fitting his body into new nooks and crannies, and climbing to sometimes dizzying heights. As the school years approach, he will be willing to take reasonable risks and try new movement challenges inspired by the give-and-take of his newly developing group play skills.

Mini- and Maxi-Milestones of Balance and Big Movements

Coordination. The coordination of the preschooler's movements is no longer dominated by reflexive, automatic responses or the young toddler's preoccupation with mastering the upright position. He shows an increasing flexibility in dissociating (separating) the movement of his body parts from each other. As he walks, his arms swing smoothly at his sides, one after the other, forward and backward, in rhythm with the movements of the leg on the opposite side of his body. This heterolateral (meaning on the opposite side) movement of the arms and legs is also evident as he runs.

These coordinated swinging movements have been helping to undo old patterns of his body's responses so that he can automatically make more new choices about which body parts to move. His two hands no longer symmetrically fly up to that "high guard" position near his shoulders seen in the early toddler years. Now one hand can hold a toy efficiently while the other does something to it—like pulling the string on a bear that talks or winding up a mechanical car—even while he is walking.

Another indication of his ability to dissociate movement of his body parts occurs when he alternates his feet on the stairs, at first while he is going up and later while he is coming down. He can climb up the rungs of a ladder or jungle gym, with feet alternating and hands helping appropriately. He learns to pedal a tricycle and a Big Wheel® toy, with his feet smoothly alternating their pushing action.

Though these reciprocal and alternating movements show considerable improvement during the preschool years, he usually cannot attain real skipping. Instead, he will learn to gallop with one foot always leading and may even "lame duck" skip for a while with a step-hop of one foot alternating with a walking step of the other foot. Girls are more adept at these preskipping activities, and boys often are not willing to be bothered trying such intricate skills requiring the close coordination of the two body sides.

Balance. These reciprocal movements are accompanied by more efficient shifting of body weight from side to side. The weight shifting is a tricky balance maneuver that develops along with other coordination skills. It allows alternating movements in the upright position. No wonder he holds onto the railing for dear life at first as he tries the new skill of going up or down the stairs with one foot on each tread. Those steps feel pretty big to the short, novice weight-shifter. Even the experienced stair-climber may revert to clutching the railing when, on one of your outings, he needs to descend the extra-wide or deep stairs at the county courthouse.

Those intricate little weight-shifting movements around the body's center of gravity aren't perfected yet, and his little body has trouble predicting when he can rely on them. He is ultracautious at first on carnival rides and on movable playground equipment such as a flat, wooden merry-go-round. Nevertheless, he keeps experimenting with his advancing balance skills, gaining confidence in their reliability. His body becomes more efficient. It learns to make appropriate postural adjustments necessary to promote fluid movements in the upright position.

The preschooler is not like a solid wooden block standing upright so that a light shove would send him clattering to the floor. Instead, the miraculous body of the developing youngster has little balancing devices inside that are flexible, not stationary, and include many parts of his body. One arm flies far out to the side to counterbalance his body's tipping in the opposite direction if he leans sideward to catch a passing lightning bug or jumps off the crossbar of his backyard swing set. One shoulder elevates slightly or a lot, depending on the degree of the challenge. One leg may fly out or bend a little and the hip may elevate or rotate. Even his toes and ankles will do their part to adjust appropriately as the body tips. If postural adjustments are unsuccessful and the brain gets a message that a fall off his tricycle is imminent, then the arms are given a different message. "Move out quickly to break the fall," the arms are told, "and prevent injury to this little guy's head or trunk." These complex mini-capabilities lay the groundwork for achieving more obvious maxi-milestones like climbing up and sliding down a tall sliding board, riding a seesaw, and leaping off a moving swing.

In the early preschool years, you will notice that these important little balance responses have developed so that he can jump off the bottom stair step. At first, he lands with a jarring and unsteady "klunk." Later he learns to land lightly with a little "give" in the knees and hips. As you would expect, a little hopping on one foot begins to emerge at this time, too.

Quickly the careful, experimental quality of his jumping and hopping skills gives way to more automatic responses. You will see him jump down out of his favorite tree-climbing perch. While he cannot "leap tall buildings in a single bound," he can at least jump easily off small boulders near your center or step successfully from rock to rock at his favorite frog-catching brook without getting *too* wet. The wide base of support he needed in the early waddling years has become narrower and narrower. Now he can walk on the curb or on the narrow railroad ties in your play yard, often jumping off the end and landing comfortably on one or both feet. He begins to learn to kick a ball with one foot while balancing precariously and briefly on the other. And now he can tiptoe quietly if he needs to get up at rest time or if his teddy bear is "napping."

Motor Planning. Other big-movement skills develop, too. The preschooler's new balance, coordination, and dissociation abilities combine with a more grown-up awareness of what his body is like. His body scheme (or internal body awareness) is becoming more accurate. It gives him an automatic sensory awareness of the location of those body parts he has been naming since the early toddler years. All the practice with pointing to his eye or knee, along with the movement experiences he has been enjoying, helps him succeed now when he threads his way through a complicated jungle gym maze. The new skills help him organize and coordinate his body to push a wagon with one foot while kneeling inside and steering accurately around obstacles or into tight "parking" places.

At a parade site, he can leave the group in the back row (with permission) and wriggle his way through the crowd of legs to a good spectator spot in the front next to another teacher. He can even do this without jabbing anybody with the little American flag he carries to wave enthusiastically in the direction of the oncoming band.

The preschooler's advancing sensory awareness of how to move the various parts of his body is helping develop a more unified whole-body concept. This concept helps him understand the relationship of his body parts to each other. It provides a recognition of how the size, shape, and location of his body relate to the space around him. Motor planning of new movements that he has never tried before results from this awareness, allowing him to create and carry out a plan for trying other new actions easily.

You probably remember the difficulty you had learning to serve a tennis ball. Every stroke was accompanied by lots of thinking and planning and telling your body parts what to do—your elbow, your wrist, your arm, your knees and feet, and your other hand. Remember how complicated it seemed until the motor plan was set and you could serve automatically?

Now imagine the difficulty the preschooler would have trying to motor plan when driving his tricycle or, even harder, a Little Tikes® garden tractor with its attached cart through a maze of bikes and tricycles and littered toys or jackets on the play area. What a maneuvering task! Many preschoolers have difficulty telling their bodies what to do when they want to get into the correct position to climb onto a bicycle, instead of a tricycle. The bike's training wheels help take care of the balance problem. However, they still have to learn to mount the bike by swinging their legs over the seat or bar, getting up on the seat, and placing their feet on the pedals accurately before they are ready to begin learning to ride.

Once he masters this big step, a preschooler will be ready to begin learning to combine the familar pedaling motor plan learned from his tricycle or a Big Wheel® toy with the new balance requirements of a two-wheeler. His first halting efforts lay the groundwork for the independent bike pedaling that will finally come during the early grade-school years.

 How to Help Develop Balance and Big Movements

- Big outdoor climbing and riding equipment is a must for the pre-schooler. Wooden outdoor sets are sturdy and hold up well for years if properly preserved. Some centers prefer strong metal sets if they feel proper treatment of the wood will be a cumbersome duty through the years. Be sure both are sturdily set in cement holes in the ground. This essential major investment must be chosen care-fully. Consider the size of your property, where the set will be placed, how many children will use it at one time, and what activities you want available. In addition to the typical swinging, rocking, spin-ning, hanging, and sliding pieces, there are marvelous creative climbing, crawling, and inventing opportunities offered with this equipment.

- Perhaps you prefer not to invest in outdoor equipment right now because your budget will not allow it or if you expect to move fairly soon. Noncommercial equipment listed in Figure 6–2 encourages outdoor big movement with a low financial investment.

- Inspect your outdoor play area regularly for potential safety hazards. Look for broken glass or rotting equipment, rusted chains or nails, and hard surfaces such as cement under swings and sliding boards. If you take the youngsters to a public playground that contains these or other hazards, notify the local recreation director.

- Unless soft grass is available, it is recommended that thick flexible outdoor mat pieces be located under swings and seesaws and at the foot of sliding boards. The pieces fit together like jigsaw puzzle pieces to make playgrounds safer. You can get information about several different manufacturers' products from General Recreation, Inc., P.O. Box 406, Newtown Square, PA 19073. Telephone (215) 353-3332.

- Many schools have indoor big-movement equipment as well, for play and exercise in wintertime or on rainy days. Fix up one area with mats and with equipment that hangs or rocks or is suitable for climbing. It is essential that this equipment be installed properly and used safely. Try roller skates, a small seesaw, a sliding board or merry-go-round, a Sit 'n Spin®, a trapeze, tires or inner tubes, foam wedges, an expanding plastic-covered tunnel, or an indoor tent (or try a table covered with a blanket or sheet that drops to the floor so that

Figure 6-2 INEXPENSIVE, NONCOMMERCIAL OUTDOOR BIG-MOVEMENT EQUIPMENT

Tire swing. Be sure the rope is strong and durable enough to withstand all weather conditions (try a boating supply store). Put a few holes in the bottom of the tire so that rainwater will drain out instead of collecting in the bottom and providing a breeding ground for mosquitoes or wet clothes. Tires can also be hung horizontally with ropes attached to huge eyebolts, one in each quadrant of the tire.

Inner tube swing. Be sure the air nozzle is flattened, covered for safety, and kept near the rope attachment at the top. Tubes are stretchy to encourage bouncing.

Wooden spool or core from electric wire cable. Call your public electric utility company if you want to pick up a free one. Various sizes are available and suitable for climbing on, jumping off, or pushing around the yard. You may need to sand and varnish yours to prevent splintering. Beware of splinters.

Railroad ties or wooden two-by-fours attached firmly on or near the ground provide a stable walking or balance beam. Again, finish carefully to avoid splintering.

Flat rocks can provide a walking or stepping-stone path. (Flagstones are a little too slippery to be safe when they are damp.)

Upright tires can be buried halfway to make a strong but flexible area for climbing through or on top, or for playing follow-the-leader.

youngsters can crawl inside and play. Bring some of the smaller riding vehicles indoors during bad weather.

- For balance indoors, buy Romper Stompers® or make tin-can stilts with rope loop handles. (To make stilts, select a large tuna fish can or a two-pound coffee can. Remove the lid, turn the can upside-down, make a hole through the two opposite sides of the can near the top, insert the cord, like a venetian blind cord, long enough to make a loop handle to midthigh height, secure the ends inside the can with knots, and replace the plastic lid on the open end to protect floors.) The taller the cans, the greater the balance requirement.

- If a child is not yet ready to walk on railroad ties, safely located curbs, or balance beams, he might enjoy having a taped line on the floor so that he can play tightrope walker or gymnast.

- When forward walking on all these narrow balancing surfaces is quite well developed, suggest walking backward on them to help children find exciting new challenges in a familiar activity. Walking sideways could be a challenge, too.

- Indoor or outdoor obstacle courses provide wonderful opportunities for carefully planning body movements for tight spaces—under a chair, over a bench or a big ball, through a tunnel or a Hoola Hoop®, or between two empty boxes. Use your ingenuity to create a variety of these temporary play environments.

- Many play activities that are suitable for the preschooler help build muscle strength and tone. The following are some examples:

    1. Pulling or pushing other children in a wagon.

    2. Carrying moderately heavy containers of blocks or beanbags.

    3. Climbing or swinging on big outdoor play equipment.

    4. Gentle arm wrestling games. (Emphasize the fun of playing together and give children turns at winning sometimes.)

    5. Wheelbarrow walking. (Begin by holding children's thighs as they walk on their hands. Later move down to the knees or ankles as arm strength increases.)

- A small, nursery-sized trampoline that is only a few inches off the ground helps preschoolers experience pressure in their joints, which compress with each jump. This helps build strength and muscle tone, too. Be careful to place it away from nearby obstacles, and instruct youngsters about the precautions that come with the directions. We recommend that an adult be present at all times when a child is using this toy. Keep it fastened in an upright position when it is not being used.

- Large cardboard "brick" blocks or big plastic interlocking blocks are a lasting, inexpensive investment. Preschool engineers can design and make buildings that are taller than they are, as well as bridges, tunnels, and even strong roadways they can walk on. These blocks are bilaterally coordinating as well as fun since they require two hands for carrying and building. Big structures can fall on top of a preschooler without hurting the child or damaging the blocks.

- Be sure to provide a variety of big-movement experiences so that they will foster growth in most of the aspects of development we have been emphasizing in this book. Figure 6–3 gives examples.

DEXTERITY AND HAND/EYE COORDINATION

The agile hands of the developing preschooler are forever piling and building, picking up and putting down, reaching, shaking, squeezing, turning, and fitting things together. The hours of exploring with fingers will help him gain skill and accuracy in fastening, inserting, dressing, and manipulating.

He will continue to use his eyes to give him feedback about what his hands are doing. As his eyes carefully monitor the accuracy of his movements, they send messages to his hands to make intricate adjustments to achieve the results he wants. With practice, the preschooler will begin to perfect catching, coloring inside lines, and copying the very simplest geometric shapes. He will begin using a pencil grasp that will provide the stability and consistency necessary to proceed later with the complex task of handwriting. By school age, many children will be able to print their names and a few other letters, particularly if they have been exposed to preschool educational settings.

Mini- and Maxi-Milestones of Dexterity and Hand/Eye Coordination

Often the preschooler's play space is littered with tiny pieces of blocks, Legos®, Duplos®, and other construction toys as well as puzzles and minuscule

Figure 6–3 BIG-MOVEMENT PLAY FOSTERS DEVELOPMENT

Socialization. Taking turns, being careful not to hurt others, feeling a sense of accomplishment, following the rules.

Imagination. Pretending that moving or climbing equipment provides transportation to nearby or distant destinations.

Language. Talking about flying or vehicular "travels" and other pretend topics.

Space Awareness. Becoming more aware of the distance and duration of movement through space and observing the size and shape of space from a bird's-eye view or while rotating or moving back and forth.

Vision. Looking at stationary toys in the play yard while moving (ocular pursuit).

Sensations. Receiving information from muscles, joints, tendons, and the movement-through-space receptors.

plastic family members and farm animals. The fact that a preschooler can become absorbed in hours of satisfying play with these tiny toys tells you that his small-movement skills are coming along nicely. With practice, he is learning not to knock down his structures or plastic figures accidentally, thereby interrupting the flow of the imaginative work that propels the play forward.

The preschool years will bring a steady refinement in a child's ability to coordinate his eyes with his hands for paper, crayon, a felt-tipped marker, pencil, and paint activities. These tabletop or on-the-floor playthings will attract the child's attention much more than they did in his younger years. He will observe the effects of his own movements as his eyes read his lines and scribbles on the paper, providing feedback to him about their accuracy. As his small-movement skills advance, the increasing accuracy of his lines and strokes will inspire him to try more and more intricate prewriting maneuvers.

It is impossible to consider the sequence of how children acquire these graphic skills without being reminded that generally total big-movement skills occur before more isolated small-movement capabilities emerge. You will recall that in the infant years a youngster used to wave his arms toward an attractive toy in a total swiping movement. Then he learned to grasp and manipulate toys, intricately separating his fingers, and finally poking one finger into an opening or accurately pinching a corner.

Think of how the child engaged in his prewriting activities during the toddler years. He held a writing implement in a rigid, fisted grip, making sweeping arm movements that covered oversized computer printout paper with wide circular and straight lines. Sometimes his whole body moved as he threw himself enthusiastically into the activity, rocking back and forth on the chair with each large up and down movement.

As he grows up to be a very young preschooler, large-movement strokes still predominate. Earliest coloring books indelibly record the colorful huge scribbles that cover the page, ignoring the constraints of the cheerful pictures underneath. Paint easels allow floor space for stepping into the creative process with whole-body movements. Spatters and paintbrush dabs on walls or curtains near the easel attest to the large, sweeping movements that have occurred.

With advancing small-movement skills, the novice prewriter begins to learn to stabilize his trunk and shoulders while freeing up a forearm to move separately. He begins making smaller, more controlled strokes, often with the arm several inches above the writing surface. This capability for dissociating (or separating) different body parts continues to progress as the preschooler learns to rest his forearm on the table. There he stabilizes it so that the wrist can be free to move and control even more careful strokes. Eventually, maturation and experience allow him to dissociate finger movements from wrist movements. He is at last ready to try experimenting with the exacting task of drawing lines to represent something—like a fat, jolly snowman. Circular, vertical, and horizontally lined shapes come first. Next he might be ready to try simple geometric shapes and even alphabet letters.

These drawing and prewriting activities show that the preschooler is ready for symbolic representation with a writing tool (now his lines and squiggles begin to mean something to him). For harder symbols, it is easiest for him if he first watches you draw them, and then he tries to imitate your lines and movements. Later he will learn to copy without imitating and eventually can copy from memory. (This explains why grade-school classrooms have alphabet letters lining the top of the chalkboard for months, or even years, after the children have already been taught to copy the letter.)

Increasingly more dissociated movements occur in the development of ball skills just as they do in prewriting activities. At first, the whole body is fairly rigid and stable. Then more small movements of the hands and fingers come into play.

As you toss a big, soft plastic ball to a young preschooler, he looks awkward as he catches or misses it clumsily with extended arms and stiff posture. He will probably trap it against his chest in a whole-arm movement before he begins to use the more intricate finger movements required to catch it with his fingertips. These minute movements will also be required to bounce and catch the ball once or twice to himself, a skill some older preschoolers master.

You will notice that ball activities do not require just big-movement skills. Try bouncing a ball three or four times with your fist or the back of your hand. It is almost impossible to keep it in control. You know that the big-ball tossing and bouncing games you play with preschoolers help prepare them for the baseball exploits of the years ahead. Did you realize they also help prepare the dexterity necessary for writing?

Cutting also helps preschoolers develop prewriting skills as well as coordination of the two hands working together, one hand turning the paper and the other hand cutting. As they advance through the preschool years, youngsters will learn to dissociate the open/close finger movements required for cutting from the commonly associated open/close mouth movements. Some school children and even adults retain remnants of this preschool tendency, and you will see that as they cut they chew on their tongues or clench and unclench their jaws.

The increasing dexterity (as well as big-movement planning) of the almost-into-kindergarten child will allow him to take on added responsibility for his dressing and other independent living skills. Many will learn to do the following:

1. Button and unbutton (unless the buttons are in the back where he can't see them).

2. Buckle up his sandals or belt.

3. Snap the waist of his pants at the top of the zipper (some snaps are too stiff for even the strongest little fingers).

4. Close the bottom of his coat zipper before zipping it.

5. Put on and remove boots and other winter clothes that are plenty big enough.

6. Brush his teeth thoroughly and wash his face and hands.

7. Blow his nose fairly neatly.

8. Dress himself completely, including all front fasteners except ties.

The fact that a youngster has developed the dexterity and motor planning necessary to learn these fairly complex tasks does not guarantee that he will make a smooth transition into accepting responsibility for them. Some children dawdle along in their dressing routine, continually distracted by toys and books that attract their attention until you may feel compelled to nag or scold. Other children purposefully use such dawdling techniques just to take advantage of you, and sometimes a little power struggle begins to develop over how well a child uses his new motor skills to take care of himself independently. For tips on how to manage such behavioral impasses if they arise, see the "Personality/Socialization" sections of this chapter (on the preschooler) and of the preceding chapter (on the toddler).

By school age, this youngster becomes a pleasant little dinner guest, capably managing the food-handling tasks that require good dexterity and the coordinated effort of both hands working together. Spoons and forks replace fingers for all appropriate foods, and even soup and peas are almost mastered. Some preschoolers are taught to use a piece of bread or a butter knife to help push hard-to-pick-up food onto the fork. Many learn to use a knife to spread soft things like mayonnaise or jelly, stabilizing the bread carefully with the other hand. Cutting soft foods like pancakes and French toast comes next and requires using tools with both hands at the same time—each one requiring a different movement, and one of them even upside-down! The kindergartner can pour his own glassful of milk accurately from a small carton or pitcher. If he has been repeatedly instructed to position his drinking cup far from the edge of the table, tipped-over glasses at the table are rare.

The common preschool play activity of tea parties or pretend mealtimes reminds us that preschoolers often act out familiar events in their play. Play also provides opportunities for practice of a newly learned or newly developing skill. In this case, the skill is fine-motor dexterity for handling small cups and saucers and for pouring accurately from a teapot or pitcher into the miniature cups. As the grade-school years approach, this dextrous little host will even be able to scribble mock invitations to his tea party, perhaps signing his name at the bottom.

 ### How to Help Develop Dexterity and Hand/Eye Coordination

• Play bubble blowing with young preschoolers. It encourages good visual following skills. Have them tap the bubbles with their pointer fingers for coordinating the eyes with the hands and observing the cause/effect relationship of what happens to the bubbles. Some older children are dextrous enough to catch a bubble on the blowing wand or even on their finger, without breaking it.

- Encourage ball skills in preschoolers by first introducing them to balloon toss or tap. Large balloons move slowly and can be tracked fairly easily by the eyes. Also try a large plastic beach ball. A Nerf® ball is a good idea for the new ball handler, too, because it is soft and unthreatening. These balls can provide a successful experience if they are tossed accurately at close range for children to catch. Keep the toss gentle at first. As skill and confidence improve, step back a few paces, still maintaining a distance that assures success, and try a firmer 8- or 9-inch playground ball (or a plastic one from the grocery or variety store).

- Beanbags are also unthreatening because they are soft. Try making a variety out of sturdy, colorful fabrics filled with navy beans, lentils, kidney beans, dried peas, lima beans, or rice. Older children enjoy guessing the contents by feel, a good sensory experience. If they have trouble guessing, let them choose from among several fillers they can see in their original packages. This visual clue will give them the information they need to make the choice.

- Make a beanbag toss game out of a sturdy cardboard box with eyes, nose, and mouth cut out of a painted face. Make sure the holes are big enough. Balls of foam, wool, stockings, or newspaper are light and easy to throw in, too.

- Encourage children to catch with their hands once they have mastered trapping balls against their bodies. To encourage the fingers to help catch, introduce a Koosh® Ball, which has soft rubber tentacles, a Gertie Ball™, or one of the soft, squishy objects mentioned above. Little fingers can curve around these surfaces that give as they catch, helping to assure success.

- Clay is wonderful for pinching, pressing, poking, and pounding. A little later, they will enjoy molding and using tongue depressors or other tools to create things they can label verbally. More coordination practice results from rolling a clay ball or snake with two hands together than with one hand pressing the clay on the table. Plastic molding sets are motivating but may reduce originality.

- Tapping and hammering toys encourage youngsters to use a tool to aim where they are looking. Empty plastic egg cartons are cheap and impermanent but fun! The twelve fairly wide targets can be made more obvious by marking a bright color on each. Children will soon discover that holding the carton with one hand helps the accuracy of hitting it with the other, thus coordinating the two hands in play as they each perform a different function.

- You may wish to present a group project by putting numbers on the twelve targets of the egg carton and encouraging older preschoolers to count out loud as they hit them, lightly at first, then harder when they are ready to break the carton. They will be learning to remember counting as well as the left-to-right progression (which helps prepare for reading) through the reinforcement of seeing the numbers, the sound of their voices, and the jarring movements of muscles and joints.

- Pegs with various-size tops provide other targets for using a mallet and are available in both pegboards and peg desk sets. The wooden cobbler's bench has fairly wide cylinders and firm resistance. Using pegs to copy an easy design helps visual perception in addition to hand/eye coordination. Lite-Brite® is an even more intriguing peg-type activity on a lighted board.

- Store pegs in plastic boxes or small Ziploc® bags so that they won't get lost and are clearly visible.

- Xylophones can be used for hammering skills, too, if children are encouraged to carefully tap one note at a time rather than pound randomly. Some children will be interested in following as you show them how to play a tune with careful hand/eye coordination. A few will have enough visual memory skill to play a short tune later.

- Sewing cards and boards are fun for enhancing color recognition and following a design, as well as hand/eye coordination. The sequence won't matter to children at first, but when they are ready to learn to correctly outline figures, you can show them other ways to try it.

- Nesting and stacking toys are wonderful for developing the logic of sequential concepts of biggest to smallest while improving hand/eye coordination. They come in colorful barrels, drums, and pyramids as well as in fascinating characters from Sesame Street® and Walt Disney.

- Lauri® crepe foam-rubber puzzles are pliable, easy to manipulate, fairly indestructible, and carefully graduated to encourage increasingly more complicated fine-motor and visual skills. Older preschoolers can use them as templates and trace around the outlines when pieces are removed.

- Show your budding gardeners how to plant seeds in cupcake holders, muffin tins, or egg cartons. They will benefit from the feel and dexterity of placing the tiny seeds into the soil. They will be thrilled when they realize their cause/effect role in the development of the little plant they watch grow.

- Notice how small action toys and dolls require dexterity and coordination when the youngsters fit the pieces, accessories, and clothes together. This creative play makes the fine-motor effort easy.

- Windup toys are a big hit with preschoolers since by then they have the dexterity to work them. Provide a few on the toy shelves. They will encourage intricate dexterity and promote cause/effect awareness as children realize their actions result in the movement of the toys.

- Allow plenty of time and space for coloring, freehand drawing, cutting, and painting on large blank paper. Also hang a chalkboard on the wall (at the right height), and provide some individual small chalkboards, peg and chalkboard desks, and easels. Coloring worksheets of single large objects and creating handmade greeting cards and seasonal decorations encourage hand/eye coordination, too.

- Encourage children at times to draw or paint pictures that represent familiar, simple objects like people, snowmen, houses, and happy faces. If a child seems interested, tell or demonstrate how to add characteristics to make the drawings more distinguishable—a hat, a chimney, or a smile. If he watches you draw a simple design or picture, it will be easier for him to reproduce it (imitation) than if he draws it from memory or from copying a picture. Your clues will enhance his attention to detail and will improve the quality of his drawing. Allow lots of free drawing time without your direction, too.

- Use large-diameter pencils and crayons if a child is having major difficulty getting comfortable with holding a pencil correctly by the time he is approaching school age. You may wish to order plastic three-sided grippers from Developmental Learning Materials to slide onto the pencils. Stetros® (they look like molded colored clay) can also help to position fingers automatically at the correct place with regular-sized pencils. (Rusko Writing Co., P.O. Box 121, Crawfordsville, IN 47933).

- If necessary, show a child how to cut with his fingers curved around the scissors (not straight) and his wrist in a straight or slightly bent up position (not bent down toward the palm). If a child bends his wrist downward, it stretches the wrong tendons and makes it much harder in the long run. Try it yourself, and you will see how hard it is.

- Provide scissors for both right- and left-handed children, or try some of the new ones, for example, those made by Crayola® that can be used by both.

- Colorforms® require fine-motor manipulations to pull the designs off the backing and place them accurately on the picture board, then later replace them carefully on their own imprinted outline on the backing. A word of encouragement from you might be enough to stimulate his interest in the perceptual challenge of putting the pieces back so that it will be ready for play the next time.

- Card games like go fish and old maid are fun but can be frustrating if a little one can't hold many cards in his hand at one time. Show him how to hold onto the bottom corner tip of each card with his thumb and "pointer" with one hand, while he spreads the top corners apart with the other hand. Start with two cards and gradually add more. Another trick is to have youngsters stand up their cards in the edge of a long, narrow aluminum-foil or wax-paper box. The box becomes the card holder, and the child is free to handle the cards one at a time.

- If this is too difficult, try card games that involve holding no cards at all—like concentration (with five to ten pairs or more) and slapjack.

- Clothes in the costume box should be easy-on, easy-off to promote independence. Tops should be loose enough so that children can easily pull them over their heads and onto their arms. Pants should be loose enough to be snapped, zipped, or buttoned readily. Elasticized waistbands should not be too tight, and magnetic clasp belts can be used rather than ones that buckle. Velcro® is also a wonderful invention! Parents can be encouraged to have their children's own clothing plenty big enough as a favor to their bid for independent dressing at home.

- Rainy- or snowy-day dressing and undressing can be made easier and quicker by putting plastic bags around the youngsters' sneakers before they put on boots. Children can then slide them on or off with less frustration. Make certain they understand that the plastic bags are only for the shoes and that they are not to play with them. It is also helpful and economical if boots are a little bit bigger than shoe size.

- Nose-blowing requires a lot of small-movement skill for fingers as well as for the muscles that surround the chest cavity. If a preschooler is having trouble blowing through his nose, have him try blowing feathers or tiny squares of tissue off your hand, first through his mouth, then through his nose. This provides him with the feedback that lets him know when he has succeeded in exhaling air. Then he can learn to repeat the action.

- A toy piano or keyboard is an excellent activity for dissociation of the fingers. Encourage children to try intricate fingering, if they are willing, rather than using just their pointer fingers to peck out the notes. If the instrument comes with simple numbered or color-coded notes, following them can be a challenging hand/eye and perceptual activity.

- *If* a preschooler *wants* to learn shoe tying and is having trouble, try the sequence and words of instruction listed in Figure 6–4. Keep instructions short and simple, and ask parents to supply long laces so that he has plenty of length to practice.

VISION

In preparation for the important visual demands of the approaching school years, the preschooler is learning three important skills. First, he is learning to keep his eyes "on target," which helps him focus his attention. Second, he is becoming more efficient at scanning, that is, searching quickly for the important things he most wants to look at. This helps prepare him to visually pluck things from the environment just when he wants to. Third, he is also steadily improving in his ability to visually discriminate things from each other. He is becoming adept at comparing things and noticing differences and similarities in the way they look.

In these important preschool years, the child's eyes are gaining in exploratory skill. Instead of just a global-looking, he now uses a planned search for distinctive features. Increased visual perceptual skill is a culmination of childhood experiences. It integrates information from all the senses. The efficient use of perceptual ability helps prepare him for one of the most important and necessary skills in today's society—reading.

Mini- and Maxi-Milestones of Vision

The movement of a child's eyes as he scans the shape and essential elements of a visual stimulus makes a major contribution to his ability to perceive and understand what he sees. The tiny little muscles around the eye coordinate its movement. The muscles also help him "read" and understand the squareness of his blocks, the roundness of his tricycle wheels, and the irregular shapes of his puzzle pieces.

Figure 6–4 SUGGESTED WORDS AND SEQUENCE FOR TEACHING SHOE TYING TO CHILDREN WHO ASK FOR HELP

1. "Pull the loops through."
   Have child pull the two final loops at the end of your sequence of steps in tying so that he achieves the feeling of success at finishing the task you started. It also helps him discriminate where those little loop ends are hiding. After he has done this part many times, he may be ready to try tying from the beginning, perfecting one step at a time as he proceeds.

2. "Make an X."
   Cross laces over each other at the beginning of the tying sequence.

3. "Go under the X."
   Take the tail of the top lace, place it under the X, and pull it tight.

4. "Make a loop."
   Make a small loop, by holding two parts of one lace close to the center X, leaving a long tail hanging.

5. "Go around the loop."
   With the other lace, make a loop around the first loop, leaving a small hole or space that will be used for the next step.

6. "Go through the hole."
   Push the middle of the second loop through the hole, leaving a long tail. This is by far the hardest step.

7. "Pull the loops."
   Pull them straight out to the sides until the knot is tight. Keep each loop pinched closed.

8. If steps 4, 5, and 6 are too hard for the child, have him try making two loops like rabbit's ears, then making an X with the two loops and proceed with steps 1 and 2.

Each visual experience relates to or changes a tiny portion of the brain, which becomes selectively sensitive. That is, the little parts learn to identify or detect a particular piece of perceptual information. Like Sherlock Holmes, the child can store each of these detecting devices away in the filing cabinets of his memory. Later, he can pull one out for identifying a particular type of perceptual feature. Scientists think the feature each detects may become permanent.

The child's increasing accuracy in analyzing distinctive features of lines, shapes, and objects in the environment is also due to other important factors. His visual acuity has improved, and by school age his eyes have achieved nearly the 20/20 vision considered to be average for adults. Color recognition expands during the preschool years from barely recognizing a couple of colors you have named, to consistently recognizing—and even naming—all the primary colors. By kindergarten, he can even name the numerous in-between hues in his huge crayon collection. In addition, his increasing language and cognitive skills allow him to apply verbal labels (names) to objects and many of their associated perceptual features. This helps him recall the information he has observed.

Spatial awareness expands to include selecting a bigger or middle-sized item when three are presented. In time, he learns to match shapes by both color and size at the same time. He also begins to notice the spatial relationships of construction toy pieces more accurately and perceives the reality of empty spaces. After learning to copy a closed pyramid with blocks lined up adjacent to each other, he begins to grasp the idea of copying an open one, with open spaces between each two blocks in the pyramid.

Any child's mental set, or state of expectancy for what he is going to see, also affects how he learns from looking. For example, when he walks into the kitchen and looks around if he is thirsty, he will notice the carton of juice that has been left on the table. If, instead, he is hungry, he will notice the peanut butter jar. If he is not thirsty or hungry, he will notice the red ball in the corner. If he has been sent there for the purpose of fetching keys from the table, he may not even notice the juice or the peanut butter or the ball.

This change in mental set allows him to select the foreground from the background of everything he sees. In his favorite book, he picks out the little spotted dog in the complicated pictures when the story's main character is Spot. But he also enjoys opportunities to peruse Richard Scarry books, randomly scanning and glancing at each fascinating detail of this author and illustrator's busy-background pictures. He learns to see from the grandstand which football player in the confusing array of players is the one with the ball. His advancing "figure/ground" perception allows him to focus attention on appropriate details or information while ignoring portions that would distract him.

The experienced little scanner automatically learns to put together individual perceptual features into a hierarchy or graded series of pattern, structure, and sequence. He no longer records in his mind new perceptual information as an isolated piece of fact. He notices visual patterns that are either more cluttered or less cluttered, colors that are closer to blue or closer to red. He observes the structure of his toy truck or doll or crayons as either rounder or squarer, or more pointed or less pointed. He sees sequences of larger and smaller toys, first and last pages in his books, taller and shorter block towers. These steps help him create a unified whole from the information he is perceiving. It is a process of synthesizing.

In addition, his visual perceptual skills and memory have matured so that he can match vertical, horizontal, and circular lines and many shapes made with them. He is even starting to be able to copy some of them. He still has trouble with oblique lines and shapes because his brain is equipped with more cells for perceiving the horizontal and the vertical than for recognizing and storing information about obliqueness. No wonder when he gets to school he will learn to write "o" and "t" before "k" and "y."

He also may still have difficulty accurately noticing or reproducing intersecting lines and adjacent or overlapping figures. These present a perceptually greater challenge. Recognizing and drawing a row of five unattached circles will be a capability of the preschooler long before he can discriminate well enough to draw the overlapping rings of the Olympics logo.

His ability to analyze individual perceptual features has become more capable. The older prekindergartner learns the language labels for "same" or "alike" and "different." He learns to accurately take note of obscure discriminating features that set things apart from each other, even when they also have a lot of similarities. When he and his friend are playing with their matching action figures, they are acutely aware of every little scratch or mark that identifies which one is their own. They can differentiate geometric shapes that resemble each other like square/rectangle or triangle/diamond, or slightly different-sized magnetic letters like "O" and "o."

New skills emerge as a result of greater analytic ability, memory, and a more unified and remembered synthesis of perceptual features. He begins to show greater "form constancy." This means the consistency in how he recalls the overall pattern and structure of things he sees that are the same except for color, size, rotation, location, or some other detail that does not change its most important overall characteristic.

The child shows many examples of his ability to retain a constancy in perception of form. Long before the preschool years, he had recognized that a ball is a ball, whether it is large or small, figured or plain, multicolored or neutral. He even had learned to recognize that his favorite stuffed Winnie the Pooh bear is a replication of the figures drawn in his books by A. A. Milne, even though the figures are smaller or in various poses. Now as he approaches the school years, he may begin to notice that the letter **"A"** on his building blocks has many of the same characteristics as the "A" on his decorated ball and the "A" in his alphabet book, even though the color, size, or details of the "A" might be different.

This form constancy applies to an awareness of the visual similarities, and does not suggest that the preschooler necessarily knows the name of this "A" letter. Some do; many do not. A few five-year-olds recognize the sequence of letters in their first name and can pick out this sequence of letters if it occurs in a newspaper headline or text of one of their books.

 How to Help Develop Vision

- Help program or preset children's visual searching skills by playing a "what-shall-we-look-for-today" game in the car or van, or around the school. Keep it light and unpressured. Be sure the things you are searching for together are easy and fun for them to find. Help them establish a "perceptual set" during today's search for a brief period of time, holding in their attention and memories the features selected. Play for five or ten minutes in the beginning. Later try "until we see the playground" (across town) or during a picnic lunch.

- For the perceptual-set game, pick a particular color or try circles or squares or triangles. Look for drawn shapes or outlines at first, and encourage language labeling the names of colors or shapes. The older preschoolers can also notice that geometric shapes form the outline of a jar lid, book, or top of an end table. When they are ready, try suggesting two features (round and red or big and square).

- Continue the sorting activities children began during the late toddler years. Try buttons, beans, wooden beads, or blocks, and sort by color, shape, or size. At first, sort by one feature (all-white beans in this container, all-red in another, all-green in a third one). Later some preschoolers may be able to consider two different features together (square red button in one container, round white button in another).

- If older youngsters are enjoying this sorting game and are ready for a new challenge, see if they can combine color, shape, and size at the same time: "Let's string all the small, square, green beads on this lace!"

- Encourage children to search for objects in the hidden picture pages in *Highlights for Children* or other children's magazines. Begin or end this search with a discussion of the meaning of the whole picture to provide practice in appropriately switching their attention from a minute search for details to a whole global awareness and vice versa.

- Beware of figure/ground problems in puzzles that have a busy background, or nearly-all-one-color overall designs. Early jigsaw puzzles should have clearly defined drawings to provide plenty of obvious color and design clues to the novice puzzle solver.

- Older preschoolers can benefit from a formboard puzzle of all the alphabet letters, each to be inserted into its own shaped hole. Perceptual awareness of their shapes will precede being able to name the letters or to use them to create words. An insert puzzle helps enhance children's recognition of the distinguishing features of each letter.

- Play card games with the children. Old maid, Go fish, and slapjack help increase the children's perceptual awareness of the discriminating features of the cards and help speed up their ability to process perceptual information quickly. Commercially available sets of these game cards with novel and entertaining designs expand the perceptual advantage of playing the games. These card games can be introduced with a partial deck to decrease the perceptual challenge and shorten the duration of the game.

- Visual memory games like concentration encourage the older preschooler to notice and remember distinctive features. You could use any playing cards that have two or more cards of the same design. If you use, for example, a bridge deck, start with a few pairs that are very different, like the ace and a picture card, or a ten and a single-digit number. Grade up to more pairs slowly as the child experiences success. Remember, if you begin with the whole deck and he does not match the pairs well, he will think the game is frustrating and not much fun. Arrange the game, instead, so that he will be good at matching the few pairs that are very different from each other.

- To further encourage a child to experience and know shapes and angles and perceptual connections among objects around him, try the ideas below. The following activities help children integrate newly acquired information and apply it to new situations. This is called "generalization."

  1. Name perceptual features as you encounter them together.

  2. Walk with your group around shapes you notice on the ground of the playground, preschool room, or city sidewalks. As you walk, name and talk about the shape you are outlining

  3. Play a clothesline game of laying the rope out in a particular shape, then walking around it.

  4. Mention similarities and make comparisons in shapes and perceptual features of familiar or novel things all of you can feel: oranges and wheels of toy cars, books and towels or washcloths, brooms and forks, ketchup squeeze bottles and cylindrical blocks, bananas and the outline of a quarter moon picture in a book. This activity helps children integrate touch sensations with vision and spatial awareness as part of a unified whole body of meaningful information.

- If you like providing prereadiness worksheets for children, make your selections carefully. Be sure they are at the right level to be fun and fairly easy. Refrain from overchallenging a preschool child with tasks of matching, circling the right answer, tracing the shapes, and other perceptual problems that might discourage him from enjoying such activities when he gets to school.

- Help preschoolers notice that they can use construction toys such as Legos®, blocks, Tinker Toys®, and Lincoln Logs® to copy very simple designs or pictures shown in the instructions or on the toys' boxes. This perceptual skill begins to emerge in the preschool years if the designs are simple enough and children do not become discouraged.

SPACE/TIME AWARENESS

By the preschool years, the blossoming young learner has heard many references to the close alliance between space and time. Adults use the term "here" to represent the spatial quality of geographical nearness (The book is here,) as well as a time concept (Summer is here). He may also have noticed the use of "first," "second," and "third" as well as "before" and "after" to mean either space locations or time sequences of events. He definitely knows that he wants to be first in the line walking to the playground or first to hold the ball for demonstration of a new group game, even though he may not be able to use the word "first" properly yet himself. Notice that his location in line is a spatial concept, and the sequence in which he receives the ball is a temporal concept. To further underscore the connection between time and space, adults around him use the term "space" to represent outer space, personal space, distance between things, and the space of an hour's time.

For the developing child, the sequencing of events in both time and space begins with a global awareness of separate notions such as roundness, squareness, daytime, and nighttime. This global awareness proceeds to more and more accurate comparisons such as fitting a small round piece into a specific formboard hole or knowing that "darkness" means it is time to go to bed. This creates a basis for an all-embracing temporal and spatial reference frame. In time, the older preschooler learns to make more exact estimates of earlier learned concepts. Slowly he develops a system of comparisons and correspondences that become increasingly more accurate.

Although the preschooler is beginning to show more consistency in his understanding of temporal/spatial information, he still only focuses on one or two pieces of this information at a time. He has only a hazy understanding of how different pieces of spatial information are related or how time spans and time sequences form a unified whole temporal picture. His reference system still has a long way to develop.

As the preschool years unfold, he learns to generalize the information he gathers. He begins to locate objects relative to each other and events that are closely connected in time. This allows him to develop a more complete understanding of space and of time.

Mini- and Maxi-Milestones of Space/Time Awareness

The preschooler's concept of nearby environmental space begins with himself as the center. In time, he learns to imagine and remember space information at a little bit of a distance, even when it is out of view. He learns to find objects when you describe their location in another room. He can bring you the sweater you tell him is in "that" corner of the room down the hall. Then he can accurately stand in one room and point toward the corner where familiar objects are located in a room down the hall. Still, he will probably be inaccurate about pointing toward the location of familiar objects upstairs. At his home, he cannot stand in his living room and point accurately toward where his toy shelves are located in his bedroom upstairs. This type of little research experiment shows us that, although distant spatial awareness is developing, he has not yet learned to combine the imagination of horizontal and vertical together.

The preschooler begins to notice what is near and far. This is called an awareness of proximity and separation. He can tell you that Colleen in his car pool lives farther away than Todd, who lives next door. He knows he can ask Andy, who is sitting next to him at lunch, to pass the mustard. However, he is smart enough to ask his teacher to pass the ketchup because it is close to her plate but far from Andy's.

Next he becomes more acutely aware of things that are inside other things, and what forms outside edges. This is called "enclosure." We notice that his drawings of people usually show at least a circle enclosing facial features, not just random lines and dots with names like "arm" or "eye." These concepts develop before he grasps the meaning of measurements, angles, parallel lines, and shapes. Only much later does he learn to coordinate these spatial qualities of proximity and enclosure along with shapes and measurements.

This ability to coordinate various pieces of spatial information into one stable reference system develops slowly but blossoms under our very eyes when we know what to watch for. For example, the preschooler learns first that the tape recorder is always stored on "that" shelf and the Mickey Mouse puzzle pieces always fit into one particular wooden puzzle board. He is noticing spatial qualities but only one at a time.

Only later does he recognize "that" shelf as the third one, the one in the middle. He also later recognizes that the puzzle board is a big rectangle with parallel sides and right angles, and that there are lots of other rectangular-shaped objects in his play space. It will require considerable effort and trial-and-error playing for the preschooler to acquire this more universal system of spatial awareness.

The recognition of a middle location or a middle size shows that concepts of size and sequence have matured. Just before he is ready for kindergarten, he will probably be able to identify a middle-sized object from among three of varying sizes, but most preschoolers cannot sequence more than three.

He loves trying out his newly developing spatial awareness by building things. In his creations, he eventually learns to notice spatial aspects well enough to copy his own or others' simple structures made of five or six blocks or more. As the existence of space as a separate entity begins to dawn on him, he can copy or design buildings with space as part of the design. He no longer focuses his attention only on the blocks themselves. He is now aware of the difference between a pyramid built with blocks touching and one built with spaces between the blocks. The empty space is real to him now.

Preschoolers named Eric or Philip or Liz will eventually learn to write the "i" in their names without meticulously making the dot touch the top of the vertical line. They will learn that the space they should have left above the line and below the dot is a real entity.

The preschooler notices and relies on fixed reference points in his environment (the puzzle piece always fits; the middle shelf remains in the middle). These reliable fixed points form the basis for establishing a more mature spatial reference system that allows him to combine even more pieces of information about spatial qualities. It helps him eventually recognize that not only do *those* pieces always fit into *that* puzzle, but *that* puzzle board is the same size as the other puzzle boards that fit into *that* puzzle rack. This is one reason a neat, orderly, consistent play environment is recommended.

We do not advocate a puritanical preoccupation with rigid cleanliness or orderliness. However, a consistent plan for storage of toys helps give the preschooler an appreciation for classifying and ordering his world. It encourages an awareness of such spatial qualities as size, shape, proximity, and enclosure.

Young preschoolers who have been asked to copy shape drawings that are too hard for them to draw often manage to get the enclosure aspect of the picture right. Circle, square, and triangle all look like a closed curve. They have a notably different quality from X and + figures that they draw with an open, unenclosed appearance. The latter look more like separate lines. Also, proximities (nearness and distance) may be exaggerated because no overall spatial reference system has developed yet for their drawings. Preschoolers often draw eyes too close to the nose when drawing a person. Only at a later age do facial features become more accurately proportioned. Kindergartners rarely center their drawings on a large sheet of paper. Instead, their spatial attention may be attracted to one edge or corner, and that is where they put their drawings.

Meanwhile, time sequences are developing, and you can see that the preschooler recognizes different periods of the day. He can tell you that breakfast, not dinner, comes after he wakes up in the morning. He knows the meal might include cereal or orange juice, not a hotdog or baloney sandwich. If his Dad comes to pick him up before lunch instead of at the usual time after his nap, you will know by the questions he asks that he recognizes the temporal change.

The sequence of understanding that develops in the child's awareness of space will also occur as he learns about time. A child understands the proximity of storytime always preceding rest-time long before he understands "There are ten days before your birthday." At first, he can only predict time sequences of events that repeatedly occur close together (that is, in close proximity, such as washing hands and then eating lunch). Only in the older child does the passage of time become more realistic. Then the sequences of these pairs of events are hooked together in the child's mind into a whole big reference system that allows comparison and prediction. While this understanding of time represents a major step forward, real calendar skills and clock reading are still a long way off.

 ### How to Help Develop Space/Time Awareness

- Preschoolers can profit from solving a large variety of puzzles since children learn most during the first few times they solve the puzzles. To expand the number available, have a puzzle-sharing day occasionally when children are encouraged to bring in their puzzles from home to share with each other.

- Here is another way to add variety to your puzzle collection. Save colorful, large pictures from the sides of cereal or cookie boxes. Cut each of these pieces of cardboard into a few puzzle pieces (depending on the children's capabilities). They will enjoy putting together these novel puzzles that remind them of good treats. They might even enjoy cutting them out if their small-movement skills are advanced enough to allow cutting of light cardboard.

- Play guessing games like "Will this little nesting block fit into that one?" and "Which spoon is bigger, this teaspoon or that soup spoon?" Verify answers by fitting things next to or inside each other.

- Dollhouses and toy play sets not only stimulate imaginative play but help clarify spatial relationships. See if children can place furniture into the dollhouse to resemble the furniture arrangement in the kitchen or story room. When purchasing dollhouse furniture from catalogs, try to include furniture that resembles your center. Buy more tables, chairs, and shelves than a family home would have so that children can sometimes approximate their school environment when playing.

- Windup toys (if they can manipulate them), friction cars, and talking toys that work with a pull string or switch may help preschoolers understand cause/effect relationships and before-and-after sequences.

- For youngsters who are not bothered by a lightweight blindfold, play a simplified game of "Pin the Tail on the Donkey," turning them only once or twice on a spot that is not too far from the donkey. They can play a similar game using a picture of a child's body, putting the head, hand, or foot where it belongs. These activities help children to visualize body image as well as to make spatial judgments about where to pin the missing part.

- Try this game blindfolded or with eyes closed. Have the children point or walk toward the location of a familiar stationary object you name. Be sure they later peek to see if they have made a correct spatial judgment. Vary the game by having children crawl or hop to the targets, or take giant steps or baby steps. Make sure there are no other obstacles in his way. It's fun and a spatial challenge.

- If a child does not feel comfortable with a blindfold, maybe he would prefer a large paper bag on his head instead. He could have the fun of drawing a face on it first. If he doesn't like the bag, he might be willing to keep his eyes closed until he gets used to the game.

- When several children are playing together, give two of them a five- or six-foot rope to hold up high so that another youngster can try to get *under* the rope without touching it. The children slowly lower it and see how low the rope can be placed before some part of the child's body touches it as he goes under. This game adds motor planning and body awareness to the spatial task. Each child waits for his turn, which is a temporal learning experience, too.

- Place the rope on the ground and ask the children to see if they can get *over* it without touching. Then have two youngsters hold the rope, one at each end, and slowly raise it. You should see that the rope is not raised too high so that no one gets hurt, and that each one gets a turn.

- Maintain a fairly consistent program schedule so that preschoolers learn to predict "before" and "after" events accurately. Help them judge time spans by counting days on a calendar or looking for a specific position of hands on a clock (although they cannot tell time or calendar dates yet).

- Let children take turns guessing what the next regularly scheduled activity will be to encourage them to focus on the temporal aspect of the day's events: "Now that we have washed our hands, what do you think we will do next?"

- When you use terms like "just a minute" and "in about an hour," be fairly accurate to help realistic time judgments develop. Also give time spans fairly accurately to the children when predicting the length of an activity, or when allotting "five minutes" for children to complete a task.

- Encourage older preschoolers to use space/quantity words once they understand them: *between, next to, high, low, beside, more than, less than, around, in front of, in back of,* for example. Also encourage temporal words such as *before, after, now, soon,* and *later.* Be sure to use them accurately.

PERSONALITY/SOCIALIZATION

The three-year-old has survived the "terrible two's" and is beginning to emerge as a more sociable little creature. As his confidence in his own autonomy and individuality soars, he begins to show an interest in making friends and interacting with one or two others in play. Still, however, the most significant people in his life are clearly the members of his family and the caretakers he sees daily.

The preschooler shows less of that scattered, boundless energy of the toddler that makes you wish you could harvest or funnel it as an energy source for solving world problems! Instead, during the preschool years, you will see this energy more focused as his attention span increases. He takes less of a shotgun approach to his toys.

He begins to work toward more long-term play goals, and this makes his activity level seem less random. As the school years approach, it will become apparent that he is becoming ready to have his inquisitive energies further focused and refined to meet the attentional demands of the classroom.

Mini- and Maxi-Milestones of Personality/Socialization

Now that the toddler years have come to a close, the developing youngster pretty well recognizes that his personal identity is different and separate from the people around him. He is ready to move a step further in establishing a realistic awareness of himself. He begins to recognize that there are gender differences and, in time, he identifies himself with adults of the same sex. You may notice more truck and car play emerging among boys, and doll and tea party play among girls. This is particularly (but not exclusively) true if children witness this type of gender difference in the interests and behaviors of the adults they know.

The preschooler recognizes that he cannot have exclusive rights to the affection of his parents or caretakers. In particular, he must emotionally untie himself from his close attachment with his primary caretaker—usually his mother. He begins to accept the necessity of sharing these special adults with others. This is a major step in his socialization process and helps him move beyond the entirely egocentric behavior that characterized him during the infant and early toddler years.

This recognition of his own gender identity and this acceptance of less exclusive caretaking from special adults in his life help prepare him for making his own social judgments. Instead of merely conforming his behavior to the watchful eye of these grown-ups because of fear or experiencing their disapproval, he begins to develop a conscience. He learns not to cross the road even if no adult is watching him. He also begins to see things from other people's points of view as he grows away from having such a self-centered view of the world. He sometimes notices when you are too busy cleaning up spilled paint to be asked to play ball. He makes great strides forward in accepting the unwritten rules of social interaction. He begins to take a critical look at his own behavior and recognizes social errors he has made. He recalls the slap he has given a friend, the toy he has grabbed away from an unsuspecting toddler, the plate he watched clatter to the floor as he reached past it for a forbidden cookie. He begins to experience feelings of shame or guilt when he knows he has done something wrong. He may hide the pieces of the broken plate or begin to cry if told that you saw him deliver the slap that he later regretted giving.

The preschooler begins to show initiative in doing things that demonstrate his increasing social responsibility for his own behavior. The initiative he takes also reflects the greater control he has over his movements, both large- and small-motor skills. He now knows that he has choices and can exercise free will to obey or not obey the rules he has learned from you. He can generalize this new awareness to social situations outside the classroom. You can trust him to visit another school without ruining their toys or endangering himself or others. He begins to integrate input regarding values or cultural standards from his school and family, his peers and their parents.

With his increasing awareness of social rules and consequences, the preschooler shows that he can wait longer than he could as a toddler. This is particularly true if pleasant distractions are entertaining him or if he knows good things will happen to him as a result of his own good behaviors. For example, he can stand to wait a little past "hungry tummy" time if a cheerful class outing delays lunchtime. He can usually control his impulses to handle everything in another classroom he is visiting or to call out during a play the group is watching. It will help him to know you will compliment his good behavior afterward or maybe even give stickers to the children who were well-behaved during the special event.

Since his concept of the passage of time is developing into a reference system he can depend on, he begins to feel secure that promised or expected rewards will, in fact, materialize. He is also developing a more realistic awareness of some of the pitfalls in everyday living. He vividly remembers objects or situations that have frightened him in the past: the unexpected fall down the stairs, the hot coffee he tipped over, the week his mother was hospitalized. The feelings he experienced with these events are often imprinted within him and may resurface when he suspects similar events may occur. He takes to heart repeated warnings about potential dangers he has not actually experienced, like being hit by a car or falling off the top of a high sliding board. He also feels the tension from the fears of those around him, even if those fears are unfounded. Some adults exude anxiety about germs, fire sirens, thunder and lightning, or deep water. A preschooler may develop a fear of the dark during these preschool years. If he has not experienced nightmares before, they may emerge now. The monsters and dragons that may appear in his play help him work out fears or insecurities that might otherwise undermine his confidence and prevent him from reaching out to socialize with other children.

"Magical thinking" is clearly evident during these years, and many children confuse fantasy with reality. They love fairy tales and make-believe activities that allow flights of fancy. Many talk with imaginary companions. The magical thinking a child may exhibit helps him cope with new fears and with his emerging individuality and gender identity.

Play. Most of the time, three-year-olds still enjoy playing alone with their toys. Each child plays by himself with his Tonka® truck or Brio® wooden train set, or next to another child playing with a similar toy (parallel play). A small glimmer of associative play emerges as he begins to show interest in playing with other children.

Once he begins to experience success in playing comfortably with one child, the preschooler experiments with playing with a small group of peers. The two or three children, playing with similar toys, will probably show more interest in each other than in the toys they are beginning to share. Initially they show no sense of group organization to reach a common goal. They may exchange a toy car or set up their dolls near each other for a pretend tea party. This associative play eventually replaces parallel play by the time preschoolers are ready to enter kindergarten.

When there are several children to choose from, the membership of the small play group changes often—sometimes amid loud eruptions of disagreement. Squabbles are forgotten quickly, and play often resumes fairly promptly. "All's well that ends well" seems to be the theme, at least until the next disagreement.

Slowly the preschooler learns to prefer group play rather than solitary play and even prefers other children to adults. His increasing interest and need for making friends motivates him to try out new play strategies for preliminary sharing and group decision-making. While some children become quite bossy or aggressive at this age, many slowly begin to establish a balance between asserting their own rights and sharing their toys. Occasional adult intervention may be required, but generally these preschoolers learn to settle their own disagreements.

With repeated success in playing associatively, the youngsters will begin to organize their small groups to achieve a goal. Someone will be appointed the "daddy" or the "baby." Sharing of ideas for block construction will commence, and they will begin to take turns for activities like making the pretend peanut butter sandwiches in the play kitchen corner or trying out the new swing on the playground.

The preschooler's play is often a fictitious representation of important features in his own life or of events he observes in his immediate environment. Because of his imagination and more advanced intellectual skills, complex representations develop. "Store" will emerge as a favorite play activity, accompanied by lots of pretend equipment, some of it quite elaborate. Play countertops and shelves may be laden with many boxes and cans of "groceries." This imaginative play will also probably involve assigning of roles ("storekeeper" and "shopper"). The play will also help reinforce the importance of honest exchange of money for goods (though accurate money concepts are not learned yet).

His play patterns will show you that he is beginning to respond to the human need for developing and understanding values. When he plays "house" or interacts with friends, he will mimic the words and attitudes toward other people that he learns at home and at school. He may use your most stern admonitions and scoldings or your terms of affection and praise if they are also prevalent in your everyday social interactions. He may be a mirror to you of your own behavior if you listen carefully. At the game table, he will learn not to cheat and how to follow rules. In his play with hero figures, he will act out the important issues having to do with dominance, submission, and personal injury.

Throughout the preschool years, play continues to have a strong effect on cognitive development. During play, he will use trial-and-error and rehearsal to acquire and perfect new skills and knowledge. For example, his block bridge may topple several times before he finally discovers that he must make the sides even if he wants the horizontal block on the top to be flat.

The play of the preschooler can continue to include the good work habits he began to acquire as early as the toddler years. He can learn to persevere with difficult constructions or drawing tasks he has invented without giving up or losing his self-control. He can be expected to clean up the toys and his personal belongings, sometimes with a measure of help when his play has left things in considerable disarray. He can organize his play activities so that he forms and carries out plans, and generally completes one activity before he begins another. He can begin to organize his awareness of time so the play experience has run its course before it's time to clean up and go home. One or two gentle reminders of the approaching end of playtime help him conclude his play comfortably on time.

Families and teachers who promote such early work-readiness skills are preparing future teenagers and adults who accept responsibility. These children are more likely to show initiative in the workplace and make well-thought-out and reasonable decisions.

 How to Help Develop Personality/Socialization

(For additional ideas about managing behavioral impasses, see the "Personality/Socialization" section already mentioned in Chapter 5.)

- Provide kind but unmistakable discipline using simple explanations and firm guidelines. Be *consistent* to help children establish and maintain a sense of security and predictability.

- Because preschoolers are at an age prone to developing fears, keep your explanations of potentially scary or unpleasant events brief and simple. Long-winded reasons for being careful of large playground equipment or for not worrying about a substitute coming in while his usual caretaker is away on a short vacation are likely to be more than preschoolers can absorb realistically. Such long explanations may set off feelings of anxiety out of proportion to the real physical or emotional dangers of the situation. Beginning to prepare youngsters too far in advance of an anticipated event, like a trip to the doctor or change in staff, may escalate concerns unnecessarily. A little forewarning can be useful. Excessive forewarning is too much of a good thing. Use your discretion.

- Allow expressions of fears and fantasies *from children*. This is particularly true for scary or unexpected circumstances like a hospitalization or lengthy separation from a parent. It may help to play dolls or house or hospital with the child. Let him be the parent or the doctor sometimes if he wants to, and you play the part of the child. Don't be tempted to overinterpret such play to the child or his parents.

- Teach children to express likes and dislikes but to do so in a courteous, respectful, maybe even pleasant manner. Their feelings and opinions are important, but so are those of others.

- Recognize that gender differences may emerge strongly in the play of preschoolers. Allow for individual differences, even if nontraditional play patterns develop. Some girls love Erector® sets, road-building equipment, and wrestlers. Many boys delight in nurturing teddy bears and may even be "baby" occasionally when playing house.

- Try to keep competition at a minimum when the children are learning new skills. If keeping score encourages a youngster to try harder, keep the score goal low enough to achieve easily. Slowly raise it as his skill increases. If possible, have him keep score against himself rather than against another child at first. It is better for him to feel good that he made more points today than he did yesterday than to feel sad that he didn't make as many points as Jeffrey.

- Introduce preschoolers to games for two or four youngsters like Sesame Street® Games for Growing or for the whole group (for example, musical chairs). This helps them learn important socialization skills like following rules, taking turns, winning, and losing. Be sure to stick to the written rules or simplified rules you have all agreed upon. That will help them learn about fairness and honesty and will prepare them for successful game playing outside the preschool center.

- While de-emphasizing the importance of competition in these games, at the same time acknowledge that a winner and a loser will, in fact, emerge. Teach the youngsters to lose gracefully, always congratulating the winner with a hearty handshake and "Nice going." Also teach them to win pleasantly and to use kind words of encouragement for the loser.

- Encourage preschoolers to develop a sense of humor by sharing with them the jokes and funny stories they begin to enjoy and initiate at this age. However, avoid the temptation to tease or kid preschoolers by making fun of their errors, shortcomings, or personality characteristics. If kidding takes place in your center, be sure the preschoolers understand the fun and benefit positively from the verbal interchange.

- If you notice that the play of your group of preschoolers is laced with far more negative social comments than positive ones, try tape-recording yourself playing with them or leading a group activity. When you get a chance, listen to your own taped remarks and see if you can teach yourself to replace any negative comments with more positive ones. Instead of "Hurry up and get ready, Jason, or you won't be ready for your car pool," try "I like the way you've started dressing, Jason. You will look handsome in that jacket and hat." Avoid negative generalizations like "You're never ready on time."

- Encouraging children to put away toys, clothing, and other objects not only fosters neatness, it also provides one of the earliest experiences in classifying and sorting. It helps children learn the idea of relation and belonging. (Books belong on the display unit, boots are related to coats and both go in cubbies, dirty paintbrushes and dishes are sorted from clean ones and put away in a different place.) These concepts are important for development of language, spatial awareness, visual discrimination—all important building blocks for learning.

• Independent dressing and care of personal belongings and toys promote good organization and time management. It also builds children's self-confidence to know that they are not dependent on others for these everyday needs. Try to set aside enough time so that you don't always have to do these jobs for them. Although it is quicker and easier for you to dress and clean up after children yourself, they will not learn as much.

• Allow children to make simple decisions so that they can feel in control of portions of their environment that affect them: "Which of these two games do you want to play?" "Which toys shall I help you pick up first, the blocks or the cars?"

• It isn't too early to select some easy jobs for the youngsters to do. Give them a choice from among several. Perhaps they can help set out snacks and napkins or feed the animals.

• Try serving *real* little sandwiches and hot chocolate on doll dishes and silver for a special occasion tea party with youngsters. You could set the table together, make the sandwiches, and you might even "dress up" for the occasion. It would be a good time to practice those fancy table manners you've begun at lunchtime. Make a big thing about folding the napkins in your laps, saying "please" and "thank you" in a dignified voice, and being extra deferential to each other. Children will love it, and those afternoons will add to their store of precious memories of the nursery school years.

LANGUAGE

The self-centered speech of the three-year-old continues through the early preschool years, and you will hear a heavy smattering of "I," "me," "mine" words. However, vocabulary is expanding beyond these pronouns and the verbs and nouns he used in the toddler years. Now his vocabularly includes many color words, adjectives, adverbs, and prepositions. In addition, the preschooler's reciting of nursery rhymes charms grandparents and other visitors at home, and provides a happy playtime and learning opportunity during his hours in the preschool.

By the time he is ready for kindergarten, the preschool conversationalist will have stopped acquiring new words at a rate that doubles his vocabulary every year, and he will never achieve that geometric progression again. Instead, his comprehension of the *meanings* of words and phrases will increase rapidly, and he will refine how he uses words to express his thoughts and feelings. He will use humor, and also colloquial expressions like "Right?" and "You know?" He will even begin to define simple words and try experimenting with word games like "I'm thinking of . . ." The preschooler's language reflects the beginnings of an interest in the use of words themselves and of the ideas they represent. The language is no longer just a way of expressing his needs and giving information related to himself and his immediate needs.

Mini- and Maxi-Milestones of Language

During the preschool years, the child continues to develop the language components of phonology, syntax, and semantics, each of which will be described in detail later. He hones each to the more mature, advanced level required for entering the grade-school classroom.

The *phonological* system of language includes the melody of stress, pauses, and intonational patterns used to modify how the speech is produced. It includes the loud yell of the overeager jungle gym climber, and the squeals and rapid staccato exclamations that occur when someone brings a turtle or pet bunny into the center. Many a preschooler returns from a class trip to the barnyard or a puppet show relating his news with recurrent "ummm" that tells you his mind is racing fast and his mouth can't quite keep up. Some show this rhythmic pattern even during quiet play or routine reports about daily activities. Most children by school age will be demonstrating lots of inflection in sentences like "It's mine!" and "Watch out!" on the playground and "Do I have to?" during cleanup time.

Phonological considerations of language are also related to the distinctive speech articulation features. Lisps and incorrectly pronounced *r*'s and *l*'s will permeate the air of any school setting for under-fives, but the oldest children in the group use clear pronounciation of nearly all other speech sounds. Reversals of sounds are common (just as they are for writing reversals of *b* and *d*, *p* and *q* for four- to six-year olds). Many preschoolers will see the noodles in the pot and announce "pisghetti" for lunch, will talk about the "aminals" in the zoo, and will report having little "engerny" when they are tired.

The phonetic approach to reading taught in many grade schools, including an emphasis on rhyming and identifying sounds associated with letters, taps into the phonological system of language development. Children who learn during the preschool years to listen accurately to each discriminating feature of speech sounds and rhythms and to articulate with clarity are learning skills that will serve them well when they open their first preprimer reading book.

Syntax is the feature of language and speech that has to do with the construction of sentences. It identifies the understanding that the hierarchy and form of words hold greater and lesser importance in each particular sentence. A child first learns single words, then whole phrases that seem to him to be single entities. By the preschool years, he understands and differentiates many of the individual parts of sentences and their functional relationships. When he gets to elementary school, he will still be fooled by new big phrases like "pledge of allegiance to the flag" and "L–M–N–O–P," which he will run together as though they were single units of speech.

Syntax also includes consideration of the prefixes and suffixes that change the meaning of the words they are attached to, like *un-*, and *-s*. The preschooler knows undressing is not the same as dressing, and "toy" represents something different from "toys." These meaningful little pieces of speech were discussed in Chapter 5 on the toddler and are called morphemes.

Preschoolers continue to generate original sentences, following syntactic rules that resemble but are not quite the same as adult rules ("I catch-ed the fish-es" six morphemes). Their sentences are longer, and structure is dramatically improved over the toddler's attempts: "Look, that red wagon bump(ed) into me." As the school years approach, sentence structure begins to include complex and compound sentences. "Please give me the picture I made in the paint corner," and "I got a bike for Christmas, and I went to my grandfather's."

The *semantic* part of any child's grammar includes his own personal internal dictionary. It is a collection of words he knows how to use, and it includes an awareness of the object or characteristic to which the words refer ("toybox," "green," or "on").

The child's semantic development reflects more than just vocabulary growth. It reflects how he is categorizing or organizing his world. It shows that he is noticing the enduring qualities, regular occurrences, and relationships in the environment and in the collection of facts he has acquired. The semantic development is accompanied by an increase in abbreviated thought processes. These become internal language and help him structure his understanding of information he is trying to sort out. The preschooler might not put his words together in such a sentence as, "You have to drive a long time to get from Maine to California." Each of these words could be in his vocabulary, but he probably hasn't quite developed the concept the sentence would be expressing. He also probably hasn't yet developed the "you have to" type of sentence formation.

In Piaget's famous conservation experiments, a preschooler certainly knows the words "glass," "water," "bigger," and so on. But the words are not enough. He cannot string the words together in sentences to explain that the tall, narrow glass does not contain more water than the short, fat one. The concept has not yet developed. In addition, he still may have only a hazy notion of how to use the words "same" and "different."

While these examples point out the immaturities in his internal thought processes, the fact is that cognitive growth is occurring rapidly and that inner language is becoming richer. For example, you can tell when the older preschooler is using real logic to figure out plots of stories, plays, and TV programs. One bright preschooler, upon hearing a reading of *The Ugly Duckling* for the first time, sat quietly for a moment, then said, "That's like the story of Rudolph the Red-Nosed Reindeer."

Measures of vocabulary size are closely allied with overall estimates of intelligence. The prekindergartner in your school who has the largest vocabulary may be identified by your staff as the child "most likely to succeed" in grade school. The reason is not because he is good at memorizing isolated words but because generally the large vocabulary is the tip of an iceberg. Underneath the surface is a deep body of comprehension: ideas, facts, concepts, interconnectedness of bits of information, novel applications, and possibly a whole range of creative thought processes. *These* are the things that will set him apart from children of normal intelligence in the years to come.

In playgroups of the very young (and still egocentric) preschooler, teachers will hear a collective soliloquy going on—each child talking "at" the others from his own point of view. "My dolly riding wagon. Oh no! She fall down. Dolly have a boo-boo." You will also hear, "You can't have mine," and "Don't do that" as each member of the group uses words to assert his independence and to reestablish possession rights.

As he approaches kindergarten age, each youngster's general socialization skills begin to help him perceive the world from other people's points of view. His speech during group play begins to reflect the more cooperative thinking that leads to real adaptive social communication. Now a real dialogue can be heard:

"Our trucks can go fast. Rmmmm. Here's the gas station."
"I'm coming to get some gas."
"Okay, I'll get gas, too. Rmmmm."

This type of reciprocal speech pattern and taking turns in conversation shows a real responding of one child to another.

Questions. The preschooler could be called "the great questioner." He generates question-making phrases and sentences, using this fairly newly developed quizzing ability hundreds of times to learn information about people and things around him.

There are many forms of questions. For each of the types of questions, the preschooler first shows that he understands the question form before he begins expressing and using that form himself. One form of questioning is made with words he has already been using. He just changes the inflection: "Am I funny?" "You can fix it?" These often seek yes or no answers. Many forms of questions use *wh*—words like *who, what, where, why,* and *when. How* is generally included with these. The *wh* questions, as they are called in the

English language, seek new information. He understands the first three types of questions, *who, what,* and *where,* even before the preschool years. Then *why* arrives on the scene with a splash, and for some children, becomes as prevalent a part of their vocabulary as "no" had been during the toddler years. *Why* may dominate these children's communication with adults for months or even years.

While the questioning period is a pleasant relief from the "no" stage experienced earlier, it brings its own frustrations as adults grapple with answers that are satisfying to the preschooler—not too complicated and not too simplistic. Another frustration occurs when the adult does not really know the answer: "Why is the sky blue?" The child's questions help him gather and integrate countless pieces of information. He needs these pieces to form the enduring reference system he is creating to help him understand the world around him. He will carry this well-informed reference system with him into the learning environment of his neighborhood grade school.

 How to Help Develop Language

- Children learn to speak by having the opportunity to listen, talk, ask questions, and explore answers. This helps increase their vocabulary and their understanding of the world. Talking out a new experience helps them solve problems and integrate information. Respect and encourage each child's verbal participation in individual conversations as well as in group activities. Let children make their own discoveries and even their own mistakes in order to learn.

- Allow children time to organize their thoughts as they speak. Do not be tempted to jump into a short period of silence to finish a child's sentence for him.

- Pay attention and respond when the children spontaneously approach to share news with you. Children actually talk more often and use longer sentences when they have initiated a topic than they do when you encourage them to talk to you about something.

- Keep your voice well modulated as you speak with the children in your care. You will be modeling speech sounds the children will copy. Avoid rapid, high-pitched, or overly nasal talking, particularly when you feel under stress.

- On the other hand, do use intonational changes in your voice to help underscore your meaning. Preschoolers use these acoustical cues to help them understand and remember what you are telling them. "Now, take your partner's hand. Be careful as we cross the street." Speak distinctly. You will be modeling careful articulation to encourage the children's accurate speech.

- Play games that encourage the children to carefully listen to and identify environmental sounds. When they are older, help them notice the sounds that occur at the beginnings of words. A few prekindergartners may be ready to point out or cut out pictures of B-words like *ball, baby,* and *balloon* and other little phonetic exercises. (Children who are ready will do this quickly in kindergarten or first grade, so you will not want to push this beyond a happy play experience now.)

- Schedule daily story time for introducing new books and reading old favorites over and over. Introduce stories with increasingly complex plots and ideas as the children grow older and their comprehension expands.

- Use nursery rhymes, songs, and reading of Dr. Seuss books aloud to help children notice speech sounds that match at the ends of words. This is an important step that helps children later learn to recognize and accurately sound out letter groupings that have matching sounds (*hat, pat, sat*).

- Play musical chairs, follow the leader with claps, Simon Says, and other games that encourage children to focus their listening (auditory figure/ground). The children must attend to one sound in the environment even while moving, hearing the sound of voices and shuffling feet, feeling the touch-pressure of chairs they are passing and children bumping into them, and so on.

- With their eyes closed or heads down, encourage children to guess which child is saying hello or what familiar object is being dropped.

- Introduce rhythm band instruments to help children learn to hear and remember sound patterns musically as a step toward hearing and using them appropriately in speech sounds that match each other.

> *e*-lephant, *No,* he can't, *Here we go.*
> versus
> Nin*tendo,* He *can't* go, I *won't* stop.

- Sensory play elicits language development. Water, sand, mud, clay, baby lotion or shaving cream, and finger paints encourage children to talk about how things feel as they use them.

- Pretend activities stimulate conversation and the language of social interactions. Examples include dolls, kitchen play equipment, and costumes. We also like dollhouses, toy furniture, and tiny figures for their unlimited play value and language stimulation. When children play they are grown up, it gives them the chance to copy adult behavior and verbal expressions. Toy barns and animals, trains and villages, airports and planes, and garages with small cars and equipment also foster language development and cooperative interactions.

• Encourage group discussions about the play possibilities for new toys and equipment that arrive at your center. Encourage vocabulary growth and question making.

• To encourage language output, especially in shy children whose speech is sparse, try puppets. Sometimes reticent children will express themselves more expansively when they speak for a puppet.

• To develop vocabulary, concepts, and internal language, provide interesting and varied science and social studies experiences in which the children can see and do things—planting seeds, visiting nearby destinations, viewing and taking care of animals or enjoying interesting visitors to the preschool (a foreign visitor in a costume, a musician with his instrument, a traveler with slides and souvenirs). Experiment with the following: Will ice melt faster in the sun or in the shade? How many beans would you guess are in the small jar?

• Encourage space-rocket play to promote counting backward, sequencing of events, language about space destinations, and rocket blast-off preparations. Plan a day when the school or one room will be turned into the inside of a rocket or space station.

• Be sure families have marked all clothing and personal possessions with children's names. This not only avoids a gigantic lost-and-found pile, but it also encourages children to "read" their own and each other's labels. Such an "incidental learning" process helps children learn to decode written symbolic information without the need for any formal teaching.

• If you notice that a child has developed the habit of asking "why" questions or making other inquiries disproportionately often, explore the reasons. If a child is insatiably curious, he is giving you verbal clues that he needs you to help fulfill his curiosity. Provide self-directed learning objects for him to play with, like magnets or carbon paper. If, instead, the child appears to be nagging for more and more attention, think about what might be making him feel neglected. Then see what changes you can bring about.

• If you have a VCR and TV available at your center, you might want to plan an *occasional* special viewing period for children on rainy days. Videotapes can be purchased or rented. You may want to select a videocassette of Mickey Mouse, Pinocchio, Winnie the Pooh, or a special holiday film about Rudolph or Frosty. Encourage the children to talk about the films afterward to help expand their vocabularies and encourage comprehension.

- Provide appropriate tapes or videocassettes along with matching books occasionally at story hour.

- We don't recommend full-sized home computer purchases for children until the youngsters are well along in elementary school. However, Coleco, Texas Instruments, and many other companies make educational computer toys. You may want to examine them and see if they could be suitable for some of the older children in your group.

- Apple® computers are popular in elementary schools and have many disks and teachers' guides available with Pre-K programs for language arts, drawing, reading, and math readiness. If you purchase or borrow a computer for your center, we suggest that children have very limited time on them. In our opinion, sensory, movement, social, and language activities are more important learning experiences during the preschool years.

IMAGINATION/CREATIVITY

The preschool period of magical thinking is a fascinating age when the imagination soars to new heights. In the toys that litter the play space and in objects and circumstances in the child's environment, the little creative thinker spies ideas and happenings that no one else knows are there. He believes earnestly and enthusiastically, and would be the first to start clapping when the audience is asked if they believe in Tinkerbell.

Of course, this imaginative impulse must be tempered with reality. Of course, the exaggerations that occur in the chatter and reporting of play experiences must stop short of fibs and actual lies. Of course, little children whose eyes are full of wonderment must eventually grow up to a realistic understanding of Santa Clause, the tooth fairy, and the fact that the grown-ups in his life are not superhuman. While it is true that this age must pass, you can observe with appreciation the faith and belief system of the little magical thinkers and their natural tendencies to generate new thought patterns and notions that never existed before. By the end of the preschool years, you will want to help foster the inclination children have toward a more realistic frame of reference without dampening the creative ability and enthusiastic imagination of the budding novelist or choreographer or muralist.

Mini- and Maxi-Milestones of Imagination/Creativity

You can tell as you watch the play of the early preschool child that he has achieved cognitive and perceptual awareness far beyond the scope of the little toddler. He also has an increased understanding of his body, feelings, and senses. He has a more accurate awareness of the physical and emotional characteristics inherent in toys, people, and fascinating events he has experienced. He has absorbed information from books, TV programs, and videos. All these things make him considerably more alert to the possibilities of what *could* be, to a much greater degree than a baby or toddler could imagine. Now he can begin to put together creative notions beyond just responding directly to an object's obvious qualities or acting out in play the behaviors he has witnessed or experienced himself.

Now his imaginative play becomes quite elaborate, and he pretends often when he is by himself or with a playmate, using toys and objects. In time, he moves from realistic to substitute objects. He is no longer as dependent on what the real properties of an "agent" might be. He can use such symbolic representations as a block for an airplane, a wastebasket for a drum, or even as farfetched an example as a stick for a house. He learns eventually to pretend an object is present without even a substitute, and when nearly school age may be heard to say, "Let's go over here to be in the castle," or "I'm coming on my horse to save you." He also learns to expand real experiences or reality play into imaginary activities: "Look at me. Now I can slide down the pole. Come on, Jimmy. Let's me and you play fireman." Or "I love peanut butter sandwiches cut up like that. Mine can pile up to be a big tower. Look, my carrot climbs up so high he can see out the top. Hey, I liked that skyscraper we saw yesterday."

Pretend play now is sustained for longer periods of time than in the toddler years. The pretending extends to a sequence of events rather than playing out a single incident (pretending a whole birthday party instead of just the blowing out of the candles). The preschooler now shows that he can plan ahead what his representational play will include. It is more premeditated, not just accidental or spontaneous pretend play.

The frequency of such imaginative play escalates through the preschool years. Dramatic play becomes a central activity for groups of children. The doll corner, kitchen corner, and costume boxes or drawers are beehives of activity. Different roles are tried out, with frequent changes of who is in the group playing and who is depicting which family member or community character. The week after the fire engine visits the preschool, all the firefighter hats and play boots and shiny badges will be in high demand! Sometimes the dramatic play erupts into wild, unfocused, almost haphazard role-playing. It may even disintegrate into silly attention-seeking. At other times, it begins to take on a more planned, almost organized flavor.

In dramatic play, the child imitates the real world, often taking the role of adults, or he pretends situations in the unreal world. As abstract thinking and social skills develop, pretend play may begin to include props or specific settings. These lend themselves to action plans and even sociodramatic scripts. These intricate dramas may require the children to break into little groups for social interaction and to take on specific roles. What a change this is from the more isolated pretending that occurs in the two- to three-year-olds. Now the children interact together, talking back and forth at length. They use pretend objects to imitate other things in imaginary actions and situations. Make-believe play also moves beyond the reality-oriented play that helps the child make connections between his world and the adult world. Princesses and strong, courageous hero figures emerge, and rockets blast off to destinations with foreign terrain and weird creatures.

Watching a group of children happily engaged in an imaginative play experience provides a useful lesson in group dynamics. Each child's ideas and creative plans can build on and expand the ideas of the other children. If each is listening to the others and allowing new ideas to emerge spontaneously, the resulting creative effort is clearly beyond the boundaries of capability of any one member of the group. For children, as for adults, the outcome of a group effort can be more than the sum of its parts—but only if no one limits the effort by trying to be the sole controlling force. The group effort is at its best if all participants are allowed to be contributing members.

Finger and hand puppets provide another popular form of dramatic play as children learn to substitute puppets for themselves or for others. A dollhouse makes use of small people figures and furniture for a creative play experience, too. Family adventures and domestic turmoil will be depicted dozens of times by children who favor this form of expression. The developing dramatist can also work out the fears prevalent at this age by playing doctor or big animals or monster, often with lots of pretend sharp needles, biting, growling, or breathing fire.

The naturally imaginative impulses of the creative preschooler are encouraged by exposure to many other commonly experienced preschool activities. These children love stories and books, and will request that their favorites be repeated often while they fill in anticipated familiar phrases for themselves. As they progress through the preschool years, they begin to create simple fictitious stories of their own, if encouraged. At first, they expand on and embellish real-life experiences they have had or stories they have heard. They love fictitious characters they have been exposed to repeatedly and may include them in the simple stories they make up. A family trip to DisneyWorld® during this period will produce hours of recapping to others of actual events that occurred. In addition, they will inevitably include Disney characters in their newly created stories, make-believe play, or artistic creations.

Painting, drawing with markers, and pasting numerous seasonal wall decorations are very important creative opportunities you have undoubtedly included in your school program. Preschoolers also love finger paints and clay for expressing decorative or representational ideas.

Music will be an important part of the preschool program, and the children will be learning songs accompanied by tapes, piano, or guitar. Their developing language capability and memory will allow them to remember words so that they can fill in the blanks (like "Old MacDonald Had a Farm") or sing the songs at home. Older preschoolers will notice rhyming words in songs and nursery rhymes, especially if you point them out or encourage making up other words to rhyme. Simple singing games and action songs will provide hours of musical entertainment and will help children develop coordination and big- or small-movement planning.

Some children will sing right on pitch from the first time a song is introduced. They will be able to hum familiar melodies or recognize them if you play them on the piano. Other children will rarely sing accurately on pitch and will be the last to recognize even "Happy Birthday" or "Mary Had a Little Lamb" if you tap it out on a xylophone.

Rhythm bands are also important preschool activities that encourage musical expression. In addition, they foster coordination of different parts of the body into a whole, unified effort. Initially, the movement of the instrument itself to resemble the rhythm will require maximum effort. Older preschoolers can learn to march and play their instruments at the same time. Some will never achieve rhythmic accuracy in following the music. Others will display an instant affinity for accurate body rhythm.

While many toys will promote creative expression in the preschooler, building blocks seem to be the favorite. Their uniqueness lies in their sturdiness, versatility, and ageless quality. By the preschool years, children have progressed through three stages: (1) just carrying the blocks around, (2) putting them in a container and dumping them out, and (3) building rows or piles or towers. Now they are ready for more technically challenging building and more symbolic representation with the blocks. Real creative expression skyrockets. You will need at least one hundred fifty wooden pieces, with ten to twenty shapes to keep four to six children happily occupied.

The preschooler's increased spatial awareness allows him to make interesting-looking bridges and enclosures. He will leave spaces between or within the block structures. He begins to notice and create designs and decorative patterns that include scale, balance, symmetry, careful composition, and sometimes color arrangement. Older preschoolers use the blocks over and over again for pretend play. Individual blocks may be "driven" or "flown around." Structures will emerge, which are given names and which serve functional purposes (garage, house, airport). Tall wooden cylinders or rectangles will "people" the structures with family members or community figures (pilot, grocer) who will be walked around and inside the structures, carrying on a meaningful dialogue as they go. Blocks will provide an extension of the dramatic play children exhibit during the make-believe, magical, and reality-testing period of the preschool years.

One characteristic of the magical-thinking age that sets this child apart from his older creative counterpart is that he is not entirely sure of the boundaries between reality and fantasy. Many children exhibit this confusion in play activities and even as they carry out their daily routine or take part in new experiences. For this reason, as a preschooler relates events that happen to him, he sometimes blurs the real with the unreal, enthusiastically exaggerating and creatively embellishing the truth of his story. He may also fabricate implausible explanations for his naughty behavior. These misunderstandings of reality at this age cannot be called "lies" in the classical sense, but the little story-teller must be gently and firmly helped to face the truth of the situation.

The magical thinker's imagination is unencumbered by the reality of how facts and isolated percepts are interrelated. For example, he is a little unsure of time, space, and size/number relationships. For the young pre-schooler, all things are possible, much as they are in the dreams of adults—where unrelated and impossible circumstances feel very real and true until the dreamer awakens. Then the dreamer can chuckle at the images and events that could not have happened in reality. Yet they seemed real during sleep and were accompanied by strong feelings of involvement: pleasure, fear, anger, joy, or awe. Upon awakening, the dreamer will never again be fooled into thinking that the particular dream could have taken place in real life. Yet he has benefited from experiencing the dream, and he can use creative powers grounded in reality to solve problems or otherwise to create while following the inspiration that may have originated in the dream.

So it is for the developing child. Once he has achieved the beginnings of a consistent cognitive framework for time, space, speed, and the relationship of simple number concepts, he will realize the impossibility of some of his earlier thoughts. By school age, he will have integrated information about feel and shape and movement well enough to categorize some concrete information on the basis of likenesses and differences. He will be able to use language to describe the percepts and concepts he is organizing into a unified reference system. It will be like awakening from a dream world characterized by the jumble of information experienced by the younger child. From then onward, his creative thinking will be based on more realistic ideas. Yet he will be indelibly imprinted by the feelings and sensory experiences and thought processes of those "unreal" earlier years.

The magical-thinking age appears to be unique in the continuum of human development. And yet the child is merely carrying out his life in a way that feels right to him based on his current body of knowledge. Isn't it true that in later life the twenty-year-old's high hopes and unrealistic dreams will amuse the forty-year-old, and that the forty-year-old's business strivings may be considered too all-consuming by the seventy-year-old? At each stage in life, we must try to understand the viewpoint of others in order to grasp the meaning of their actions. We must respond to those actions with respect and interest, even in circumstances where we feel obliged to try to gently guide the underlying thinking to new levels. We must present our case without dashing the hopes and goals that keep them going.

The adult responsible for the care of a disarmingly trusting, believing magical thinker bears a particular responsibility. Such an adult will want to promote play growth and experimentation with creative thinking. At the same time, he will want to encourage the maturing of a child's understanding of reality. No one can predict which of these imaginative young ones will grow up to envision and take steps to create world peace or to write an insightful best seller, or to devise a completely new approach to architectural design.

How to Help Develop Imagination/Creativity

- Express interest in artwork, ideas, songs, or poetry children spontaneously create. Write them down, and keep them in individual or group-creativity books. Send copies home to the parents. This will help the children know that you consider their creative endeavors important and will encourage other such creations to emerge.

- Encourage each child to talk about his own drawings, paintings, and constructions. However, do not force ideas on him about what to make and how to make it or how to improve its authenticity and accuracy. If you choose to suggest he copy your simple models to enhance visual perception (see "How to Help Develop Vision"), be sure to give equal time to his creative energies and express lots of interest in the models he has created.

- As spontaneous imaginative play emerges, you may need to intervene if you observe that one or two children continuously dominate the play experience to the detriment of the other children's creative expression. Quietly help the dominating children learn to listen to ideas from the others without discouraging their own possibly superior creative impulses. Help the other children learn to be more assertive by giving them time to express and carry out their ideas.

Dramatic Play

- Collect hats or insignia representing firefighters, police officers, nurses, and so on, and other portions of uniforms like a nurse's cap, a doctor's stethoscope, or a jockey's jodhpurs. Put them in your costume box along with old blouses, handbags, gloves, suit jackets, jewelry, and so on. Short skirts can be added to become floor-length gowns without the risk of trips and falls. Big flat shoes or plastic Jellies® can be used instead of high heels.

- Encourage children to check how their costumes look in the unbreakable full-length mirrors near the dress-up corner. This not only reinforces their imaginative play, but it also encourages awareness of body image, which can help development of big-movement planning.

- Have the youngsters look at the mirror while making funny, sad, scary, or silly faces. They can watch themselves while they dance or move forward or backward. If you have a second mirror, they can even see what is in back of them.

- Puppets are wonderful tools for encouraging language and creativity. Young children are spontaneously attracted to making puppets come alive. Your youngsters might enjoy creating a puppet play, drawing pictures for scenery, and adding props.

- Try a craft activity of making finger or sock puppets, hand puppets of papier-mâché, or tongue depressor/Popsicle® stick figures. Perhaps begin by drawing simple facial features on their finger or hand with washable paint (be sure it is washable). Or put a hanky on each child's hand and tie it at the wrist to make a ghost. Encourage the use of the finished products in group play or informally staged productions.

- Preschool-age children love sitting at pegboard and chalkboard desks where they can pretend to be school students, a teacher, or a grown-up doing desk work. If you do not have a peg desk, they can use a small table or a cardboard box.

- Enrich the preschoolers' play environment with large play kitchen appliances and equipment, structures that are or can become a grocery store, a telephone booth, a playhouse, a post office, or other community environments.

- Simple cooking activities are also creative and fun. Youngsters learn to follow sequential instructions and wait for the finished edible product. Parents of various ethnic backgrounds might be willing to come in to teach an unusual, delicious new dish. This type of creative activity also helps impart early social studies concepts.

- Present an array of nontoy objects to a group of children and encourage them to create make-believe play with them. Try kitchen utensils, an empty paper towel cardboard cylinder, leaves, coffee cans, or empty boxes. Watch the creative wheels turn as they play, and gently encourage everyone in the group to share ideas in order to expand the scope of the creative experience.

Arts and Crafts

- Maintain a wide variety of creative art supplies. Introduce charcoal, pastels, or the new finger crayons as well as the usual felt-tipped markers, paints, crayons, paste, and so on.

- Use tempera powder to mix bright, cheerful, primary paint colors, not pale, watered-down shades. A touch of liquid detergent in the water makes a thick, creamy consistency that will not run down the page on the budding artist's easel. Store the extra paint in baby-food jars or in other small containers with tight-fitting lids.

- Finger painting on shiny shelf paper is a creative and sensory experience for little hands, fingers, wrists, and even elbows. Or use tongue depressors, sponges, combs, cotton, or Popsicle® sticks to create designs by drawing on the wet paint. Put a small amount of blue and red paint on opposite sides of the paper so that children can discover how to mix the colors. (Red and blue make purple.)

- After he is used to the feel of finger paints and when the novelty is wearing off, try sprinkling various textures onto the painted paper: sand, sawdust, shavings from the end of a coarse rope, and so on.

- Try putting a drop of tempera paint on paper; then have children blow it around the paper with a straw.

- Have children create an interesting texture design by rubbing the side of a crayon over a coin, leaf, brick, wood, or even an old zipper.

- For a stretchy, soft, smooth-textured play material that feels wet and cool and that encourages big movement and coordination of the two hands, try this recipe: Add liquid laundry starch a little at a time to Elmer's® washable white glue until it is the consistency of Silly Putty®. Wrap in plastic wrap for storage.

- For experienced clay molders who have had numerous opportunities to make and keep their creations ("It's mine"), try introducing a group project where each child makes an object or idea from a familiar story you have read together over and over. Assemble the resulting clay depictions into a scene or series of scenes representing the story—perhaps just in time for a parent meeting or in a location by the door where all the parents can see it if they come inside to pick up their children. Encourage children to tell the story to their parents at home, recounting the events represented by the group clay creation.

- Glue small objects onto a crayon drawing or watercolor painting to add extra interest, or create a "collage"—a new word for this budding artist.

- Paste made of flour dampened with water is an effective sticking agent but can get lumpy. If you buy white glue, be sure it is water soluble and nontoxic.

- String macaroni or large colored beads on a long sneaker shoelace. Or make a lace with masking tape wrapped around the end of a piece of yarn to be a firm "needle."

- Dust washable powdered colors onto sand in a tray or cookie sheet for a novel drawing surface. Also try sprinkling talcum powder on a table or corner of the floor. The children will enjoy drawing designs in it— a good sensory experience that also encourages hand/eye coordination.

- We have included Figure 6–5 to stimulate many creative ideas.

Figure 6–5 CREATIVE MATERIALS FOR CRAFT PROJECTS

Keep a high shelf available for baskets of these creative materials:

acorns	pasta shapes	small mirrors
beads	picture stamps	stars
beans	stickers	straws
buttons	pinecones	string
empty spools	pipe cleaners	tape
eye droppers	craftsticks	tongue depressors
laces	rubber bands	wood scraps
leaves	seeds	yarn
	Shells	

Papers you might want to collect could include:

paper bags	crepe	newsprint
carbon	envelopes	paper plates
cardboard	foil	plastic
cellophane	glazed	playing cards
computer	holiday cards	printed newspaper
construction	Kleenex®	tissue
Con-Tact®	magazines	wax
corrugated	manila	wrapping

Other materials could include:

fabric scraps
feathers
fur
upholstery and rug samples

Nature

- The world of nature provides a perfect source for instruction and appreciation that you can use in your work with preschoolers. An outdoor nature walk or a through-the-window observation of a nearby ancient oak tree can be a fine source of programming for creative activities. After such a visit, try leaf prints, paintings or drawings of woods or single trees, or try acting out the growth process, from being curled up as a seed or bulb to standing at full height with outstretched branches, stems, and leaves.

- Bring small fallen branches inside, and have children decorate them with colored flowers cut out of construction or tissue paper.

- To increase awareness of novel and creative uses of things in the everyday environment, go on a "sound hunt," listening carefully for background sounds that usually go unnoticed. For example, suggest that children tape-record a few sounds and play "sound quiz" with the group.

- Help children be aware of and appreciate their bodies as wonderful creations, with senses of sight, hearing, smell, taste, touch, and movement. Refer to the "How to Help Develop Awareness of Sensations" section of this chapter and of previous chapters for ideas for developing this appreciation.

- Children love both to trace their own hands and to outline the bodies of their playmates. They may enjoy coloring in the outlines. If you put the drawings away, they can do the tracing again in several months to see how much they've grown.

- A three-dimensional body can be made with a double thickness of heavy paper. Cut out a child's body outline. Stuff crumpled paper between, stapling along the outside edges as you stuff for a three-dimensional facsimile of the youngster.

Stories

- During circle time, encourage older preschoolers to create original group stories. Each child in turn adds a sentence or idea, building on the story created by members of the group who participated before him. Rather than taking turns in sequence around the circle, try letting each child make his contribution as creative notions come to him, until everyone who wants to has participated at least once.

- Try tape-recording a group story-making occasion as it occurs, stopping the tape during lengthy periods of "ummm" while a child is organizing his thoughts. You can ask such a child to tell you when he is ready to turn the recorder back on. Following the session and on subsequent days, you can play the recording so that the children can listen to their voices and to their creation.

- Have children illustrate different parts of the story with dark or bright colors, then photocopy the resulting artwork and create a book for each child to remind him of the story the group created and to encourage each to tell the story to his parents.

- If a child's relating of actual events steps too far beyond the boundaries of reality, be prepared to acknowledge your interest in and appreciation of his telling of the story. At the same time, however, remind him in a pleasant way of the portions that are pretend or a strong wish.

- For a child who tends to exaggerate truths and to use little white lies to control adults, verify the information but then refuse to be convinced of his untrue version of reality. Privately relate to the storyteller your understanding of the realities involved. Briefly present supporting evidence ("I see that your writing is quite different from your mother's so you could not have written this little note"). However, be prepared to recognize that the child's somewhat hazy awareness of reality allows for conflicting facts to exist simultaneously. If the exaggerations occur rarely, let them pass. If they persist or dominate a child's interactions, look for underlying causes of insecurity or make the family aware of the problem.

Constructions

- Before disassembling large, complex, and interesting creations made with blocks, Legos®, or other construction toys, snap a photograph of the creators next to the structure to emphasize your interest in their work and to promote self-confidence and recognition of the creative impulse.

- Take the photos from different heights so that you get a variety of viewpoints, including those of the children. If a large, complex construction project seems to be underway, you might even want to take pictures while the building efforts are taking place. Then the children can create a kind of journal of the event.

- Enforce the rules that no one may destroy or rearrange someone else's building block creation and that everyone helps with cleanup (but one or two finished or partially finished structures may be left standing until the next day).

- See if the youngsters can invent different ways to transport the blocks back to the shelves. Perhaps they can pile some on a scooter board or use some small blocks as cargo on a longer block "ferryboat" or "truck."

- Share these books with your staff members:

   Building Block Art by Judy Herman (1986)
   Please Touch Museum Education Store
   210 North 21, Philadelphia, PA 19103

   The Block Book, revised edition, by E. S. Hirsch (1984)
   National Association for the Education of Young Children
   Washington, D.C. 20009-5786

Special Events, Games, and Original Musical Activities

- Children would love the excitement of putting on a playground carnival. They can plan games and decorate different booths like a face-painting booth or a puppet-show booth. They might even put on a short play, have a songfest, or exhibit their art. It does not have to be an elaborate affair, and it is always nice for parents to have a chance to see their children in action.

- Help preschoolers make novel noisemakers. Try gravel, rice, beans, dried peas, paper clips, or bobby pins. Put them into empty plastic milk or detergent bottles, coffee cans, or bowls. Let the older children shake or rap on the containers with a wooden spoon, a wire whisk, or their knuckles. If two or three containers are similar, the bigger one will make a lower sound. Many kinds of receptacles and noisy inserts will make a delightful sound if you are creative in your selections. Caution: Be certain the top is taped on securely so that the little pieces will not spill out and accidentally be eaten by younger children.

- Musical games and songs will be an important part of the curriculum of your school program. They will enhance rhyming, memory, and other language skills as well as body rhythms. They may also increase big-movement skills, sensory awareness, and fine-motor dexterity. Dozens of books are on the market that present suggestions of finger plays (musical and nonmusical), action songs, and games. Here is one book we suggest:

  Songs in Action, second edition by R. Phyllis Gelineau (1988)
  Parker Publishing Company

  This book presents songs for children of all ages with tips for accompaniment on a guitar, ukelele, or autoharp.

- One series, The Brite Music Program, offers tapes that combine music with social development. The delightful songs are fun for children to learn and feature different subjects: character building, personal safety, interpersonal relationships, patriotism, and nutrition. Order from:
  Brite Music Enterprises
  P.O. Box 9191
  Salt Lake City, UT 84109

- Below are listed songs we have created and tried out with numerous groups of young learners. They are listed more or less in order of difficulty. Use songs requiring right-left discrimination only for your oldest children. Or you could try modifying the words to eliminate confusion, or identify right and left before the song begins by marking right hands with a sticker, dot, or red ribbon. Remember to use your opposite hand for right- and left-hand words if you are facing the children in a line. Original tunes follow in Figure 6–6.

• Figure 6–7 shows qualities of child development that may be helped by familiar action songs or games. Figure 6–8 shows the benefits of our original action songs included in this chapter. Of course, each activity will also promote language development and social interaction among the children. In addition, because they are *action* activities they all also help children experience and perfect new motor-planning opportunities.

Figure 6–6 SUGGESTED TUNES FOR ORIGINAL SONGS

LARGE ONE, SMALL ONE

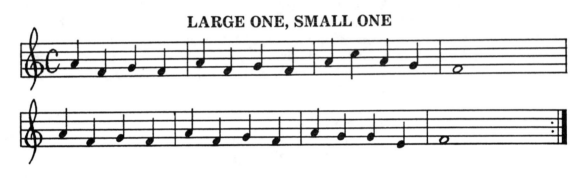

THE TRAVELING BEANBAG SONG

RED HEART

LARGE ONE, SMALL ONE
Tune: See Figure 6–6 for optional suggestion

Stanza 1: Sing and make motions while children hold large paper circles in left hands, and small circles in right hands. You face children and hold circles in your opposite hands.

LARGE ONE,
> (Move your big circle past your left shoulder.
> Children mirror your movements across midline.)

SMALL ONE,
> (Move your small circle past your right shoulder.)

LARGE ONE, SMALL ONE,
> (Repeat movements.)

WHERE IS CIRCLE BIG?
> (Two hands behind back.)

LARGE ONE, SMALL ONE, LARGE ONE, SMALL ONE,
> (Repeat movements.)

THERE IS CIRCLE BIG.
> (Big-circle hand out in front of face.)

Stanza 2: Discard circles by having everyone put them temporarily on the floor in front of them.

LARGE ONE,   SMALL ONE,
> (Stand, arms up) (Squat)

LARGE ONE, SMALL ONE,
> (Repeat movements.)

AM I GROWING BIG?
> (Slowly grow to arms-up full height.)

LARGE ONE, SMALL ONE, LARGE ONE, SMALL ONE,
> (Repeat movements)

I AM GROWING BIG.
> (Slowly grow to arms-up full height.)

Stanza 3: (Include this stanza if children can do this fine-dexterity movement.)

LARGE ONE,   SMALL ONE,
> (Raise index finger, then pinky alternately.)

LARGE ONE, SMALL ONE,
> (Repeat movements.)

WHERE IS FINGER BIG?
> (Two hands behind back.)

LARGE ONE, SMALL ONE, LARGE ONE, SMALL ONE,
> (Repeat movements.)

THERE IS FINGER BIG.
> (Point index finger up.)

WOOO!
> (Tap this finger with other index finger.)

THE TRAVELING BEANBAG SONG
Tune: See Figure 6–6 for optional suggestion
(Each person holds beanbag in two hands and sits on floor with legs out in front of them. Place beanbag in each position as you sing it.)

NEAR ME,   FAR;
    (In front)   (far in front)
ON ME,   UNDER
    (On head) (sit on beanbag, holding up empty hands)
THERE YOU ARE OVERHEAD,
    (Elbows straight, hands overhead) (Then retrieve beanbag)
NEXT TO ME,
    (Next to)
HIGHER,
    (In front at shoulder height or higher)
LOWER,
    (In front near floor)
PUT IT IN BETWEEN INSTEAD.
    (Beanbag between two feet. Hold hands up to show empty.)

MAGIC BOX
Tune: "Pop Goes the Weasel"
(With exaggerated movements, distribute pretend "boxes" to each child before beginning song—or have a child distribute them. Place one imaginary box in front of each person.)

WE PUT INSIDE OUR ANKLES AND KNEES
OUR THIGHS, OUR HIPS, OUR WAIST
OUR WRISTS AND ELBOWS, SHOULDERS AND HEAD,
POP GOES THE WEASEL.
    (With each line of song, everyone places hands on the body parts named, and places the body parts inside the box. Use large movements for pretending to step in, then slowly stoop as each upper part is touched until, by "... shoulders and head," everyone is crouched completely, head tucked, arms encircling head. On word "POP," leap upward, pushing off imaginary top of box, arms outstretched high above head.)

LET'S MOVE FASTER

Tune: "London Bridge"

(Everyone sits cross-legged, doing rapid alternating movements listed in song. Repeat each verse once—second time faster—as children perfect accuracy of movements, or begin each verse slowly and sing each line progressively faster.)

Stanza 1:

PUT YOUR RIGHT HAND UNDER—ON, UNDER—ON, UNDER—ON,
PUT YOUR RIGHT HAND UNDER—ON, LET'S MOVE FASTER.

Place left hand, palm up, in front, and leave it there throughout the first verse of the song. Place palm of other hand *under* then *on top of* the stationary hand. Alternate turning palm over and back throughout the song.

Stanza 2: Same as the first with hands reversed.

Stanza 3:

PUT YOUR LEFT FOOT FAR AND NEAR,
FAR AND NEAR, FAR AND NEAR.
PUT YOUR LEFT FOOT FAR AND NEAR, LET'S MOVE FASTER.

(The knee straightens and bends so that the foot goes far from body and near.)

Stanza 4: Same as third but with right foot.

Add other verses:

SHRUG YOUR SHOULDERS UP AND DOWN
BEND YOUR BODY SIDE TO SIDE or
MOVE YOUR ELBOWS IN AND OUT, etc.

THE WRAP GAME

Tune: Football Cheer, "Hooray for Our School"

(Give a 12- to 18-inch piece of yarn to each child, who wraps it around each body part as named.)

WRAP UP YOUR THUMB.
WRAP UP YOUR WRIST.
WRAP UP YOUR ELBOW.
WRAP UP YOUR SHOULDER.
   ONE,   TWO,   THREE,   FOUR
(Tap thumb) (wrist) (elbow) (shoulder)
    LET'S WRAP   FOUR MORE
  (Arms over head) (Cross arms over head)
WRAP GAME, WHAT FUN.
    (Uncross arms)

WRAP UP YOUR ANKLE.
WRAP UP YOUR KNEE.
WRAP UP YOUR HIP.
WRAP UP YOUR WAIST.
   ONE,   TWO,   THREE,   FOUR
(Tap ankle) (knee)   (hip)   (waist)
   LET'S WRAP   FOUR MORE
(Arms over head) (Cross arms over head)
WRAP GAME, WHAT FUN.
   (Uncross arms)

RED HEART

Tune: See Figure 6–6 for optional suggestion
(Everyone holds a small paper heart in *both* hands, moving it as described in each line of the song.)

PUT YOUR RED HEART UP,
   (High in front of you)
PUT YOUR RED HEART DOWN,
   (Near floor in front of you)
PUT YOUR RED HEART IN AND OUT,
   (Make circle with fingers of one hand; with other hand, put heart "in and out" of that enclosure)
PUT YOUR VALENTINE NEAR A FRIEND OF MINE,
   (two hands move heart near adjacent child on one side, then on the other)
SAY "I LOVE YOU"   SHOUT RIGHT OUT.
   (Loudly, with cupped hands) (Quietly)

PUT YOUR HEART IN FRONT,
   (Directly in front of you)
PUT YOUR HEART IN BACK,
   (Behind)
PUT IT OVER, UNDER, NEAR,
   (Make horizontal platform with one hand; with other hand, put heart over it, under it, then close to front middle of body)
PUT IT RIGHT BESIDE, PUT IT LEFT BESIDE,
   (Twist trunk to place heart to right of body, then left)
SAY "I LOVE YOU"   LOUD AND CLEAR.
   (Loudly, with cupped hands)   (Quietly)

ELBOWS ON YOUR KNEES
Tune: "Turkey in the Straw"
(Everybody sings while sitting on the floor with legs out in front of them, making each motion in sequence as they sing the words. Speed up the words and motions as children master them.)

PUT YOUR ELBOWS ON YOUR KNEES,
AND YOUR ANKLE ON YOUR TOES,
PUT YOUR RIGHT HAND BACK,
AND YOUR WRIST ON YOUR NOSE,
PUT YOUR CHIN ON YOUR SHOULDER,
THEN YOUR SHOULDER ON THE FLOOR,
PUT YOUR ELBOWS ON YOUR KNEES,
LIKE YOU DID — BE ... FORE.
          (Clap) (Clap) (Clap)
(Leave plenty of room between children so that they can safely put their shoulders on the floor.)

Figure 6-7 ALPHABETICAL LIST OF ACTION SONGS AND GAMES AND THEIR BENEFITS FOR CHILD DEVELOPMENT

	Sensation	Balance	Bilateral Coordination	Midline Crossing	Body Image	Dexterity	Space Awareness	Imagination
Did You Ever See a Fishy?			✔					✔
Did You Ever See a Lassie?		?	?	?		?		
Do Your Ears Hang Low?			✔					✔
Flag Drill (Distribute pretend signal flags)			✔	✔				✔
Follow the Leader	?	?	?	?		?	?	
Go In and Out the Window							✔	
Hokey Pokey	✔	✔			✔		✔	
If You're Happy and You Know It	✔				✔			
I'm a Little Tea Pot			✔					✔
Inky Dinky Spider			✔			✔		✔
Lion Hunt			✔					✔
Little Cottage in the Wood			✔					✔
Looby Loo	✔	✔			✔		✔	
Mulberry Bush			✔	✔				✔
My Hat It Has Three Corners			✔					
One Finger, One Thumb, Keep Moving	✔	✔	✔		✔	✔		
Peas Porridge Hot			✔	✔				
Ring Around the Rosy	✔	✔						
School Cheers (Pretend being cheer leaders)			✔	✔				
Simon Says	?	?	?	?	?	?	?	
Simplified Charades								✔
Ten Little Indians			✔			✔		
Two Little Ducks That I Once Knew			✔					✔

Figure 6–8 SKILLS FOSTERED BY ORIGINAL SONGS

	Sensation	Balance	Bilateral Coordination	Midline Crossing	Body Image	Dexterity	Space Awareness	Imagination
Large One, Small One		✔		✔		✔	✔	✔
The Traveling Beanbag Song	✔			✔			✔	✔
Magic Box	✔	✔			✔		✔	✔
Let's Move Faster					✔		✔	
The Wrap Game	✔		✔	✔	✔	✔		
Red Heart				✔			✔	
Elbows on Your Knees		✔	✔	✔	✔			

TOY CHART

In the chart on the next pages are examples of good toys. They are divided into ten categories that are listed alphabetically. Toys in each category are presented approximately developmentally. All the toys provide learning experiences and, therefore, are educational. The most important aspects of child development that can be stimulated by each toy are marked in columns on the right. The reasons for some marks may not be immediately obvious, and they should encourage you to notice wider possibilities the toys offer. Toys mentioned in the text are not necessarily repeated in the chart.

The toys listed show examples of the attributes a particular type of toy should have. If you experience difficulty finding the toy listed, there will generally be toys of similar quality in catalogs or on the toy-store shelf that will accomplish the same goals.

EXAMPLES OF TOYS FOR THE PRESCHOOLER: THREE TO FIVE YEARS	Awareness of Sensation	Balance and Big Movements	Dexterity and Hand/Eye Coord.	Vision	Space/Time Awareness	Personality/ Socialization	Language	Imagination/ Creativity
ARTS AND CRAFTS *Crayola® Crayons.* Binney & Smith®. *Finger Crayons.* Battat. 6 plastic crayons. *Soap Crayons.* Coleco.	●	●	●	●	●	●	●	●
Finger Paints. Tempera Paints. Cray Pas (oil colors in sticks.) *Watercolors. Magic Markers:* Crayola®. *Soft and Light Markers.* Binney & Smith®. *Face Paints.* Galt®. Washable.	●	●	●	●	●	●	●	●
Papers, Chalk, Pastels, Paste, Pipe Cleaners, Brushes, Sponges, Sand, Straws, Sand Paper.	●	●	●	●	●	●	●	●
Scissors. Rose Art®. Crayola®. Each pair for either right or left hands.			●	●	●		●	●
Clays: Colorplast. Bright colors. Air dry to harden. *Caran D'Ache.* Soft modeling clay. 5 bright colors. *Play Doh®.* Kenner ®.	●	●	●	●	●		●	●
Adjustable Wooden Double Easel and Paint Trays.	●	●	●	●	●		●	●
Flannel Board. 24" x 30". Precut story sets, dinosaurs, farm animals, etc.			●	●			●	●
Lights Alive®. Tomy®. Draw or print with 6 various tools. Change colors by moving a dial.			●	●	●			●
Magna Doodle®. Ideal™. Drawing pen and disks are magnetic. Create pictures, words, games. Then erase with "magic" eraser.			●	●	●			●
Silly Putty®. Binney & Smith®. Pliable, comes in plastic egg to make shapes.	●		●		●		●	●
Spirotot® Design Toy. Kenner®. 4 pattern gears make designs when used with colored pens.		●	●	●	●			●
BIG EQUIPMENT *Variplay House-Gym and Slide.* Community Playthings. Wooden, sturdy. Attaches at various heights and arrangements.	●	●			●	●		
Giant Waffle™ Blocks. Little Tikes®. 14" square, unbreakable plastic. Indoors and out.		●		●	●	●	●	●
Building Bricks. Large, sturdy, corrugated fiberboard bricks.		●			●	●	●	●
Merry-go-round. Today's Kids. Durable plastic.	●	●				●	●	

EXAMPLES OF TOYS FOR THE PRESCHOOLER: THREE TO FIVE YEARS	Awareness of Sensation	Balance and Big Movements	Dexterity and Hand/Eye Coord.	Vision	Space/Time Awareness	Personality/ Socialization	Language	Imagination/ Creativity
Playall. Childcraft®. 3 curved sections of unbreakable polyethylene. Join to make circle, seesaw, various shapes to walk, crawl, or roll in.	●	●			●			
Giant Tumble Balls. See catalogs. 16" up. Climb, ride on, sometimes with help.	●	●						
Gymboree® Gymmat. Connor Toys. Folding mat.	●	●			●			
Pipeworks®. Playskool®. Indoors and out. Excellent building, climbing, inventive toy.	●	●			●	●	●	●
Jungle Gym. All heights. See catalogs.	●	●			●	●	●	
Rainbow School Parachute. Holcomb's Educational Materials. 12' wide, 10 nylon handholds.	●	●	●		●	●	●	
Bugs Bunny™ Bop Bag. Largo. 36" inflatable toy. Weighted base, bounces back.	●	●	●	●	●			
Big Teeter Totter. Little Tykes®. 5' seesaw, wide-angle base.	●	●				●	●	
Sand and Water Table. See catalogs. Cover, drain, adjustable, portable.	●	●	●	●	●	●	●	●
Scooter Board with Handles. Holcomb's Educational Materials. 11" square on swivel casters to roll, scoot around, sitting, tummy.	●	●		●	●			
Slide. Swings. Rings. Climbing Set. See catalogs.	●	●	●	●	●	●	●	●
Junior Jumper. Community Playthings. 32" x 44" trampoline with steel-tubing handle. Supervise.	●	●			●			
BOOKS *Hand Rhymes.* Marc Brown. E.P. Dutton. 14 poems, illustrated with hand games to play.	●		●	●		●	●	●
Cars and Trucks and Things. Richard Scarry. Random House.				●		●	●	●
A Farmer's Alphabet. Mary Azarian. Godine. Woodcuts, rural subjects representing letters.				●		●	●	●
Babar's ABC. Laurent de Brunhoff. Random House. Only 2–3 pictures on each page of this book of elephant characters. 15 other Babar books.				●		●	●	●

EXAMPLES OF TOYS FOR THE PRESCHOOLER: THREE TO FIVE YEARS	Awareness of Sensation	Balance and Big Movements	Dexterity and Hand/Eye Coord.	Vision	Space/Time Awareness	Personality/ Socialization	Language	Imagination/ Creativity
Cat in the Hat and *To Think That I Saw It on Mulberry Street*. Theodore Seuss Geisel (Dr. Seuss). Random House.				●		●	●	●
Make Way for Ducklings. Robert McCloskey. Puffin. Soft copy.				●		●	●	●
Curious George. H.A. Rey. Houghton Mifflin. Series for 2 years and up.				●		●	●	●
A Is for Angry. Sandra Boynton. Workman. Animal and adjective alphabet book.				●		●	●	●
Crafts. Jean Warren. Monday Morning. Early craft activities, easy to follow.								
(Use *The Caldecott Medal* annual award list for children's books.)								
CONSTRUCTION *Jumbo Wood Beads*. Playskool®. 5 shapes, nontoxic colored beads.		●	●					
Nursery Set. Community Playthings. 276 blocks, 11 shapes for 10–12 children.		●	●	●	●	●	●	●
Hollow Blocks. Community Playthings. Open-ended, wood squares, double and half squares, ramp, long and short boards. Indoors or out.	●	●	●	●	●	●	●	●
Basic Building Set. Lego®. Interlocking plastic blocks.			●	●	●	●	●	●
Pre-School Building Set. Tyco®. Interlocking colored plastic pieces with storage bucket.			●	●	●	●	●	●
Magnetic Crane, Wagon, Block Set. ABC School Supply, Inc. Working crane.	●	●	●	●	●	●	●	●
Lincoln Logs®. Playskool®. Real wood.		●	●	●	●	●	●	●
Tinkertoy®. Playskool®. Interchangeable wood and plastic pieces.		●	●	●	●	●	●	●
GAMES *Animal Dominoes*. ABC School Supply Inc. 30 colorful pictures to match.			●	●		●	●	
Play 'n Fit. Lauri Enterprises™. Textured rubber, smooth on one side, rough on the other. Lotto, puzzle, stencil for tracing, too.	●		●	●	●			

EXAMPLES OF TOYS FOR THE PRESCHOOLER: THREE TO FIVE YEARS	Awareness of Sensation	Balance and Big Movements	Dexterity and Hand/Eye Coord.	Vision	Space/Time Awareness	Personality/ Socialization	Language	Imagination/ Creativity
Early Discoveries. Discovery Toys. 4 board games, colors, shapes, sequencing, counting.			●	●	●	●	●	
Magnetic Fish Pond. Spears. Pond picture, poles. Catch fish with magnets.	●		●			●	●	●
Candy Land®. Milton Bradley®. Board game, need color recognition, no reading.			●	●		●	●	
Cootie®. Schaper®. No reading, teaches colors, numbers, as body parts are added to bug.			●	●		●	●	
Chutes and Ladders®. Milton Bradley®. Board game, spinner and pieces. 2–4 players. No reading.			●	●		●	●	
Fronts and Backs Memory. 39 illustrated cards, match fronts with backs. *Animal Families Memory.* Milton Bradley®. Matching card game.			●	●	●	●	●	●
Adjustable Hurdles. Childcraft®. 12"–21", crawl, jump over, under, around, obstacle course.	●	●			●	●	●	
Happy Hoops Croquet. Fisher-Price®. Each hoop has different action when ball goes through after being hit by mallet.	●	●	●		●	●	●	
All Pro Dunk-It. Ideal™. Basketball set. Weighted base. Adjustable height.		●	●	●	●	●	●	
Ring Toss. Holcomb's Educational Materials. 2 stable 11" wood posts, 6 rings.		●	●	●	●	●	●	
IMITATIVE PLAYTHINGS *Dolls. Stuffed Animals.* All styles to love, dress, talk to, etc. Washable.	●		●			●	●	●
My Buddy™. Playskool®. Soft 23" dressed boy doll to cuddle.	●		●			●	●	●
Huggable Puppet. Fisher-Price®.	●		●			●	●	●
Teach & Play Carpenter. Amtoy®. Doll with real zipper, buttons, snaps, laces, buckle.	●		●	●	●		●	●
Mighty Dump. Tonka®. Realistic, sturdy truck. Many good, tough trucks to choose.		●	●		●		●	●
Tea Set. Creative Playthings. Firm and not too tiny, has play food in set.			●			●	●	●

EXAMPLES OF TOYS FOR THE PRESCHOOLER: THREE TO FIVE YEARS	Awareness of Sensation	Balance and Big Movements	Dexterity and Hand/Eye Coord.	Vision	Space/Time Awareness	Personality/ Socialization	Language	Imagination/ Creativity
Mickey Mouse or *Big Bird Talking Telephone.* Playskool®. Talk, 6 Sesame Street® characters talk back. Push buttons. "D" battery needed.			●		●		●	●
Party Kitchen. Little Tikes®. All-in-one kitchen: sink, range, table.			●			●	●	●
Action Garage. Fisher-Price®. Garage, ramp, elevator, cars, people.			●		●	●	●	●
Medical Kit. Fisher-Price®. Stethoscope works.	●		●			●	●	●
Play Family Jetport. Fisher-Price®. Airport terminal, crank-operated heliport. Helicopter with propellers that spin. Jumbo jet with motor-like sound, wheels turn, crew, 4 passengers, etc. *Farm Set*, etc.			●	●	●	●	●	●
Wooden Railway System. Brio®. Engine, cars, tracks. Add separate parts.			●	●	●	●	●	●
Camera. Fisher-Price®. Not necessary to close one eye to see. 27 different zoo animals through a hole when button is pressed. Look through another hole, see real view. Press button, pretend to take picture.			●	●	●			●
Puppet Stage/Play Store. Kaplan School Supply Corp. 3 chalkboard folding panels, center flaps down for creative play.		●	●	●	●	●	●	●
Play Housekeeping Furniture. See catalogs. Wood lasts, but needs storage space. Heavy cardboard folds to put away.		●	●	●	●	●	●	●
Wooden Workbench with Tools. See catalogs.	●	●	●	●	●			●
Rosewood Manor™ Doll House. Today's Kids. Sturdy, furnished with 30 pieces.			●	●	●	●	●	●
MANIPULATIVE *Nerf® Ball.* Parker Brothers®. Soft foam ball, various sizes.	●	●	●	●		●	●	
Koosh™ Ball. Oddzon Products, Inc. Squishy, rubber-tentacled ball. Easy to catch. Does not roll.	●	●	●	●		●	●	
Shakerball. Chicco. See-through. Marbles inside move to various levels when shaken.	●	●	●	●	●			

EXAMPLES OF TOYS FOR THE PRESCHOOLER: THREE TO FIVE YEARS	Awareness of Sensation	Balance and Big Movements	Dexterity and Hand/Eye Coord.	Vision	Space/Time Awareness	Personality/ Socialization	Language	Imagination/ Creativity
Crunch Ball. CAP™ Toys. Washable, textured, light. Good to squeeze, throw, kick.	●	●	●			●	●	
Slinky®. James Industries, Inc. Coil moves continuously in hands, on tables, etc.	●	●	●	●	●			
Popples™ Sewing Cards. Colorforms®. Firm design boards with strong laces.		●	●	●				
Jumbo Wood Beads. Playskool®. 5 nontoxic, colored shapes with strong laces.		●	●	●				
Shape Stack™. Playskool®. Shapes inside disks must be matched to build tower.			●	●				
Gazoobo. Chicco. 12 shapes fit into openings of keyhouse. Color-coded keys unlock doors to play.			●	●	●			
Colorforms®. Flat vinyl shapes stick to vinyl-covered cardboard. Variety of story themes.			●	●	●		●	●
Puzzles. Battat, Judy, Lakeshore, Lauri, Puzzle People, Simplex, etc. Puzzles of wood, plastic, rubber, heavy cardboard. Interlocking puzzles more difficult.			●	●	●		●	●
Mr. Potato Head®. Playskool®. Bendable arms, posable body. All pieces store in head.	●		●		●			●
Lite Brite®. Milton Bradley. Create pictures with lights, pegs. Electric, not under 4.			●	●	●			●
Parquetry Blocks. Playskool®. Diamond, circle, square-shaped blocks make designs.			●	●	●			●
Block Clock. Amloid™. 12 different plastic, shaped numbers fit clock spots. Take apart, put together puzzle.			●	●	●		●	
Deluxe Magnetic Board. Magnetic Letters. Fisher-Price®. Upper- and lower-case boxes.	●		●	●			●	●
Roller Coaster. Anatex Enterprises. Child moves various-shaped wooden beads along curved winding wires attached to wooden base.		●	●	●	●			
Alphie® II. Playskool®. "Robot" computer. 6 programs: matching, music, color, memory. Math, spelling later. 4 "AA" batteries needed.			●	●	●		●	●

EXAMPLES OF TOYS FOR THE PRESCHOOLER: THREE TO FIVE YEARS	Awareness of Sensation	Balance and Big Movements	Dexterity and Hand/Eye Coord.	Vision	Space/Time Awareness	Personality/ Socialization	Language	Imagination/ Creativity
MUSICAL/LISTENING								
Tuneyville Choo Choo®. Tomy®. Plays 11 tunes with 4 records as it moves.		●			●		●	
Rhythm Instruments: See catalogs. Bells, blocks, cymbals, drums, sticks, tambourines, triangles.	●	●	●		●	●	●	●
Tap-A-Tune™ Piano. Playskool®. 2 levels. Bottom has nicely spaced colored keys for fingers; top is xylophone. Color-coded songbook.	●		●	●	●		●	●
Tapes and Book Sets. Fisher-Price®, others. Many different subjects, some with music.					●	●	●	
Tape Recorder. Fisher-Price®. Activities to be recorded, storybook, tapes, and music. Batteries needed.						●	●	●
Talk 'n Play. Playskool®. Pictures, cassette, and push buttons. Batteries needed.			●	●	●			
Record Player. Fisher-Price®. 2 speed. To be used only by adults at this age.								
RIDING								
Large Horse. Flexible Flyer®. Horse bounces on springs.	●	●					●	●
Wagon. Radio® Flyer. Heavy-gauge steel body with play-safe edges.		●		●	●			
Tricycle. Angeles. Well-balanced, sturdy, good for outdoors.		●		●	●			
Scooter. Little Tikes®. Double rear wheels for stability.		●	●	●				
Hoppity Hop™. Sun Products Corp. Inflatable, heavy rubber ball with hand grasp to sit on, bounce, and move.	●	●		●	●			
Roller Skates. Fisher-Price®. Wheel control for beginners, adjustable 6–12 shoe sizes.	●	●		●	●			
Garden Cart. Tractor. Little Tikes®. Cart attaches to tractor. Pedals. Steering fun.		●	●	●	●			
WATER PLAY								
Lawn Shower. H.G. Toys, Inc. Attach vertical pole to hose with 25' diameter spray.	●	●				●	●	

EXAMPLES OF TOYS FOR THE PRESCHOOLER: THREE TO FIVE YEARS	Awareness of Sensation	Balance and Big Movements	Dexterity and Hand/Eye Coord.	Vision	Space/Time Awareness	Personality/ Socialization	Language	Imagination/ Creativity
Turtle Sandbox. Little Tikes®. Molded polyethylene sand box. Top swings open to play.	●	●	●			●	●	
Beach and Garden Set. Fisher-Price®. 6 pieces, watering can, rake, nozzle, trowel, pots.	●	●	●		●	●	●	
Castle Molds. H.G. Industries. 4 different molded, shaped castles for play in sand.	●		●		●		●	●

GLOSSARY

Analysis. Visual analysis includes recognition of distinctive features. Example: Noticing a teddy bear on a book page and recognizing its body features and also its relationship to a familiar beloved teddy bear. Includes fine-spatial features, position of the figure in space, and form discrimination. See *synthesis.*

Bilateral. Both sides. Example: Ball play often requires the use of two hands.

Body scheme. Internal body awareness. An automatic sensory awareness of the location of body parts and their relationship to each other. A unified whole-body concept.

Cephalocaudad. Head to toe (or, literally, head to tail). The sequence in which most full-term babies develop new-movement capabilities.

Cognition. Application of intellect as opposed to feelings/affect in mental processes.

Dissociation. Separation of the movement of one body part from other body parts. Example: Fine-finger dexterity without inappropriate movements of the wrist or of the fingers of the other hand.

Distal. Away from the center of the body. The more peripheral portions of the body, like the hands and feet.

Extension. Straight position of the body. Example: Standing up straight, arms at sides, or lying flat on the floor.

Figure/ground perception. Ability to appropriately shift attention from particular fine detail of a stimulus to global awareness. Example: Being able to see "the forest for the trees" and vice versa. Noticing "It's a cow" versus noticing "It's a farmyard scene."

Flexion. Bending. Example: Putting an elbow in "make-a-muscle" bent position, or curling the whole body up into a ball.

Formboard. A puzzle in which the pieces insert into a specific shape opening rather than interlock with other pieces.

Form constancy. Consistency in recalling the overall pattern and structure of visual stimuli. Noticing that the most important overall characteristic of something seen remains the same in spite of differences in color, size, rotation, location, angle of vision, or some other detail. Example: All tricycles are tricycles, even when viewed from a distance or pictorially represented in a book.

Generalization. Integration of newly acquired information and application of it to new situations.

Habituation. Gradual adaptation to a stimulus. Becoming accustomed to something because of frequent exposure to it. Example: Not noticing the sound of the furnace running or the pressure of shoes on the feet.

Heterolateral. On the opposite side. Contralateral. Example: Right arm and left leg.

High-guard. Position of the hands and arms of the novice walker at shoulder height that helps with balance and stability.

Incidental learning. Information gleaned in the course of play or other informal activities without the need for any specific teaching.

Internal representation. Understanding of and appreciation for the function of an object.

Kinesthesia. Ability to consciously perceive and judge through muscle and joint sensations the extent or direction of weight or movement.

Midline. An imaginary line from the center of the forehead to the space between the feet. The coordination of a child's movements across this imaginary line suggests the brain is working as a motoric whole.

Motor planning. The figuring out and executing of a sequence of new, nonhabitual movements. Examples: Climbing through an unfamiliar obstacle course, or learning to remove a sweatshirt or to tie a bow. Once the sequence is learned, it no longer requires motor planning to repeat it.

Myelination. A process in which a sheath or covering automatically grows around some nerves, allowing them to function faster and more efficiently.

Object permanence. Recognition of the existence of an object, even after all or part of it is out of sight. Example: Baby shows he has object permanence when he starts to enjoy playing hide-and-seek with toys. Until then, when you hide his toy, he loses interest. Peekaboo is an early game to help baby begin to develop object permanence.

Optical righting reaction. Automatic movement of the baby's body to keep the head vertically aligned. This orientation to being right-side-up promotes balance and orientation to vertical space as a point of reference from which to develop other concepts of spatial awareness.

Perception. Mental awareness that includes multisensory and feeling (affective) appreciation of objects or situations in the environment, and that integrates a new piece of information with patterns of ideas held in memory. The ability to make sense out of a new stimulus by associating it with things experienced before.

Phonological system of language. The melody of stress, pauses, and intonational patterns used to modify how speech is produced, and also the distinctive articulation features of speech.

Pincer grasp. Position of the tip of the thumb and forefinger in opposition to each other when holding an object.

Prone. Position of the body when lying on the stomach.

Proprioception. Sensation stimulated by action of the organism itself. Example: Internal awareness of movements of joints, tendons, and muscles.

Proximal. Closer to the trunk.

Reciprocal. Alternating. Example: Leg movement while pedaling a Big Wheel® toy.

Reflex. Involuntary automatic actions.

Rotation. Turning on the axis. Example: Rolling over or turning the body to the side in preparation for sitting or standing.

Semantic. Relating to the meanings or significance of words.

Supine. Position of the body when lying on the back.

Symbolic representation. Use of one object to pretend it is another. Example: A wastebasket for a drum, a block for an airplane, or later even as farfetched as a stick for a house. The representation is not necessarily dependent on the real properties of the objects.

Symmetrical. The same on both sides of the midline of the body. Mirror image. Bilaterally symmetrical actions—both sides of the body working together doing the same thing at the same time. Examples: Clapping and baby-so-big.

Syntax. The arrangement of words in speech. The construction of sentences.

Synthesis. Visual synthesis is the ability to perceive individual features as a unified whole or to place them in a hierarchy of pattern, structure, or sequence. Example: Noticing that a teddy bear picture is located in a particular favorite book, and that that particular picture is on the last page of the book and it is located on the top of the page. See *analysis.*

Tactile. Having to do with the sense of touch.

Temporal. Having to do with the passage of time.

Vestibular system. Pertaining to the parts of the brain that receive, sort, and transmit information about the head's movement through position and movement through space and how the body should respond to it.

Index

(code for Figure – f)
(code for Glossary – GL)
(code for Toy Chart – TC)